HISTORICAL
DRAMA

y como siempre ha sido
lo que más ha alegrado y divertido
la representación bien aplaudida,
y es representación la humana vida,
una comedia sea
la que hoy el cielo en tu teatro vea.

The Maker to the World, in Calderón,
El gran teatro del mundo

Und jetzt an des Jahrhunderts ernstem Ende,
Wo selbst die Wirklichkeit zur Dichtung wird . . .

Schiller, Prologue to *Wallenstein*

Vergangenes historisch artikulieren heisst nicht, es erkennen "wie es denn eigentlich gewesen ist." Es heisst, sich einer Erinnerung bemächtigen, wie sie im Augenblick einer Gefahr aufblitzt.

Walter Benjamin, "Geschichtsphilosophische Thesen"

HERBERT LINDENBERGER

HISTORICAL DRAMA

The Relation of Literature and Reality

THE UNIVERSITY OF CHICAGO PRESS
CHICAGO AND LONDON

HERBERT LINDENBERGER is Avalon Foundation Professor of Humanities in Comparative Literature and English and chairman of the Comparative Literature program at Stanford University.

THE UNIVERSITY OF CHICAGO PRESS, CHICAGO 60637
THE UNIVERSITY OF CHICAGO PRESS, LTD., LONDON

© 1975 by The University of Chicago
All rights reserved. Published 1975
Printed in the United States of America

Library of Congress Cataloging in Publication Data

Lindenberger, Herbert Samuel, 1929–
    Historical drama.

    Includes bibliographical references and index.
    1. Historical drama.   I. Title.
PN1872.L5   809.2'51   74-11630
ISBN 0-226-48239-1

TO MICHAEL AND ELIZABETH
ON WHOSE NEARBY NOISE THIS BOOK
SOMEHOW THRIVED

CONTENTS

PREFACE

I may as well start with an explanation of what this book is not trying to be. It is not, for instance, a study of the development of historical drama as a genre. If I had tried to write a history of this (or any) genre, my mental hands would have been tied by a constant search for continuities and for explanations as to why this particular form flourished in certain eras and not in others. Even if I had avoided chronological organization, I should quickly have found myself bogged down in the process of contriving and defending workable definitions of the genre. Is Racine's *Athalie*, deriving as it does from a short, little-known passage in the Old Testament, properly speaking a history play? What is one to do with the Greeks, who did not share our particular modern distinction between myth and history? As in so many genre studies, much of one's intellectual energy would have been expended on setting appropriate limits on what precisely constitutes the genre and then defending one's use of the examples one has chosen. I might as well admit that by a strict definition one cannot categorize historical drama as a genre at all, though one can speak of specific forms of historical plays which prevailed at certain moments in history — for instance the medieval mystery cycles, the English chronicle plays of the 1590s, German historical tragedies during the age of Goethe, or documentary dramas of the 1960s.

Given the limitations inherent both in a chronological account and in generic description, I might have fallen back on that most favored means (during the last generation at least) of avoiding the difficulties of history and theory — that is, I could have conceived this book as a close reading of representative great texts. Although I briefly considered this mode of organization, I recognized that the greatness of a text does not insure that it is representative of anything except literary greatness; moreover, close reading (for all its pedagogical value, as well as the value it had in helping me reach an understanding of the subject I was marking out for myself) would have demanded that the texts I chose to discuss would be read chiefly in isolation from one another, and that the need to treat each text with the thoroughness it deserved would prevent my giving a proper emphasis to the problems which most concerned me.

As it turned out, I found I could best organize the book around the problems themselves, for example the ways that dramatists have perceived history at different times and the changing responses of readers and audiences to historical plays of the past. At an early stage of my thinking I realized that I was no longer able to look at texts quite as I had been taught by the literary historians and formalist critics I had worked with in graduate school many years ago, that in fact the process with which we perceive a text, or by which a writer perceives the historical matter he is translating into dramatic terms, is fundamental to any understanding of these texts.

It even occurred to me that my fascination with historical plays derived partly from the fact that these plays provide a special opportunity to examine the transactions between imaginative literature and the external world, which literature variously attempts to imitate, to attack, to influence, and to transcend: for historical writings, whether we classify them simply as history or among the traditional literary forms, make a greater pretense at engaging with reality than do writings whose fictiveness we accept from the start. The very term "historical drama" suggests the nature of this engagement, with the first word qualifying the fictiveness of the second, the second questioning the reality of the first. By concentrating on historical drama, moreover, I hope I may be able to make some statements applicable to all dramatic literature. As I shall show, the boundaries between historical drama and recognizable genres such as tragedy and romance are often quite fluid; and one might remember that every major dramatist from Marlowe through Brecht (with the exception of a few, like Molière, who specialized in comedy) was also a writer of history plays. I should also like to think that this book is a contribution to that continuing discussion within the criticism of our century which seeks to determine the ways in which literary utterances and forms differ from and parallel nonliterary types of discourse; unlike that significant body of recent work which approaches these questions by means of the linguistic model, it is not so much working toward general definitions as exploring the ways that readers and audiences experience what they take to be literature and reality.

Although I chose neither to trace the development of a genre nor to provide analyses of individual works, I have introduced particular historical plays by means of what one reader, Naomi Lebowitz, has called a "horizontal" approach, that is, by discussing a work briefly within each of a number of separate contexts. My chief examples, works such as the major historical plays of Shakespeare, Corneille, Racine, Goethe, Schiller, Büchner, and Brecht, appear in each chapter, some examples in fact within virtually every subchapter. Since each chapter is designed to approach historical drama from a distinct point of view, the repeated use of the same play (occasionally even the same scenes and aspects of a play) from chapter to chapter is a way of utilizing a limited body of major texts to help define and clarify the various problems with which the book is concerned. By means of this method, moreover, I can approach a play from different angles of vision according to the changing contexts in which it is discussed. The horizontal approach thus makes possible a kind of critical middle ground between straight theoretical argument and the close reading of texts, for it provides a way at once of shedding light on the individual work and of buttressing the speculations that are the subject of a particular chapter.

The first chapter is built around the problems we meet in postulating and describing relationships between drama and reality. The second attempts to isolate three characteristic shapes — those of the conspiracy, the tyrant, and the martyr play — which have persisted over the centuries (though in varying guises) among plays which purport to deal with history. The third chapter, reinterpreting the ancient distinction between poetry and history for my present purposes, treats history as a magnifying agent that creates specialized perspectives through which we experience such forms as tragedy, ceremonial plays, opera, and film. The use of other literary genres and other media in this chapter is intended to help define those qualities which audiences and readers (as well as dramatists) perceive as "historical" and "dramatic" and to show how the conventions of different genres and media cause us to experience these qualities in significantly different ways.

The fourth chapter, using Shakespeare's histories as a model, tries to locate a particular imaginative area — characterized by a skepticism toward absolutes, a tendency to mediate between extremes, and an absorption in the relationship of private and public experience — which most of the great historical dramas since the Renaissance have occupied. The final chapter treats historical drama as an attempt to approximate certain diverse modes of historical thought, for instance to render a sense of historical process and to express the fascination with power common among those who do not themselves hold power. What unity this book achieves lies not in any single conclusion toward which it drives but rather in the kinds of questions it raises about the relation of drama and the external world, above all in the exploratory attitude and the spirit of intellectual play which I have tried to maintain and which, I trust, have enabled me to develop a critical approach adequate to the complexity of these questions.

Although I am stressing the questions and problems which the great historical dramas suggest, I by no means deny the intrinsic pleasure which I continually find in the plays themselves. Indeed, my preoccupation with the plays over the years has allowed these questions gradually to emerge out of my reading. Many of the English and French plays I discuss have engaged my interest since my school days, the German plays since graduate school. I first tried to organize some ideas on the subject in an exercise on genre which my advisor, Jackson Mathews, helped me formulate for my doctoral examination at the University of Washington two decades ago. An undergraduate seminar I gave at the University of California, Riverside, in 1957 demonstrated both the promise of the subject and the unripeness of my ideas. I was forced to rethink some of these ideas five years later while writing a chapter on *Dantons Tod* for my book on Büchner: here, I discovered, was a major drama which renewed some central attitudes and conventions within Shakespeare's histories, yet which also opened up possibilities that a modern writer such as Brecht could exploit powerfully.

I did not, however, commit myself to a sustained inquiry on the subject until a Guggenheim Fellowship, awarded in 1968, allowed me to reread the plays and to reconsider the ideas I had carried with me over the years. I gave some of these ideas a trial run in a paper, *"Danton's Death* and the Conventions of Historical Drama," delivered at Cornell and Stanford Universities in late 1968 and early 1969 and published in *Comparative Drama* in summer, 1969; although the central notions of the paper were later left behind, I was able to adapt a few sentences for this book. A seminar I gave on historical drama at Stanford in early 1970 convinced me once and for all that organizing my material around individual texts (a necessity in a seminar) would keep me from getting to the problems that principally interested me. In a talk I gave to the Western Shakespeare Conference in Berkeley, California, in early 1971, I was fortunately forced to articulate what I was doing in general terms at a time when I felt myself immersed in details which were not yet sufficiently connected to one another. Some four or five pages of a paper prepared for a series on pastoral at the English Institute in the summer of 1971 found their way into the fourth chapter — with the result that I felt encouraged to explore history as an imaginative mode which defines itself in individual works through its opposition to other modes such as pastoral and romance (this paper, entitled "The Idyllic Moment: On Pastoral and Romanticism," appeared in *College English*, December 1972, and I am reprinting its opening pages with the permission of the National Council of Teachers of English).

Among the many distinguished critical works that stimulated my thinking and helped clarify the questions I was asking, I should single out Georg Lukács' *Der historische Roman,* especially the chapter "Historischer Roman und historisches Drama," which, with its Hegelian categories and movements of thought, encouraged me to approach the subject on a more theoretical level than has been common in Anglo-American criticism. Walter Benjamin's *Ursprung des deutschen Trauerspiels* taught me that historical plays do not simply "reflect" an external world but that they interact in intricate and fundamental ways both with this world and with the intellectual systems of the readers and audiences who experience them. Perhaps no work of literary criticism, however, affected my thinking in so fundamental a way as E. H. Gombrich's *Art and Illusion,* above all through its stress on the viewer's relationship to a work of art and through its superb way of moving between concrete example and theoretical statement. More distantly, though no less pervasively, I must acknowledge the influence and stimulation (in this and earlier books) of critics such as Erich Auerbach, Kenneth Burke, Northrop Frye, Renato Poggioli, and Leo Spitzer: their example serves as a constant admonition that the understanding of a particular literary work must involve an understanding of the whole literary tradition — not to speak of an understanding of what life is all about! I also suspect that living through the political tensions of the late 1960s and early 1970s helped sharpen my eye for the dramatic element in history and demonstrated how powerfully the pressure of present events can affect one's apprehension of the past — both the past which is history and that which is embedded in literary works that claim to be historical.

My deepest gratitude is due to the many colleagues in various fields of literature who were willing to read and comment on the manuscript before it reached its final version. Since I was brash enough to attempt a project which, in one way or another, involves all periods of Western literature (especially from the Renaissance onwards), I had a special need to be heard by persons more knowledgeable than I in the particular areas from which I drew my examples. I mention John B. Bender, Edward J. Brown, Joaquim-Francisco Coelho, Jean Franco, David G. Halliburton, John Loftis, Charles R. Lyons, and David Riggs of Stanford University; Albert Cook of the State University of New York, Buffalo; Liselotte Dieckmann, Naomi Lebowitz, and Egon Schwarz of Washington University, St. Louis; Thomas R. Edwards, Jr., of Rutgers University; Donald R. Howard of Johns Hopkins University; Norman Rabkin and Ralph W. Rader of the University of California, Berkeley; Ada Haussmann Schmidt, Riverside, California; Walter H. Sokel of the University of Virginia; Timothy J. Wiles of Indiana University; and Andrzej Wirth of the City University of New York. I am grateful to them, as well as to my wife, Claire F. Lindenberger, for saving me from errors, misunderstandings, and infelicities — and also for encouraging me, on occasion, to speak out more boldly that I had first dared. Since I have sometimes adopted ideas and even phrases from their annotations into my final manuscript, I hope they will accept the fact that a list of acknowledgments within a preface is at best an inadequate means of indicating one's debts. I take full responsibility, of course, for whatever errors and weaknesses remain.

I should also like to thank M. H. Abrams, Herbert Dieckmann, and Baxter Hathaway of Cornell University; C. L. Barber of the University of California, Santa Cruz; Henry Breitrose, Gordon A. Craig, George Dekker, John B. Foster, Jr., Anne K. Mellor, Kurt Müller-Vollmer, Lawrence V. Ryan, and Wesley Trimpi of Stanford University; Lionel Gossman of Johns Hopkins University; Peter U. Hohendahl of Washington University; David Levin of the University of Virginia; Edgar Lohner of the University of Mainz; Arthur F. Marotti of Wayne State University; Milton Miller of the University of

California, Riverside; and Rose Zimbardo of the State University of New York, Stony Brook, for their willingness to chat with me about various aspects of the project and to offer suggestions, information, and ideas.

I wish to express my gratitude, as well, to the John Simon Guggenheim Memorial Foundation for its generous fellowship; to Washington University, St. Louis, for granting me a sabbatical leave early in the project; to Stanford University for funds for typing and photocopying; to Evelyn Barnes and Jo Guttadauro for patiently and accurately typing the manuscript; and to the Comparative Literature secretary at Stanford, Mrs. Gloria Spitzer, for her usual persistence and skill in supervising its difficult early and final stages.

FREQUENTLY CITED EDITIONS

The following works will be cited in the notes by the author's name and volume number alone.

Brecht, Bertolt. *Stücke.* 12 vols. Berlin and Frankfurt: Suhrkamp, 1953–59. Citations are from the reprint of 1961–62.

Büchner, Georg. *Sämtliche Werke und Briefe.* Ed. Werner R. Lehmann. 4 vols (still incomplete). Hamburg: Wegner, 1967–.

Corneille, Pierre. *Théâtre.* Ed. Pierre Lièvre and Roger Caillois. Paris: Bibliothèque de la Pléiade, 1950. Since all citations are from volume 1, the volume number will not be given in the notes.

Goethe, Johann Wolfgang. *Werke,* Hamburger-Ausgabe. Ed. Erich Trunz et al. 14 vols. Hamburg: Wegner, 1948–60.

Racine, Jean. *Oeuvres complètes.* Ed. Raymond Picard. Paris: Bibliothèque de la Pléiade, 1950. Since all citations are from volume 1, the volume number will not be given in the notes.

Schiller, Friedrich. *Werke,* Nationalausgabe. Ed. Julius Petersen et al. 44 vols (still incomplete). Weimar: Böhlau, 1943–.

Quotations from Shakespeare will be identified in the text rather than in notes; they are based on the New Arden edition, ed. Una Ellis-Fermor et al. (London: Methuen, 1951–). Quotations from *Coriolanus, Hamlet,* and *Richard III,* which had not yet appeared in the New Arden at the time of writing, are from the New Cambridge edition, ed. John Dover Wilson (Cambridge: Cambridge University Press, editions of 1958, 1954, and 1959 respectively).

ONE

HISTORICAL DRAMA AND HISTORICAL REALITY

LEVELS OF REALITY

Before you study the history study the historian. . . . Before you study the historian, study his historical and social environment.
E. H. Carr, *What Is History?*

Die Geschichte objektiv denken ist die stille Arbeit des Dramatikers; nämlich alles aneinander denken, das Vereinzelte zum Ganzen weben: überall mit der Voraussetzung, dass eine Einheit des Planes in die Dinge gelegt werden müsse, wenn sie nicht darinnen sei.
Nietzsche, "Vom Nutzen und Nachteil der Historie für das Leben"

If historical fact establishes a work's claim to represent reality, historical drama should be the most realistic of dramatic forms. The much-vaunted realism of writers such as Ibsen and Chekhov is, after all, built out of imagined characters going their fictional rounds; an audience's acceptance of their worlds as "real" must be based on its faith that the everyday problems and household objects with which these dramatists are concerned present a more plausible, or intense, or significant version of reality than the public issues traditional to historical plays. What we accept as "real" differs widely from age to age: a serious mind of the late nineteenth century would have felt it could better experience reality in *Ghosts* or *The Father* than in those highly rhetorical performances of Edwin Booth or Henry Irving impersonating Richard III.

The issue of whether or not we experience "reality" in a literary work (an issue present in one form or another since Plato) has become especially intense during recent generations. Throughout most of the Western tradition, writers (or at least their critics) made verisimilitude rather than reality itself the goal toward which they strove. They could thus present a historical character or action within a broad framework of accepted notions. Historical material had the same status as myth: both belonged to what Horace called "publicly known matters" ("publica materies")[1] and both depended—indeed, still do depend—on an audience's willingness to assimilate the portrayal of a

1

familiar story or personage to the knowledge it already brings to the theater.[2] Achilles must be portrayed as "restless, irascible, unyielding, and hard," Horace tells us, and Medea as "fierce and invincible."[3]

In publicly known matters, reality or plausibility exists essentially within the consciousness of the audience. Commentators on the first part of *Henry VI* never tire of reminding us that Shakespeare's audience knew Joan of Arc only as an evil force. In the twentieth century her story has become generally known to the point that any writer is forced to recognize and cope with those aspects of her career which we are all familiar with—her voices, her death at the stake, her heroic role in battle. If he wishes to secularize her voices, or bring her back, as Shaw does, to face her friends or enemies after death, he is still working within the system of meanings we attach to her. Schiller, writing of her before she had entered the popular consciousness to the degree she has in our own century, could allow her to die actively in battle instead of passively at the stake, and we allow him this freedom (as we allow Shakespeare to blacken her name) through our historical sense that even the most public stories change their meanings from one era to another. A playwright writing about George Washington for an American audience today could doubtless portray a measure of Machiavellianism beneath Washington's noble exterior, and he could even endow him with a sizable group of imaginary children; yet given our consciousness of at least the existence, if not the precise personality of Martha Washington, under no circumstances could he make him a bachelor. A poet is better off never having met his historical characters, said Goethe, referring to Egmont, whom he presented as an amorous bachelor instead of a husband with a dozen children as his sources indicated.[4] What a spectator doesn't know, to take off from the old saying, will not harm his response.

"Where the event of a great action is left doubtful, there the Poet is left Master," Dryden wrote in his preface to *Don Sebastian*, a play whose historical background was sufficiently thin to leave Dryden's imagination ample room for creativity.[5] Dryden was, of course, living at a time when people had begun to distinguish carefully between truth and legend, but when the doctrine of verisimilitude still forced one to think twice about falsifying known or even obscure facts.[6] Getting one's dates wrong could make a writer especially vulnerable in seventeenth-century France—far more so than inventing a love interest for a character when none was known to exist. Racine, already under fire for some minor anachronisms in *Britannicus*, in his preface to the play anticipates an objection which he had not yet heard, but which he feared might arise when the play was read rather than seen: "I have made Junie join the vestal order, to which, according to Aulus-Gellius, no one under six years of age, or over ten, was received. But the people here take Junie under their protection, and I thought that in consideration of her birth, her virtue, and her misfortune, they would dispense with the legal age limits, as they have dispensed with age limits for the consulate in the case of so

2

many deserving great men."[7] Racine's defensiveness, clothed in what seems to us an absurd legalism, is an extreme instance in the long and complex conflict between poetry and history which has been a central issue in criticism since Aristotle. I might add that we today would be concerned not with the legal propriety of Junie's becoming a vestal virgin but with its dramatic propriety: since it is difficult for us to share the seventeenth century's conception of the convent as a proper refuge for a raped woman, we can all too easily view Junie's flight as the only inauthentic action within what is otherwise one of the greatest of historical dramas.

Although we may be considerably less literal-minded than the seventeenth century in evaluating a dramatist's use of history, we retain considerable awareness of the relationship of a play to its source. Our modern prefaces to older historical plays generally expend a goodly amount of space on how the writer used the chronicles he was working from; often, in fact, the relevant source material is reprinted in an appendix. Although our tendency to stress the importance of sources is doubtless a product of the "positivistic" mode of scholarship which dominated literary study earlier in our century, it is also, I think, a kind of "common-sense" attitude which we have learned to take for granted: our first notion in reflecting about a history play is not to view it as an imaginative structure in its own right but to ask how it deals with its historical materials. Thus, we have learned to marvel at the way famous passages such as Enobarbus's description of Cleopatra on her barge and Volumnia's final plea to Coriolanus utilize much of the diction and even syntax of their sources, or at the fact that about one-sixth of *Dantons Tod* (*Danton's Death*) consists of close paraphrase or translation of Büchner's sources.[8] Conversely, we marvel at the way Corneille built *Cinna* out of a mere three pages each in Seneca and Montaigne, or how Racine, as he himself boasts in his preface, created *Bérénice* out of even sparser materials — a line or two in Suetonius;[9] or at how such youthful-seeming heroes as Shakespeare's Hotspur, Goethe's Egmont, and Kleist's Prince Friedrich von Homburg would all have been portrayed as middle-aged if their authors had been sticklers for accuracy. Whether we stress a work's closeness to or independence from its sources, we are thinking within a framework based on a play's relationship to the external historical reality it purports to imitate. I might add that, if the reality of a historical figure or context is defined according to the standards of contemporary academic historical writing, all but a few historical plays of the past would seem scandalously inaccurate; to cite one of the most flagrant examples, Shakespeare's depiction of Richard III, deriving as it does from Thomas More and the Tudor historians, bears little resemblance to the portrait which Paul Murray Kendall gives in his modern biography of the king.[10]

However a critic defines the relationship of poetry to history, in one sense or another he always acknowledges that the two forms of writing follow their own rules and conventions. Although Ben Jonson (at least from the evidence

3

of his two historical plays) took himself more seriously as a historian than any other Renaissance dramatist, he did not hesitate to alter a characterization (for instance, his Agrippina, who is a more favorable character in *Sejanus* than in Tacitus) whenever it suited the moral design of his play.[11] Jonson's often pedantic display of learning, coupled as it is with the transformations to which he subjected his material, illustrates in an extreme way a phenomenon characteristic of historical dramatists of most eras — on the one hand, the pretense that they are rendering historical reality as such; on the other hand, an acknowledgment that a play creates its own world with a closed, internal system of references.[12]

But these two extremes by no means exhaust the images we form of history plays. One could argue that the sources of many plays consist less of the historical materials on which they are purportedly based than on the theatrical conventions which give them their essential form. In reading through the English historical dramas of the romantic and Victorian poets, from Blake's *Edward III* fragment to Tennyson's sprawling plays about Becket and Mary Tudor, one often feels less aware of the "history" being depicted than of the overpowering presence of Shakespeare, whose language and stage conventions they sought (without much success) to imitate. To cite an "eclectic" play whose greatness nobody would dispute today, *Dantons Tod*, for all its faithfulness to the histories of the French Revolution which Büchner used, not only is based on an Elizabethan conception of dramatic form, but its very texture — for example, its crowd scenes out of *Julius Caesar* and *Coriolanus*, the Juliet-like death of Danton's wife, and the clowning of the carters taking the Dantonists to the guillotine — evokes a specifically Shakespearean world as much as it does the world of the Revolution; and on a less obvious level *Dantons Tod* parodies Schiller's much more heroic conception of what a history play should be. In a persuasive essay on *Edward II*, David M. Bevington has argued that many of the "complexities" and "inconsistencies" we have read into Marlowe's characters stem from the fact that the play has two, often conflicting, sources: the "real" history of Holinshed's chronicle and the theatrical conventions that derive from the morality-play tradition.[13]

The neoclassical conventions determine the kind of history we experience in plays written in seventeenth-century France: the need for decorum eliminates the possibility of surging crowds on the streets, of battle scenes, indeed of virtually all the forms of local color which Elizabethan and Spanish drama so assiduously cultivated, while the temporal and spatial compression created through the observance of the unities occasions an image of the past as essentially a moment of crisis instead of the gradually developing historical processes which we witness in plays such as *Richard II* and Goethe's *Götz von Berlichingen*.[14] Since the seventeenth century it has been customary to remark that the characters in a French play are more like contemporary Frenchmen (one remembers Dryden's snide remark about Racine's Monsieur

Hippolyte)[15] than like the historical or mythological personages they represent. But this is not the most precise way of describing the phenomenon: I doubt, for instance, that many of Louis XIV's courtiers spoke in anything resembling Racine's Alexandrines. Rather, instead of saying that a Turk has been turned into a seventeenth-century Frenchman (which is what Racine's enemies apparently said of *Bajazet* when the play was first performed)[16] or, for that matter, a medieval English feudal lord into an Elizabethan courtier, one should speak of the translation of a historical source into a contemporary dramatic convention, one which, by its very nature, implies its own system of character relationships, poetic language, and dramatic progressions in time. The seeming discrepancy between source and contemporary dramatic treatment is perhaps at its most conspicuous in neoclassical versions of certain folkloric Old Testament passages, for instance Milton's translation of Samson's adventures into what he took to be the form of Greek tragedy, or Alfieri's of the event-laden story of Saul into the rarefied and lofty inward action to which all his work aspired.

But the contemporary meaning of a historical play cannot be defined simply in terms of the dramatic conventions within which it is expressed. It has long been a commonplace that historical plays are at least as much a comment on the playwright's own times as on the periods about which they are ostensibly written. Whether or not we accept the recent theory that Jonson's *Catiline* was intended as a *drame à clef* about the Gunpowder Plot of 1605,[17] no one would deny that both his historical plays, for all their vast learning about ancient Rome, tell us a good deal about politics and society in London in the early seventeenth century. Shakespeare's English history plays, as Lily B. Campbell and other scholars have been at pains to show, allude to such specifically Elizabethan problems as the succession to the crown and the danger of Catholic subversion and invasion.[18] If such matters need to be pointed out to us, it is not simply because the modern reader would not catch the allusions which were probably obvious to their first audiences, but also because we are no longer in the habit — as our culture has been until recently — of scanning history primarily for the lessons it can afford the present. On one level *Götz von Berlichingen* is of course "about" the early sixteenth century, but on another level it attempts to restore certain medieval virtues which Goethe found lacking in eighteenth-century civilization (on still another level, one might add, its deliberately Shakespearean chronicle form serves as a critique of the neoclassical form which, for the young Goethe, characterized that civilization). Kleist's last two plays, *Die Hermannsschlacht* (*Hermann's Battle*) and *Prinz Friedrich von Homburg,* are of course in one sense about Roman and seventeenth-century Germany respectively; yet in another sense which is more obvious to us than it is with Shakespeare's English histories, they are "about" the present in which they were written, namely, French-occupied Prussia of 1808-11. But the word "about" implies that they merely reflect their environment; much more fundamentally, they are meant to exhort the author's contemporaries to political action.[19] If academic historians since Ranke have attempted to break the ancient tie which linked past theme with present-day matter, modern historical dramatists have been as shameless as their predecessors in reading the present into the past; to cite one of the more memorable examples, witness Brecht's rewriting of *Leben des Galilei* (*Life of Galilei*) in response to the dropping of the first atomic bomb.

The continuity between past and present is a central assertion in history plays of all times and styles. One of the simplest ways a writer can achieve such continuity is to play on the audience's knowledge of what has happened in history since the time of the play. At Richard II's deposition the bishop of Carlisle can solemnly warn of future disorders (IV.i.134-49) which the audience knows will ultimately take the form of the War of the Roses (disorders, moreover, which Shakespeare had already described in detail in the *Henry VI* plays and *Richard III*). The aged Horace in Corneille's *Horace* goes to great rhetorical effort to predict the future Roman glory which we all know is to come true.[20] When Racine's Agrippine tells her son Nero "Et ton nom paraîtra, dans la race future, / Aux plus cruels tyrans une cruelle injure,"[21] the author can rest assured the audience will know what he is talking about. Büchner's Danton can predict that Robespierre will follow him to the guillotine before six months are up.[22] In one sense, of course, such statements provide an easy means of asserting the historical reality of what is happening on stage, but in another sense they serve as a way of breaking the illusion, at least to the extent that we see the events on stage spilling over into a historical continuum with which we are already familiar. And although they help break the illusion, such statements also increase our participation in the play, for through our hindsight about how things eventually worked themselves out in history, we flatter ourselves that we, in effect, can sit like demigods presiding omnisciently over the action.

To the degree that a segment of the past is intended to link up with the present-day reality of the audience, the latter's own national past has a special status among thematic materials. Coleridge attempted to distinguish Shakespeare's English history plays from his other works with a relatively simple test: "In order that a drama may be properly historical," he wrote, "it is necessary that it should be the history of the people to whom it is addressed."[23] Coleridge's words "to whom it is addressed" suggest the active relationship which a drama on national history can establish with its audience. The possibilities of interchange between audience and drama are endless: a play can work to confirm or kindle patriotic feelings (*Henry V*), it can warn a ruler of possible dangers (*Gorboduc*), flatter a ruler (*Macbeth*), or, for that matter, attempt to undermine a ruler or powerful figure in the audience's eyes (*The Crucible*). In our earliest history play, *The Persians*, Aeschylus depicts the *hybris* of the invaders who had been defeated at Salamis only a few years before in order to warn his victorious fellow Greeks of their own *hybris*. In one of the most recent of famous history plays, *Der Stellvertreter* (*The Deputy*), Rolf Hochhuth was willing to court aesthetic disaster in order to arouse the maximum degree of guilt within his fellow Germans for their crimes during World War II. In Lope de Vega's *Fuenteovejuna* even a foreign reader can sense the symbolic authority which Ferdinand and Isabella exercise during their brief appearance — and he is equally aware that they lack such authority when they appear in Dryden's *Conquest of Granada*. The powerful effect that a drama on a people's own national history can exert is often lost when it is presented in a foreign environment, for this effect is predicated on the audience's awareness that it is witnessing the enactment of its own past.[24] Except for Shakespeare's histories, scarcely any national plays have been able to acclimate themselves abroad (one suspects that today even in England Shakespeare's histories, except during wartime, are appreciated for other than national reasons). Ibsen's and Strindberg's national dramas, fine though some of them are, are not played, in fact scarcely read, outside their respective countries. *Prinz Friedrich von Homberg* was successful in post-World War II Paris in spite of its German nationalist sentiments and only because of the existentialist statements its audiences discovered in it.

Yet among the distinguished historical dramas one could name, perhaps only a minority are actually based on "national" materials. Indeed, literary historians have generally attributed the "inspiration" for these plays to moments of intense national consciousness; whatever the truth of such statements, it remains a fact that nearly all the great English history plays were written during the decade following the defeat of the Armada. The few significant plays on German history coincide with the awakening of the German national past during the age of Goethe. Another group of fine plays — for instance, Grillparzer's *König Ottokars Glück und Ende* (*King Ottokar's Rise and Fall*) and *Ein Bruderzwist in Habsburg* (*A Hapsburg Fraternal Quarrel*), Pushkin's *Boris Godounov* and Mickiewicz's *Forefathers Eve* — can be tied in one way or another to the upsurge of nationalism during the post-Napoleonic period. Despite the aggressively nationalistic foreign policy of France during the seventeenth century, French drama is notoriously lacking in French themes: the analogy between past and present which is characteristic of all historical drama could better be served by Roman history than by what must have seemed a much too "rude" French national past. Under an authoritarian regime national themes, though they may serve patriotic purposes (as they did in the Elizabethan period and the Spanish Golden Age), are often too touchy for an author to risk. It is significant, for instance, that no play within Shakespeare's English cycle was set in the time of the Tudors; *Henry VIII*, moreover, was not only written during the Stuart reign, but it is far less "political" in content and method than the pre-Tudor plays. With a few exceptions such as the anonymous plays on Thomas More and Thomas Cromwell, Elizabethan plays on recent history were normally set in foreign places, most notably France. Chapman's *Bussy D'Ambois* and

Byron allowed their author to play on the audience's knowledge of very recent historical events without risking local political consequences.[25] The events of Marlowe's crude propaganda play, *The Massacre at Paris*, were so recent that Henry of Navarre could be presented as a Protestant hero, though his real-life prototype was to render the play obsolete soon after through his conversion to Catholicism. Whatever the setting, Elizabethans could be expected to give a "foreign" play a local application, as one gathers from Thomas Heywood's statement of 1612, "If wee present a forreigne History, the subject is so intended, that in the liues of *Romans, Grecians,* or others, either the vertues of our Country-men are extolled, or their vices reproued."[26]

If national history has enjoyed a special status, so too has ancient, particularly Roman, history. Roman history, after all, is a part of the national consciousness of all modern Europe: not only did the events of ancient Rome have the exemplary function indicated by Heywood's statement, but to feel historical continuity between the present and the ancient Roman imperium was to endow one's own history with a measure of dignity. When Casca, directly after the murder of Julius Caesar, speaks these lines—

> How many ages hence
> Shall this our lofty scene be acted over,
> In states unborn, and accents yet unknown!
>
> (III.i.111–13)

we are aware both of the exemplary nature of the action (exemplary, as always with Shakespeare, in a very complex sense, especially through the irony with which we read the words "lofty" and "acted") and of the continuity between Roman greatness and the Elizabethan present. The first audience of *Cinna*, while listening to Augustus's speeches on the grandeur of the state he was consolidating, must surely have felt both the analogy and the continuity between the achievements of the first Roman emperor and those of Richelieu.

At particular moments in history, subjects other than Rome or one's own national past can establish analogies and continuities between a play's overt subject and the audience's present. As partisans of Protestantism and the Enlightenment, Goethe and Schiller could utilize an anti-Spanish and an antiabsolutist perspective in *Egmont* and *Don Carlos*, and thus achieve something of the effect of national drama. One might add that both writers felt the lack of appropriate German materials for their plays: Schiller, for instance, in his notes toward his brilliant fragment from Russian history, *Demetrius*, listed the lack of a German subject as one of the disadvantages of his project,[27] while Goethe, reading through Scott's novels during his old age, complained of the "poverty" of German in comparison with English history (ironically enough, the historical method of Scott's fiction owes a good bit to the fact that Scott had translated *Götz von Berlichingen* in his youth!).[28] For a radical such as Georg Büchner nothing within German history could have

8

had the immediacy or relevance of the history of the French Revolution; the lines he wrote to his fiancée during the year before the composition of *Dantons Tod* — "I was studying the history of the Revolution. I felt myself as though crushed under the frightful fatalism of history. . . . The individual a mere froth on the wave, greatness a mere chance, the dominance of genius a puppet's game, a ridiculous struggling against an iron law, the recognition of which is the highest achievement, but which to control is impossible"[29] — reveal an intensity of identification with the past such as no dramatist reading his own national history can ever have surpassed.

To the degree that Hegelian and/or Marxist approaches to history have created a new sense of continuity during the past century, "universal" history has been able to address itself to an audience with something of the immediacy which was formerly the province of national history. Among nonnational subjects, only Roman history could convince Elizabethan or French seventeenth-century audiences of its essential continuity with their own civilization. But once every era anywhere — at least within Western culture and its Near Eastern appendages — could be interpreted as part of an ongoing historical process which must culminate in the audience's present, even the most remote historical contexts might be expected to reveal their relevance. During the composition of *Emperor and Galilean*, his long panoramic drama on the life of Julian the Apostate, Ibsen wrote to Edmund Gosse justifying his choice of so "remote" a theme: "The historical theme I have chosen . . . has a closer connection with the currents of our own age than one might at first think. This I regard as an essential demand to be made of any modern treatment of material so remote, if it is, as a work of literature, to be able to rouse any interest."[30] The dramatist could thus seek out eras whose essential conflicts seemed to point forward, in fact to anticipate those later stages of the historical process with which the audience might experience some emotional identification. Ibsen in his world-historical fable could address himself to the mid-nineteenth-century conflict between what Arnold, writing about the same time, called Hebraism and Hellenism.

Indeed, writers could seek out periods in which an older, reactionary view of life was colliding with some newer, more attractive dispensation: by identifying with the proponents of the new, the audience not only would feel it was experiencing the force of historical continuity, but it could flatter itself for being on the side of progress. The collision (to use an appropriately Hegelian term) between Oriental callousness and Christian compassion which Hebbel depicted in *Herodes und Mariamne*, or between medieval Catholic authoritarianism and Protestant free-spiritedness which Shaw made the central issue in *Saint Joan*, is presented in such a way that the audience cannot help but sympathize with the values of the new era, while at the same time the playwright can remind his public not to resist the historical process which is still going on in their own world. Brecht, though a firm enough believer in the historical process, managed to complicate the scheme in *Galileo*: in the collision between ecclesiastical authoritarianism and scientific freedom which he presents, we are unable to align ourselves wholeheartedly with the newer values once we see how Galileo has sold out to the churchmen and helped bring on our present woes.

Thus far I have stressed three levels of reality which shape our consciousness as we experience a history play: first, the historical materials which the play derives from its sources ("correct" or not) and which it purports to reenact; second, the theatrical conventions into which these materials are recast; and third, the sense of historical continuity which the author gives to that segment of the past which he has dramatized. But there is still another aspect to our experience with every *older* work — namely, the influence of our present situation on our interpretation of the work. Like history itself, a history play changes its meaning for us according to the shifting historical winds.[31] When *Richard II* (minus its explosive deposition scene) was revived in London during the Essex Rebellion of 1601, it had obviously become charged with more meanings than those which its first audience would have seen in it a mere six years before.[32] All great literary works, of course, acquire new meanings for us with changing times: to cite some famous extreme readings, one need only mention the weak, introspective Hamlet of Goethe and Coleridge or the post-Beckett Lear of Jan Kott and Peter Brook.[33] But history plays, to the extent that they concern themselves with politics and power, enjoy a more intense relationship with reality than other works; an audience which is led to view *Richard II* (not to speak of *Richard III*) as a portrait of its current ruler will experience a political thrill distinct from the psychological or ideological titillation of, say, a juvenile delinquent Hamlet, or a racially victimized Othello.

The political events of history plays have a way of "repeating" themselves in a more readily interpretable manner than private, psychological events. The various forms of political unrest and change — riots, conspiracies, coups, as well as most types of repression — do not, despite improvements in the technology with which they are put into effect, change their basic configurations from one age to another. When Goethe, while finishing *Egmont* in Rome, heard news of the Belgian revolution of 1787, he remarked that the early scenes he had written years before about the unrest in Brussels in the 1560s were now being enacted on that city's streets; since his drama had already achieved a new level of significance before it was even complete, he expressed the fear that it might be interpreted as a lampoon.[34] In his play *Die Plebejer proben den Aufstand* (*The Plebeians Rehearse the Uprising*), a sharp attack on Brecht's refusal to support the East Berlin riots of 1953, Günter Grass found an apt literary analogy in the crowd scenes of *Coriolanus*, which he could tie specifically to his protagonist through the fact that Brecht had

10

recently adapted Shakespeare's tragedy for his theatrical company. Whatever relationship, if any, *Coriolanus* had to the food riots of 1607, it has proved a potent force in generating later meanings, as one might note in the near-riots occasioned by the rightist adaptation performed in Paris in 1934, or in Brecht's Marxist version, which managed to ennoble the tribunes and the crowd and to make the hero even more unpleasant than he is in the original play. Some plays, of course, fail to generate new meanings once their initial relevance has worn off. Jonson's *Catiline*, despite the fascination it may have had for contemporary audiences who knew how to read its intended political meanings, by 1668 could elicit Samuel Pepys's comment that it was "the least diverting" play he had ever seen.[35] Occasionally a play cultivates sufficient ambiguity to keep its political meanings unclear even in its own time: Addison's *Cato*, for instance, was espoused by both Whigs and Tories as partial to each — the Whigs casting Marlborough as the hero Cato, while the Tories preferred to see him as the tyrant Caesar.[36]

In an attempt to place *Fuenteovejuna* in its original historical context, Joaquín Casalduero distinguished between a play's interpretability by theater directors and by critics: whereas the former must attempt to capture a play's present-day meanings, the latter must isolate what the play would have meant to its initial audience.[37] Casalduero's essay on Lope's play, which depicts the successful uprising of a small town against its tyrannical local feudal ruler, is an attempt to correct those interpretations (represented, for instance, by the late nineteenth-century "liberal" critic Menéndez y Pelayo and by contemporary radical theater directors) which stress the play's revolutionary content. Our modern conceptions of "left" and "right," which go back to the struggle against absolute monarchy that began in the Enlightenment, have little, if any, applicability to Spanish politics of the sixteenth century, a period in which the monarchy sought to consolidate its position by allying itself with the peasantry against the feudal nobility. Critics who exalt what they take to be "popular revolution" in plays such as *Fuenteovejuna* or Calderón's *El alcalde de Zalamea* (*The Mayor of Zalamea*) must cope with the fact that the Spanish dramatists of the Golden Age were able to combine hostility toward feudalism with unbending loyalty to absolute monarchy and to the Catholic religion.[38]

If critics run into problems transferring a political category to a period in which it does not fit, they encounter another type of problem in approaching writers to whom they feel so ideologically akin that they are incapable of distinguishing between what is actually "in" the work and what they take to be the writer's ideology. Brecht's plays are notoriously dangerous subjects for Marxist critics of any but the shrewdest and most flexible sort. Even Georg Lukács, who could be marvelously acute in approaching conservative writers such as Scott or Balzac, went awry with a hero of the German radical tradition such as Georg Büchner: in writing about *Dantons Tod*, Lukács could

11

insist (with the perversity characteristic of a critic whose ideological commitments might otherwise be threatened) that Büchner was not only attacking Danton's passivity but also arguing for the continuance of the Revolution.[39]

Liberal and Marxist critics, of course, wear their biases more openly than those historical scholars who, in our century, have taken it upon themselves to demodernize the literature of the past. Although literary history has shown considerable success in ridding us of the kind of "unhistorical" readings which Casalduero exposed in his essay on *Fuenteovejuna*, it is unable to avoid a more subtle sort of bias. For literary historians, no more than the political and social historians whose supposed objectivity they seek to attain, are themselves thoroughly immersed in the attitudes toward the past which prevail in their own time. Anybody who has followed the course of American historical writing during the twentieth century is aware of a succession of changing frameworks through which the American past has been viewed: the so-called "progressive" historians of the early part of the century gave way to the "consensus" historians at the end of World War II, and these, in turn, have been challenged by the "revisionists" since the mid-1960s. One need only look at the shifting image of the early years of the American republic as one moves (to cite some extreme examples) from Charles A. Beard to Daniel J. Boorstin and thence to Staughton Lynd to note that a man's view of the past cannot be separated from the political and social milieu in which he works and thinks.[40]

If academic historians are influenced by their immediate environments, it is hardly surprising if critics of historical drama have a hard time escaping the preconceptions of their own worlds. It is easy enough today to attack a statement such as the following written a century ago by Edward Dowden in his once-influential book on Shakespeare: "Brutus is the political Girondin. He is placed in contrast with his brother-in-law Cassius, the political Jacobin."[41] We can look condescendingly at such lines because of the very obviousness with which Dowden reads *Julius Caesar* according to late eighteenth- and early nineteenth-century political categories—categories, moreover, which impose their own, peculiarly modern, coloring on a historical world completely foreign to them.

But even the more "responsible" approaches to literary history which have been developed during our own century are, despite their insistence on documentation and their commitment to placing a work within its own time, unable to escape the biases of their practitioners' own time. When I was a graduate student in the early 1950s, it seemed as though the last and, in fact, *only* word on Shakespeare's English histories had been uttered by Lily B. Campbell and E. M. W. Tillyard, both of whom saw the plays as expressions of official Elizabethan attitudes toward order and rebellion, indeed as a dramatization of the so-called Tudor myth which Shakespeare would have absorbed from the various historians he had read. Despite much useful information in their work, we can no longer accept their interpretations as

12

either the last or only word; indeed, with a quarter century's distance between them and us, we can easily see how each manages to make Shakespeare look like a spokesman for patriotism and authority: Miss Campbell, reading Shakespeare through the perspective of the Elizabethan books and pamphlets she found at the Huntington Library, naturally stressed the plays' relationships with the official attitudes that prevailed in the various nonliterary texts circulating during Shakespeare's time, while Tillyard just as naturally stressed what one would expect of a conservative Cambridge don writing in a beleaguered England during World War II. Tillyard, in fact, displayed his bias quite openly when he defended his reading of *Henry IV* as an expression of the Elizabethan doctrine of order:

> The school of criticism that furnished [Falstaff] with a tender heart and condemned the Prince for brutality in turning him away was deluded. Its delusions will probably be accounted for in later years through the facts of history. The sense of security created in nineteenth century England by the predominance of the British navy induced men to rate that very security too cheaply and to exalt the instinct of rebellion above its legitimate station. They forgot the threat of disorder which was ever present with the Elizabethans. Schooled by recent events we should have no difficulty now in taking Falstaff as the Elizabethans took him.[42]

If the nineteenth-century British navy encouraged too soft a view of Falstaff, the "recent" events which "schooled" Tillyard perhaps encourage an unduly harsh view of him. During the last decade or two critics have come to make a crucial distinction between the ideas which stand behind a play and their actual embodiment within the work. The most eloquent statement of what later became a characteristic point of view is that of A. P. Rossiter, whose public lectures on Shakespeare, though written soon after Tillyard's book, did not become generally known until after their posthumous publication in 1961:

> ...the Tudor myth system of Order, Degree, etc. was too rigid, too black-and-white, too doctrinaire and narrowly moral for Shakespeare's mind: it falsified his fuller expression of men. Consequently, while employing it as FRAME, he had to undermine it, to qualify it with equivocations: to vex its applications with sly or subtle ambiguities: to cast doubts on its ultimate human validity, even in situations where its principles seemed most completely applicable. His intuition told him it was *morally* inadequate.[43]

One does not need to take a thoroughgoing Marxist view of a critic's relation to his own age to note that during the decade in which Rossiter's statement seemed a satisfying statement of Shakespeare's relationship to the ideas of his time our culture has developed an increasingly skeptical attitude toward the kind of order and authority which Shakespeare had been thought to espouse only shortly before. Indeed, by the early 1970s the tension that Rossiter noted between Elizabethan ideas of order and the statements the plays were making began to give way to a more radical skepticism which questions how seriously the Elizabethans (not to speak of their dramas) ever entertained these ideas. When Robert Ornstein, for instance, claims that the "Tudor myth system" was never taken seriously by Shakespeare's contemporaries, or when J. W. Lever writes that "the so-called 'chain of being' was in an advanced state of rust by the end of the sixteenth century,"[44] we recognize that within less than a generation the view of Elizabethan history and drama enunciated by Campbell and Tillyard has been turned into its opposite. The reality of the past is at best a slippery thing.

APPREHENDING REALITY

> ...can this cockpit hold
> The vasty fields of France? or may we cram
> Within this wooden O the very casques
> That did affright the air at Agincourt?
>
> *Henry V*, Prologue

Slippery though it may be, reality (above all, its relation to the theatrical illusion the audience is witnessing) has remained a traditional problem within historical plays, and, in fact, has often emerged as one of their central themes. The relation Shakespeare sets up in the lines quoted above takes the most simple form which a statement about illusion and reality can take: at the start of each act the Chorus comes forward to exhort the audience to accept the theatrical illusion as real.

> O, do but think
> You stand upon the rivage and behold
> A city on th' inconstant billows dancing....
>
> (III. Chorus. 13-15)
>
> Work, work your thoughts, and therein see a siege....
>
> (III. Chorus. 25)
>
> But now behold,
> In the quick forge and working-house of thought,
> How London doth pour out her citizens.
>
> (V. Chorus. 22-25)

As the Chorus works upon our collective imagination, the historical world of distant, past expeditions, battles, and homecomings gradually comes into focus and assumes a reality of its own — only to disappear temporarily as he returns to remind us of the illusory nature of the action and to exhort us once more to believe in the theatrical illusion. Shakespeare's insistence on maintaining an explicit distinction between illusion and reality is in one sense quite unnecessary, for anybody who bothers going to the theater surely knows that a play is just a play. To cite Dr. Johnson's famous defense of Shakespeare against those who held his "violation" of the unities against him—

> The truth is, that the spectators are always in their senses, and know, from the first act to the last, that the stage is only a stage, and that the players are only players.... An action must be in some place; but the different actions that compleat a story may be in places very remote from each other; and where is the absurdity of allowing that space to represent first Athens, and then Sicily, which was always known to be neither Sicily nor Athens, but a modern theatre.[45]

Johnson's statement, as one might expect, makes superb common sense, but it by no means exhausts the relationships our minds set up between drama and reality. For the notion of theatrical reality as an illusion is as thoroughly built into the history of drama as the notion of novelistic reality as an illusion has been an essential part of the history of fiction at least since *Don Quijote*. Within literature written since the Enlightenment, the problem has characteristically manifested itself in terms of the writer's self-consciousness, of his skepticism about the possibility of rendering external reality in adequate artistic terms. Thus, Schiller introduces the central historical action of *Wallenstein* with an elaborate series of devices which serve to keep the hero and his problems out of view, first by a lengthy prologue in which the poet addresses the audience and then by the curtain raiser, *Wallensteins Lager* (*Wallenstein's Camp*), which is virtually a play in its own right. "In jenes Krieges Mitte stellt euch jetzt / Der Dichter," Schiller writes in his prologue and then proceeds to guide us into the historical past in something of the manner of Shakespeare's Chorus in *Henry V*:

> Sechzehn Jahre der Verwüstung,
> Des Raubs, des Elends sind dahingeflohn,
> In trüben Massen gäret noch die Welt,
> Und keine Friedenshoffnung strahlt von fern.
> Ein Tummelplatz von Waffen ist das Reich,
> Verödet sind die Städte, Magdeburg
> Ist Schutt....[46]

It is as though a piling up of concrete detail about looting, weapons, and debris can conjure up a past whose existence an audience would otherwise be loath to accept.

Schiller proceeds with a long description of his hero but suddenly interrupts it with the reminder that Wallenstein will not even appear in the first night's play: "Nicht *er* ists, der auf dieser Bühne heut / Erscheinen wird." Instead, the audience is to see him first from a distance through the eyes of his followers:

> Doch in den kühnen Scharen,
> Die sein Befehl gewaltig lenkt, sein Geist
> Beseelt, wird euch sein Schattenbild begegnen,
> Bis ihn die scheue Muse selbst vor euch
> Zu stellen wagt in lebender Gestalt.... [47]

Schiller's image of the "shy muse" who waits before she "dare" bring forth the hero "in living form" is emblematic of the hesitation of the modern poet who holds back through fear that the reality he wishes to apprehend may elude him. Forgive the poet for delaying, he asks his audience:

> Darum verzeiht dem Dichter, wenn er euch
> Nicht raschen Schritts mit *einem* Mal ans Ziel
> Der Handlung reisst.... [48]

Before he can move to his main drama, he must first present a series of scenes of low life in which the great personages and events can be seen, as it were, from below. It is as though the poet can only gain a foothold on the "higher" political realities he will present if he focuses first on the "lower" realities of the peasants, hawkers, soldiers, and itinerants surrounding Wallenstein's camp. As far as the action of the main drama is concerned, *Wallensteins Lager* contributes little more than a picture of the loyalty that the hero's soldiers feel toward him; more important, however, the introductory play works to establish a concrete reality within which the more lofty sentiments of the main drama can take root. Written as it is in *Knittelvers*, that form of doggerel which automatically rings folk-like to the German ear, *Wallensteins Lager* contrasts sharply with the trilogy's two succeeding plays, both of which evoke an elevated world defined by the formal language of blank verse and an essentially classical structure.

I have deliberately cited the example of Schiller, for in his essay *Ueber naive und sentimentalische Dichtung* (*On Naive and Sentimental Poetry*), written in 1795, shortly before *Wallenstein*, Schiller provided the first great statement of a problem peculiar to the modern writer, namely his inability to apprehend reality (for which he used the characteristically eighteenth-century term "nature") with the directness of vision and the immediacy that many writers of the past such as Homer and Shakespeare possessed. Unlike the "naive" writers of the past (as well as Schiller's contemporary Goethe, whose successful example caused Schiller to speculate about his own dilemma), the modern or "sentimental" writer must employ a conscious effort of the will to render that reality which, he believes, came all too naturally to the naive writer. Although Schiller was writing specifically about the relation of a writer to the external world which he attempts to apprehend, his essay, by implication, extends to the relation of readers or audiences to the world which they see depicted.[49] If

16

a writer despairs of his ability to render a world adequately, he does so precisely because he fears his audience will lend neither its credulity nor its curiosity to the world he is creating. The self-consciousness of the modern writer is essentially a crisis of confidence—a fear, first, that an audience will refuse to suspend its disbelief in, let alone its indifference to, this imagined world, and, in its more radical form, a fear that no significant communication between author and public can take place at all. What Schiller, in his great theoretical essay, saw as a problem between the author and an external world out of which he shapes his creation has come to manifest itself as a problem between the author and an external world which he desperately hopes may be willing to accept his creation as credible, perhaps even (if he is fortunate) as significant.

Consider the problem of a writer today who sets out to write a play about, say, Savonarola. Even if his initial motive is his fascination with Florence in the late fifteenth century, he cannot count on a serious modern audience either to share this fascination or even to allow itself to be persuaded toward such a fascination. The presence of local historical color as a central object of interest was possible only in the nineteenth century, and even then much more appropriately in fiction than in drama. If immersion in history is doomed to leave an audience indifferent, the audience might at least be tricked into finding some interest in the character of the hero. But sympathy for Savonarola would be hard to summon up, unless the author shaped his material to present his hero as a martyr to an evil political machine; even then the author would be forced to deemphasize those characteristics of his hero which could not awaken a favorable modern response—his vituperations against luxury, for instance, or the traditional Christian terms within which he expressed his mission. Despairing in his search for a viable hero, the author could shift his center of interest to some issue which the audience might find relevant to contemporary needs. Thus, Florentine problems of the 1490s could be "translated" into some paradigm of political confrontation—between a callous ruling elite and a lower order seeking an adequate political voice, or, if one prefers a more specifically economic interpretation, between the affluence of the Medicis and the relative poverty of a deprived class.

But even if the play is centered around issues rather than characters, the author would quickly recognize that Savonarola's hell-fire-and-brimstone piety cannot be translated into political or economic terms without a violent and quite conspicuous distortion of what we normally consider historical fact. Thinking simply of character or issues is not enough to recreate the past within a present-day context. The dramatic convention within which the author works is even more fundamental than either character or issues in shaping his material. The only contemporary convention which seems generally viable for historical matters is Brechtian epic theater, which, with

17

its constant reminders to the audience not to lend too wholehearted a credence to the events depicted on stage, creates a kind of frame through which we can view the past from an unashamedly present-day vantage point. Indeed, Brecht's famous "alienation effect," whereby an audience is encouraged not to identify with the characters and actions it witnesses, provides the perfect accommodation between an author's and audience's desire for a "real" historical world and their desire to invest this world with contemporary meaning. Like the many other devices in post-Enlightenment literature that question the separation of fiction and reality (the "irony" cultivated by the German romantics, Pirandello's constant testing of dramatic illusion, not to speak of the countless novels and poems which purport to tell us about the process of writing novels and poems), the alienation effect is a means of coping with the problem of self-consciousness — not merely the self-consciousness of the author who fears the rejection of the fiction he is trying to present, but also that of the audience which feels inhibited about suspending its disbelief without some explicit coaxing or manipulation. Unless it is reminded, by some technique or other, that what it witnesses is illusory, a present-day audience could scarcely, in fact, be expected to display much interest in the characters or the action.

If written within the convention of the epic theater, a play about Savonarola could be created with a maximum of imaginative freedom: with his frank admission that he is writing from the point of view of the present, the author could shape his events within most any philosophy of history which might suit his needs. He might, for instance, interpret Savonarola's movement as a regression toward a static, medieval view of life, one that was "doomed" to fail because it rejected the "progressive" tendencies of Renaissance culture; or he might view this regression positively, as an assertion of certain "higher" values which the Florentine Renaissance had come to neglect. Or he might interpret the movement as progressive rather than regressive, and the heretic priest as a harbinger of the Reformation. Like Shaw's Saint Joan, Savonarola could thus play the role of one who was "tragically" born before his appropriate time; or he could be seen as foolish rather than tragic, a potential hero of progress who misused his historical opportunity by clothing his mission in theological rather than economic or social terms. One could even conceive of a play which would utilize all these theories and, in a veritable triumph of self-consciousness, attempt to explore how we go about making historical judgments and generalizations. It may well be, however, that at our present moment in history both author and audience have come to see the Brechtian mode as just another cliché, a convention which has outworn its potential to the point that self-consciousness will work to inhibit the very self-consciousness of its devices. Indeed, one could imagine a Savonarola play which is essentially a parody of these devices just as the play that Max Beerbohm inserted into the story of " 'Savonarola'

18

Brown" parodies the essential unself-consciousness inherent in the sublime style of the pseudo-Shakespearean historical dramas of the nineteenth century.[50]

The Brechtian mode, of course, has parody, if not necessarily self-parody, built into its very method. The parody is directed, among less specifically literary targets, at German classical dramas, especially those of Schiller, which for Brecht evoked the smugly held middle-class values of typical culture-hungry German theatergoers. Thus, *Die heilige Johanna der Schlacthöfe* (*Saint Joan of the Stockyards*) and *Arturo Ui*, are both written in a Schiller-like rhymed verse that at virtually every moment (no matter what social or economic matters are on the author's mind) calls our attention to the pomposities of an earlier theatrical mode which for Brecht did not have sufficient self-consciousness about itself. (It is a typical irony of German literary history that Germany's greatest modern dramatist should direct his attack at that earlier dramatist who provided the first powerful statement of the problem of self-consciousness in modern art.) The extremity of its parodistic impulse ultimately works to detract from, rather than enhance, the seriousness with which one can accept a play such as *Arturo Ui* as a vision of history. Throughout the play Brecht attempts to maintain four levels of historical reality: first, through the play's overt narrative, the Chicago gangster-world of the 1920s; second, through its language, the world of Goethe's and Schiller's plays and everything that their place in subsequent German culture suggests; third, through the structure of a number of individual scenes which it imitates, the world of Shakespeare's *Richard III*; and fourth, through the obvious allegorical meaning toward which all the levels are designed to point, the world of Adolf Hitler's rise to power and, even more fundamentally, the idea expressed by the play's full title, *Der aufhaltsame Aufstieg des Arturo Ui* (*The Resistible Rise of Arturo Ui*)—that recent German history might have been different if anybody had bothered to stop Hitler early enough.

As though vying with Brecht at the same time that he questioned his integrity, Günter Grass built his play *Die Plebejer proben den Aufstand* out of a similarly complicated network of historical perspectives: ancient Rome and Elizabethan London, as suggested by *Coriolanus*, the play-within-a-play which is being rehearsed in the course of Grass's play; the world of the early 1950s, suggested on one level by Brecht's adaptation of Shakespeare, with its Marxist lessons for the masses, and on another by the ideological rigidity which results in his refusal to shelter workers during the Berlin uprising; finally, the world of the 1960s, as portrayed through the indirect presence of the author, who, as everybody in the audience knows, is exhibiting his own literary and political pretensions while questioning those of his predecessor.[51] (Attacking one's literary fathers in the most blatant possible way has been traditional within the German cultural system.)

19

In theory, at least, the so-called documentary dramas of the 1960s (among which Grass's play is generally classified) should afford the closest approximation to historical reality conceivable in drama. These plays have usually concerned themselves with recent history — with persons and situations still existing within their audiences' living memory: the extermination camps of *Der Stellvertreter* and of Peter Weiss's *Die Ermittlung (The Investigation)*; the American political atmosphere in the plays about the Chicago and Catonsville trials. A writer who can depend on an audience's knowledge of what are virtually current events does not need to expend much effort on "exposition" or most of the traditional devices necessary to coax an audience into the world of the play: in documentary drama the problem of self-consciousness, from the point of view of both audience and author, should not exist at all. To the extent that many of these plays purport to be drawn from documents — the Heinar Kipphardt play from the transcripts of the Oppenheimer security-clearance hearing (*In der Sache J. Robert Oppenheimer — In the Matter of J. Robert Oppenheimer*), the Weiss play from those of the Frankfurt war-crimes trials of 1963-65 — the audience can be expected to think itself present at the reenactment of events whose proximity to reality it is willing to accept from the start. The accommodation of theatrical to historical reality would seem virtually complete in those reenactments of the Chicago Eight trial which were planned in 1970 to employ seven of the actual defendants as actors (since the eighth, Bobby Seale, was still in prison, his part was to be taken by his brother). Only one more step would be necessary to create a total fusion of theatrical and historical reality: arousing the consciousness of those who participate in the public world so that they see themselves playing roles on some great stage of history (those who have witnessed the history of recent years — for example, the spectacle of an American president secretly tape-recording events within the highest councils of government while he is himself a participant — may well have wondered if a significant demarcation line between theater and reality still exists).

Despite its pretensions about apprehending reality directly, documentary drama, like any form of drama, offers a very selective view of history. Indeed, the documentary plays of the 1960s are notable for the high degree of manipulation which their authors — or "arrangers" — have applied to the documents from which the plays are drawn. *Die Ermittlung*, despite the fact that its words are drawn from trial testimony, was originally shaped as an oratorio, which was to establish from the start the religious aura within which the play could be experienced. The carefully paired lawyers and witnesses in Kipphardt's play about the Oppenheimer case are conceived with an absoluteness and a symmetry which remind one of the virtues and vices in morality plays. Documentary plays are scarcely "dramatic literature" in the traditional sense (some which were much in the public mind while I was thinking out this book were quite forgotten by the time I got to my final

20

revisions).[52] Most, in fact, seem dead on the printed page, for they depend for their effects on their ability to establish a sense of community with their audiences. To cite an extreme example, the projected Chicago Eight play has been described in the following terms: "Each performance in each city is looked upon as a huge 'cell meeting' for the movement in that city."[53] The communal experience that emerges from performance has become the central goal of such drama; even Brecht, for all his attempts to achieve a powerful theatrical and political effect at once, seems very much a "literary" dramatist when compared to his documentary successors. Indeed, performances need not even be professional in any traditional sense, as one can conclude from the following advertisement in a radical newspaper:

> People's Actors Needed: Want to give People's acting a try? We're getting a play together on the Stanford Hospital struggle and the People's Medical Center in Redwood City. No acting experience necessary—just a Dare to Struggle attitude.[54]

Finally, one suspects, we reach the point of drama as therapy, as in that play-within-a-play about recent political history staged by the inmates of Charenton in Weiss's *Marat/Sade*. (Audiences, for that matter, are no longer essential to our conception of drama: in view of such contemporary phenomena as the "psychodrama" practiced in ordinary therapy, or the role-playing that popular psychiatric books tell us we constantly engage in, we are fast coming to define our everyday lives in dramatic terms; if drama once justified itself through its ability to imitate life, in certain contemporary contexts life justifies itself by the quality and intensity of its drama.)[55]

Rhetorically, documentary plays generally attempt to shame some character or group (Pius XII and Churchill in Hochhuth's plays, Judge Julius Hoffman in the various plays built around the Chicago conspiracy trial, the United States in Weiss's *Viet Nam Diskurs*, Stanford University in the play announced in the advertisement above) and/or to celebrate the victim or opponent of those who are being shamed; at the same time they try to shame or compliment the audience to the extent that the audience's sympathies have been faulty or correct. Structurally, documentary plays tend to take the form of trials—either actual trials, as in the plays on Oppenheimer and the extermination-camp personnel, or symbolic trials in which the audience is expected to serve as judge of whatever villains and/or martyrs the author has set up.

Trials have been a persistent element in the history of drama. One thinks of such "actual" trials as that of Orestes in *The Eumenides*, of Shylock, of Adam in Kleist's *Der zerbrochene Krug*, of Shaw's Joan, or of such essentially "trial-like" plays as *Oedipus Rex* and Strindberg's *To Damascus*. Indeed, one could speak of a natural affinity between drama and trials, an affinity that is in no way exhausted by such a journalistic cliché as "courtroom drama." A trial is, for one thing, an abstraction of reality in which issues become sharply dichotomized and reduced to essentials. Details which are not relevant to the central issues are ruthlessly expunged so that opposing forces may confront one another with an absoluteness that allows for no consideration of other viewpoints. Like a well-made play, a trial attempts to move unalterably toward the uncovering of some truth which, in one way or another, was hidden at the start. (The notion of a trial as a mode of action is suggested in those European languages which designate a trial with cognates of the English word "process.") In most of the great trial-plays of the past, despite the strongly antagonistic attitudes which are voiced throughout, the audience's sympathies are directed not to the espousal of a single side of the conflict but to a recognition of human complexity: Shylock, though he loses his case in Portia's court, has, after all, remained a considerable problem for the play's interpreters, while Kleist's Adam, though guilty in any legal sense, is, like his biblical namesake, situated ethically some place between good and evil. What starts as an attempt to uncover a single truth culminates in the insight that final positions are ultimately equivocal (indeed, not even final).

Yet the trial-like plays of the 1960s are notable for their refusal to argue for human complexity — which is only to say, of course, that they served as expressions of the political tensions within the Western world during that period. Despite the claims that documentary plays have made about their faithfulness to reality, their real intent and effect cannot be described in traditional mimetic terms. Rather than being "imitative" they often attempt to be explosive. "Putting Pius XII on stage at all is a highly charged act," Eric Bentley wrote of Der Stellvertreter, "and, so far from being illegitimate, a feeling of shock that he was put on stage is part of the game, and was on the cards from the beginning."[56] One could develop Bentley's observation to show that there is a difference in kind between the impersonation of "real" people and that of characters whom the audience recognizes to be fictional. If the situation in Hochhuth's play had been fictionalized and the recent pope transformed into an imaginary spiritual leader in some distant time and place, the play would surely have failed in that explosive effect which is its principal reason for being. An audience which knows that real historical personages are being represented on stage is willing not only to grant a high degree of credence to the events it sees, but it also allows itself to be worked upon with relative ease by the author's persuasiveness. (A potentially explosive dramatic situation greatly lessens the need for "good writing" — a fact that becomes quite evident to anyone who has tried to read a number of documentary plays.) Given its explosive intent, documentary drama quite naturally seeks out recent rather that more distant history: as long as he remains within an audience's living memory, a Lyndon Johnson or a Richard Nixon will retain a far greater explosive potential than a George Washington.

As the central (if also behind-the-scenes) figure of the televised Watergate hearings of 1973, Nixon far surpasses in public interest the various heroes, martyrs, and villains of documentary plays of the 1960s. Like the Joseph McCarthy hearings of 1954, the Watergate investigation would seem the "ultimate" in documentary drama. We not only witness real political personages who impersonate themselves, but their actions are also thoroughly improvisatory in nature, for they are busy making history in the very process of acting. Like much drama, such hearings are retrospective, for the "real" events—McCarthy's attempts to keep a favorite from being drafted by the Army, Nixon's presumed knowledge of, or collusion in, the Watergate burglary and its subsequent coverup—took place in a past whose exact nature the drama seeks to determine. And again, like much drama, these hearings employ the structural principle of the trial, though less rigorously (and thus more colorfully) than in actual court trials. During the drama itself neither the audience nor the actors can know the outcome—whether McCarthy or Nixon will be vindicated or thrown from power; indeed, one suspects that the outcome to some degree depends on the public opinion generated within the audience in the course of each hearing.

The relation of investigation to audience, as in much drama, is a complex one; there are, for instance, three audiences, each participating in and helping motivate the action in a different way: first, the "audience" of investigators who listen to and draw out each witness; second, the audience which is visible and audible within the hearing chamber and whose laughter and occasional applause serve as signals as to how the action is to be evaluated; and third, the vast audience of television watchers whose shifting allegiances to the actors are regularly sampled by the opinion polls. One could even postulate a fourth audience in the Watergate hearings, namely, Nixon himself, whose reactions while viewing the hearings—if he viewed them at all—are continually present within the imagination of the other three audiences. (If televised hearings such as these should become a permanent way of political life in our culture, they may well succeed in rendering all earlier modes of political and dramatic action, even documentary drama, obsolete.)

The documentary plays of the 1960s attempted not only to shock their audiences but also to inspire them, often, indeed, in the same play. In *Der Stellvertreter*, Pius XII may well, because of the shock effect he creates, be the most memorable character, but the example of Kurt Gerstein, the heroic young German who joined the SS to subvert the Nazi regime from within, is meant to provide the audience with a positive example they should emulate (or feel guilty about, at their inability to emulate). If the scientists and bureaucrats who attempt to remove Oppenheimer's security clearance are to horrify us at the lengths that America will go to oppress its dissenters, the

23

figure of Oppenheimer himself is designed to inspire us with the exemplary force characteristic of martyr plays since the Middle Ages. The inspirational power which the represented actions of great and famous men can exercise on an audience has long been used as a defense against those who (doubtless with some right) fear the disruptive power of the theater; thus, Thomas Heywood, in the same defense of the stage from which I quoted earlier, wrote:

> To turne our domesticke hystories, what English blood seeing the person of any bold English man presented and doth not hugge his fame, and hunnye at his valor, pursuing him in his enterprise with his best wishes, and as beeing wrapt in contemplation, offers to him in his hart all prosperous performance, as if the Personater were the man Personated, so bewitching a thing is liuely and well spirited action, that it hath power to new mold the harts of the spectators and fashion them to the shape of any noble and notable attempt.[57]

If Heywood were correct about the "bewitching power" in the impersonation of a great man, one might hope to see the world redeemed by theater.

But the representation of "real" situations, despite the power it can exert, in one sense is also a limiting factor on the effects which a dramatist can achieve. Whenever an audience is aware that it is watching real people and events on the stage, it remains conscious that what it experiences is essentially the reenactment rather than the enactment of an action. The historical past becomes a kind of closed book, one which is to be reenacted much as a religious ritual reenacts some hallowed myth. We retain a double view of the action, participating in its reality at the same time that we recognize its actors as "only" actors; the true reality is one which the representation can at best point to but never fully embody. (The open-endedness of televised political investigations such as the McCarthy-Army and the Watergate hearings has given us a special awareness that historical drama, even of a documentary kind, is at best a reenactment.) In a fictive action the only reality is the one enacted before us; the actor, instead of being "only" an actor, is much more likely to "become" the personage whom he claims to represent. Timothy J. Wiles, in a seminar paper, has written of the "tendency [of historical plays] to make their characters actors who reenact rather than act — they set up ideal and cyclic models which each new set of *dramatis personae* fulfill, rather than positing unique and undetermined histories with open futures which the characters can still effect." The closed character of the action creates a certain distance between the action and audience, at least to the extent that we know in advance the central points through which the action must progress and the goal toward which it must move. Our interest tends to shift from the *what* to the *how*: how, for instance, will author and actors approach the killing of Caesar, or how will they play on the image we already possess of a monstrous Richard III or Robespierre, or, for that matter, a heroic Henry V or Cid? How will they go about using materials we are already familiar with to shock or inspire us? And how will they succeed in winning the spectator so that, to echo the passage from Heywood above, the spectator will want to "offer to [the actor] in his hart all prosperous performance, as if the Personator were the man Personated"? The issues with which any well-known historical subject can deal are strictly limited by the audience's previous knowledge. Historical matter, in fact, restricts a writer's imaginative freedom even in those problems traditional to history plays. To introduce Octavius's or Antony's legitimacy of succession as a central problem in a play about Antony and Cleopatra would be to risk irrelevance, while to treat the Passion as Christ's neurotic rebellion against the social order would be to risk parody (though such parody is itself a dramatic subgenre, and, for that matter, a play of this sort is quite conceivable in our own day).

If documentary drama stands at one extreme in the bond it claims with actual historical occurrences, at the other extreme once can cite a type of play which is centrally concerned with historical issues without being based on any "real" history at all. I do not refer to any traditional or even readily definable genre, but to a particular way of approaching history which one can find in such a "fictional" work as Hofmannsthal's *Der Turm* (*The Tower*); one could, for lack of any known term, describe such a work as an "unhistorical history play." By freeing itself from the limitations imposed by a familiar historical action, a play of this sort can focus on the thematic content of history without bondage to the day-by-day political events which are the customary material of political plays. Some mythological plays have, in fact, been able to get at the central stuff of history more powerfully than many overtly historical dramas. Shelley created a more potent image of a political oppressor in the Jupiter of *Prometheus Unbound* than he did in the title character of his more conventional (though uncompleted) historical play, *Charles I*. In the final act of *Faust, Part 2*, the hero's destruction of a pastoral idyll in the name of economic and technological progress provides a model — as it took a Marxist critic such as Lukács to remind us[58] — of the conflict between the modern industrial world and the traditional culture which it has displaced. A writer can improvise upon a myth such as Prometheus or Faust with far greater imaginative ease than he can upon a well-known historical action.

In *Der Turm*, Hofmannsthal was able to accommodate within his fiction such themes traditional to historical drama as the growth and education of a ruler, the nature and continuity of power, and the threat of rebellion to established authority — yet in a manner that seems particularly relevant to the world of the early twentieth century. Hofmannsthal's play is the dramatic equivalent of works such as *The Waste Land* and *Ulysses*, both of which, with a similar comprehensiveness of scope, employ older myths which, to use Eliot's words in his review of Joyce's book, provide "a way of controlling, of

25

ordering, of giving a shape and a significance to the immense panorama of futility and anarchy which is contemporary history."[59] Indeed, in writing years later about *Der Turm*, Eliot spoke of Hofmannsthal's "loading this play, in symbolism which perhaps has more than one level of significance, with all the burden of his [Hofmannsthal's] feelings about the catastrophe of the Europe to which he belonged, the Europe which went down in the wreck of empires between 1914 and 1918."[60] Despite all its obvious contemporary relevance, *Der Turm* is set in a deliberately archaic world (a seventeenth-century Poland that seems more mythical than historical) which, with its central plot situation—the sudden maturing of a ruler who had spent his youth imprisoned in a tower in animal-like isolation—is borrowed from Calderón's *La vida es sueño* (*Life Is a Dream*). The contemporary meanings, in fact, emerge with all the more clarity through the archaic setting, with its age-old hierarchies and its rule by divine right: it is as though Hofmannsthal's deeply conservative concerns could find their most appropriate expression when translated into an overtly fictional form without the intrusion of those distracting facts which might compromise either the absoluteness or the complexity of his vision. Moreover, by improvising on an old fiction, Hofmannsthal could manipulate his view of history according to the dictates of his experience: in the play's earlier version (1925), he was able to temper his disillusionment with a measure of apocalyptic hope, while in the final version (1927), he voiced an equally apocalyptic sense of doom.

The contemporary reality which the play attempts to express is less properly a historical than an ideological reality, one which stands at an opposite extreme, for instance, from that of another great "unhistorical history play" of our time, Brecht's *Mutter Courage*. Like *Der Turm*, Brecht's play is based on a seventeenth-century fiction, one which provides it more with a concrete historical milieu than with the kind of history centered around famous personages and public events. With its leftist bias *Mutter Courage* deliberately turns its back on that conception of history which attributes the highest significance to the doings of the great; as the heroine puts it when she hears General Tilly's funeral described as a "historical moment," "For me, it's a historical moment that they've wounded my daughter in the forehead."[61]

Standing though they do at opposite ends of the political spectrum, *Der Turm* and *Mutter Courage* both present heroes who are to serve as representative portraits of humanity: Sigismund, the visionary whose downfall signifies the fragility of good in a permanently evil world; Mother Courage, the mean and grasping vendor whose callousness in her desperate attempt to survive is meant to tell us that an economic change could create a better human being. Whereas the conservative play is essentially elegiac, telling its readers, in effect, to join in mourning for a lost world (and also to defend what little is left of its values), the radical play exhorts its readers and audiences to look closely at the capitalist system it is depicting (though in seventeenth-century

26

dress) and then go out and change the system. And if *Der Turm*, especially in its second version, places its faith in the power of the human spirit regardless, even in spite of, a devouring historical process, *Mutter Courage* denies such spiritual values and places its faith in the possibility of an economic order which does not reduce the human being to a predatory struggle (like that of the heroine) for survival. If I confess myself to be equally — and powerfully — moved by both plays, I recognize that my response relegates me to the political limbo of the uncommitted (though it may also indicate my distance in time from the world of the twenties and thirties). Yet the sharp ideological gap which separates these two plays can help remind us that the historical vision which each of them propounds is itself a fiction which the reader can experience like any other. Through the high valuation which we have learned to place on complexity and ambivalence in our reading of fictions during the last generation, we automatically try to read highly charged ideological works from an aesthetic rather than a political point of view; as I shall argue in more detail in a later chapter, history has achieved the status of an imaginative as well as an actual place for us.

Yet one can easily demonstrate a consciousness of the fictive quality of history within the texts of many historical dramas. Reinhold Grimm, in a recent study of plays about revolution from *Dantons Tod* to *Marat/Sade*, has described "the structure of a play-within-a-play and the dialectic of theater and reality" as central to these plays.[62] If *Marat/Sade* quite specifically takes the form of a play-within-a-play in which a moment of recent history is reenacted, *Dantons Tod*, despite its apparently straightforward realism, is full of talk about theater, games, and role-playing. Such talk is, of course, to be expected in any serious narrative about revolution, if only because in revolutions, as in other tense political situations, persons do not communicate their most intimate selves but resort instead to theatrical gestures and the more ostentatious forms of rhetoric to achieve their ends. The writer who desires to face his material honestly is forced to note the discrepancies between a character's political and authentic self, or between an "official" and a "real" view of a political event. Theater thus becomes a metaphor for those aspects of character and action that deviate from the more "normal" or at least less agitated aspects.

But theater as a metaphor within drama goes well beyond plays about revolution. In the quotation from *Henry V* which stands at the head of this section Shakespeare admits the illusory nature of his play as a means of establishing the "reality" of the events he wishes to portray; the theatrical metaphor, at least from a modern point of view, becomes a way of overcoming self-consciousness. In *Richard III* Shakespeare assigns to the title character the multiple roles of playwright, stage manager, and intermediary between the audience and the play; from his opening soliloquy, Richard takes us into his confidence and, in effect, works in collusion with us to stage the bloody events out of which the play is built. Not only does the relationship he establishes with us make these events (as well as Richard himself) plausible, but they cause us to see the play from an unexpected and special angle, one which, by virtue of the fact that we have temporarily joined forces with a character whom we know from the start to be morally reprehensible, forces us to reexamine our conventional ways of looking at reality.

The theatrical metaphors with which *Richard II* is suffused work not only to "expose" the king's histrionics, they also help him regain a measure of sympathy from the audience. Though we recognize the playacting in which he engages in his great speeches for what it is, through our very act of recognition our critical faculties are satisfied, and we can allow ourselves to share something of the pity he lavishes upon himself. "Thus play I in one person many people, / And none contented" (V.v.31–32), he tells us in the last and most reflective of his soliloquies, by which time he has come to see the uselessness of the roles he had tried out earlier. As we watch him assume his final role, that of "being nothing" (V.v.41), we recognize that a theatrical role is a poor but at least dignified substitute for a role in the "real" world. Similarly with Racine's Bérénice, who, after her rejection by Titus, takes her leave in the play's next-to-last lines with a thoroughly theatrical flourish:

> Adieu: servons tous trois d'exemple à l'univers
> De l'amour la plus tendre et la plus malheureuse
> Dont il puisse garder l'histoire douloureuse.
>   Tout est prêt. On m'attend. Ne suivez point mes pas.
>   Pour la dernière fois, adieu, Seigneur.[63]

As actress, she runs the gamut from the grand, impersonal rhetoric of the first three lines to the feigned urgency (with its clipped, conversation-like sentences) of the fourth line. Having been robbed of an active role in the historical world, she consoles herself by viewing herself retrospectively as a character in history. (Only Antiochus, with his famous "Hélas!" which ends the play, is fully taken in by her theater-making.) When Shakespeare's Cleopatra expresses her horror at seeing her story enacted upon the Roman stage ("and I shall see / Some squeaking Cleopatra boy my greatness / I' the posture of a whore" — V.ii.218-220), she (or at least her author) is implicitly commenting on the attitudinizing in which she (or at least the boy who is playing her role) has engaged throughout the play — and, in fact, is about to resume in her death scene.

Theater and theatricality are of course the natural themes through which a play can express its consciousness of itself. In much the same way, novels habitually discourse about other books, as in a succession of novels from *Don Quijote* to *Les Faux-Monnayeurs* (and a multitude of successors), and poems can talk about poetry and the idea of a poem, as in a succession of poems from the *Eclogues* to the work of Wallace Stevens. One of the explicit conventions of the classical epic is the relation of the individual poem to the tradition as a whole. Every genre can turn back upon itself as a means of escaping the simplemindedness which ultimately destroys one's belief in the illusions which art creates. Illusions must constantly be tested or broken in order to reassert and sustain themselves. What one might call "generic self-consciousness" is one of a number of rhetorical instruments which an artist employs to give an appropriate complexity and resonance to the human materials which he takes it upon himself to work. The self-consciousness which Schiller saw as the dilemma of the modern artist is perhaps only a special instance of the self-consciousness which feeds on great art at all times. (It is significant, I think, that Schiller was unable to restrict his discussion of the problem to modern artists, but pointed to Euripides, Horace, and Milton as examples of "sentimental" as against "naive" artists.)[64]

If the idea of theater and theatricality has been particularly relevant to historical drama, it has also enjoyed a peculiar affinity with the writing of history itself. When history becomes self-conscious of itself, it often expresses itself in theatrical terms. Stanley Cavell, in a brilliant exploration of the nature of theatrical representation, has written of "the all but inescapable temptation to think of the past in terms of theater. (For a while I kept a list of the times I read that some past war or revolution was a great drama or that some historical figure was a tragic character on the stage of history. But the list got too long.)"[65] Behind all Cavell's examples there stands the great traditional figure of the *theatrum mundi*, which in the long list of instances which Ernst Robert Curtius gives from Plato to Hofmannsthal,[66] has proved itself one of the most imaginatively potent images in Western culture. When history invokes theater, it can, like Richard II or Bérénice, console itself, elevate itself, assert its essential dignity in the face of those who would suggest its meaninglessness. To the extent that continuity and progression are of the essence in Hegel's philosophy of history, the theater, with its sustained plotting within a specified site, provides an ideal image for his portrayal of historical development; thus Hegel can write of "the theater—that of world history—in which we observe spirit in its most concrete reality."[67] It is no accident, moreover, that the word "collision" ("Kollision"), which figures so prominently in Hegel's theory of tragedy (as in the "collision" of Antigone and Creon) is also used to describe the conflicts which take place in the historical process itself.[68] The philosopher of history views and reflects upon the spectacle of history much as an audience views and experiences a theatrical spectacle.[69] The dramatizations of history found in Hegel and other philosophers of history are only a more lofty and spun-out version of the journalistic clichés which Cavell finally gave up trying to list. But the theatrical analogy in historical writing can work in two ways: though it purports to give dignity and animation to history, as well as to assert its continuities, by its very nature it also suggests the ultimate disparagement—that history reveals itself *merely* (though also movingly) as theater.

TWO

HISTORY AND THE STRUCTURE
OF DRAMATIC ACTION

CONSPIRACY PLAYS

When we have feared three years we know not what,
Till witnesses begin to die o' th' rot,
What made our poet meddle with a plot?
Otway's Venice Preserved, Prologue

There's a mighty plot afoot.
Arthur Miller's The Crucible

When Dryden claimed that the Popish Plot engineered by Titus Oates in 1678 had swallowed up all the lesser plots of the stage, he was suggesting a connection between politics and art with a wider applicability than he may have suspected.[1] For conspiracies provide the central fable shaping the vast majority of historical dramas. The close relation between conspiracy and dramatic plot is perhaps at its most obvious in Ben Jonson's two historical tragedies, *Sejanus* and *Catiline*, for only the thinnest of generic lines separates the conspiracies central to these plays from the plotting that goes on in Jonson's comedies. Thus, like the servant Mosca in *Volpone*, Sejanus, the emperor Tiberius's favorite, plots against all who stand in the way of his power — against a succession of victims as well as against his master, who, as it turns out, ultimately learns of the plot against him and turns the tables on his servant. When Sejanus's victims describe themselves as "prey to greedy vultures and vile spies,"[2] we recognize the essential affinity between the worlds of Jonsonian tragedy and comedy. Yet in this affinity we also recognize our dissatisfaction with his tragedies, for Jonson's plotters are conceived with such spirited brashness that we find it difficult to grant their distinctly unspirited victims the sympathy which Jonson intended for them.

In comedy we expect the artifice of plot and, in fact, often reserve our highest admiration for works such as *Twelfth Night* and *The Alchemist* which, in their varying ways, display their artifice with a maximum of virtuosity. In historical drama (and in Renaissance tragedy, which in its basic premise claimed to be historical) we accept conspiracy as a central device because the play, after all, purports to be telling what actually happened. Conspiracy, moreover, is that aspect of the historical process which most readily lends itself to dramatic treatment. The subtle pressures that are constantly brought on rulers, the time-consuming tasks of effecting compromises among dissident parties, the everyday paper work necessary to keep a government going — these do not make for the striking dramatic effect which a writer can achieve by presenting a group of conspirators (like those, say, in Brutus's garden at night) who meet to plot the overthrow of a regime. Drama is less concerned with the continuities of history than with its disruptions. The two to four hours which encompass the performance of a play do not, like the dozen or more hours which a reader puts into a novel, allow much dwelling on local historical color. Since drama, by its nature, must at least pretend to be moving toward some discernible goal, conspiracies provide a kind of metaphor for the dramatic action within the historical process.

A conspiracy does not simply depict a historical moment; rather, it creates the means by which one group clashes, or resolves its differences, with another group. Most of the great historical dramas are centrally concerned either with the transfer of power from one force to another (for example, *Richard II* and Grillparzer's *König Ottokars Glück und Ende*) or with the means by which a force already in power manages to stabilize itself against the onslaught of contending forces (*Henry IV*, *Dantons Tod*). The ideal situation for a play about conspiracy is a regime that shows one or more weaknesses which could prove fatal to its continuance — a regime characterized, for instance, by its ineptness (*Richard II*), fears about its legitimacy or security (*Richard III*, *Egmont*), or a display of tyranny which awakens an "idealistic" challenge from its subjects (*Julius Caesar, Cinna*). Conspiracy can best be dramatized in situations where both the ruling authority and its opponents are visible to the audience; thus, monarchies, dictatorships, and oligarchies (for instance, those of Venice or late republican Rome) lend themselves much more readily to conspiracy plays than does a modern democracy. Although the concept of conspiracy is often enough applied to the shifts of power that take place within a democracy, the relatively wide distribution of power within a democratic government, as well as the layers of authority through which pressure against the government must be brought to bear, makes it difficult to create sufficiently dramatic confrontations between conspirators and their opponents. Conspiracy in democratic cultures is dramatically viable only at times of emergency — like those depicted in Miller's *The Crucible* and Kipphardt's *In der Sache J. Robert Oppenheimer* — when the community reaches the point of paranoia about dissidents plotting its overthrow.

Conspiracy plays have flourished best in those earlier periods which conceived of history as essentially the story of rulers — their rise, their fall, and their attempts to hold power in the face of various challenges. One need merely leaf through those historians — Holinshed, Plutarch, Tacitus, the Abbé de Saint-Réal — who supplied the materials for the major historical dramas to recognize to what a high degree each narrative consists of a string of conspiracies. If scholars have often marveled at the extent to which

31

Shakespeare followed his historical sources, this is only to say that the content of these sources consorted well with the dramatic forms which Shakespeare was developing. The multitude of conspiracies which Shakespeare found in Holinshed provided him a way of achieving at least the outward means of unity within individual plays. Although his larger concerns in *Henry IV* go considerably beyond the conspiracies he depicts, the two plays are centrally organized around a series of threats to Henry's right to hold the throne. *Richard III* and *Henry VIII* are built out of a succession of conspiracies (as often imaginary as real) which these monarchs, or their henchmen, use to consolidate their rule. *King John* and *Henry V*, in turn, are directed less to internal than to external conspiracies against the English monarchy. By choosing to write about kings who were either ineffectual or whose legitimacy was suspect, Shakespeare obviously had ready-made situations for conspiracy. From the point of view of a ruler trying to stabilize a shaky regime, any challenge, whether real or potential, will smack of conspiracy.

Moreover, in drama as in life, those who look for conspiracies can find them almost anywhere; by the same token, one conspiracy awakens reciprocal action from those who feel themselves conspired against. Thus, conspiracy plays often show two conspiracies moving against one another. A classic instance is *Wallenstein*, whose hero, while laying the groundwork for possible conspiracy against the Austrian emperor, finds himself overwhelmed by a counterconspiracy directed by those of his men who remain loyal to the emperor. A tyrant such as Richard III conspires with his henchmen against all those he thinks might conspire against him. Jonson's Catiline claims that his conspiracy was motivated by the Senate's plotting against his advancement, while the Senate, in turn, is forced to act conspiratorially against Catiline's threat. In *The Crucible*, with its multiplicity both of authority figures and victims, each side experiences the fear of mass conspiracy directed against itself. More than any other literary genre, drama lends itself to projecting the mutual fears and antagonisms of forces which are pitted against one another; the dramatist chooses conspiracy situations from history not so much, one suspects, for their own sake as for the opportunities they give him to represent the clashing of these forces. Since the audience in the theater is constantly aware of the physical absence of those being plotted against, the dramatist also has the opportunity of bringing the audience into collusion, as it were, with the conspirators, whose secrets the audience comes to share. In the development of its dramatic action the conspiracy typically moves through a succession of stages: first, the audience, but not the intended victim, knows of the conspiracy; second, the victim learns of the plot and initiates a counterplot, of which the audience, but not the original conspirators, becomes aware; third, the contending parties come to share each other's knowledge as they clash and bring the conflict to some sort of resolution. Like the "real" events they reenact, the actions of conspiracy plays easily assume predictable patterns.

As a form of symbolic action, conspiracy is of course deeply rooted in Christian tradition. Although the word "conspiracy" does not always occur in the titles of conspiracy plays, a play entitled simply *The Conspiracy*, in which Judas sells Christ for thirty pence, appears in several versions of the English Corpus Christi cycle. Morality plays can be called conspiracy plays in the sense that the devil, the bad angels, and the various allegorized sins band together to tempt man from God's path. And behind all conspiracies there stands that archetypal conspiracy which brought about man's fall. Within the larger providential view of history which gives shape to Shakespeare's English historical cycle, the many individual conspiracies distantly echo the paradox of the fortunate fall: though they temporarily plunge England into chaos, they ultimately contribute to the new order instituted by the Tudors. When we look at the story of the fall as it appears in medieval drama, we find a conspiracy situation in its simplest form, one which suggests at least two closely related features of secular conspiracy plays—first, that a conspiracy must involve more than a single character (Satan, after all, does not approach Adam directly but only through Eve's mediation) and, second, that these characters are related to one another dramatically as tempter and convert. A colorful event such as Charlotte Corday's assassination of Marat would scarcely seem suited to a conspiracy play, for the whole point of her action was that she did it alone; only in a self-conscious contemporary work such as Weiss's *Marat/Sade*, which subjects her doings to elaborate parody, can her act be developed into a full-length drama.

Within secular drama the relation of temptation to conspiracy is perhaps most beautifully realized in that model of conspiracy plays, *Julius Caesar*. In the course of less than two hundred lines during the play's second scene, Cassius succeeds in rousing Brutus out of his lethargy and tempting him to the point where he has all but resolved upon his conspiracy. In such lines as these—

> Brutus, I do observe you now of late:
> I have not from your eyes that gentleness
> And show of love as I was wont to have.

(I.ii.31–33)

we recognize the traditional insinuations of the tempter, who plays mercilessly on his victim's particular propensities to convert him to his desired end. When Brutus later asks Cassius,

> Into what dangers would you lead me, Cassius,
> That you would have me seek into myself
> For that which is not in me?

(62–64)

33

he shows himself at that stage of the temptation process where, though conscious that he is entering dangerous territory, he thinks he is standing his ground far more firmly than we recognize him to be. In Cassius's reply—

> And since you know you cannot see yourself
> So well as by reflection, I, your glass,
> Will modestly discover to yourself
> That of yourself which you yet know not of.
>
> (66-69)

we are aware that, long before Brutus has worked out his actual plot in his mind, the tempter has achieved effective control of his victim. When Brutus has left the stage, the words of Cassius's soliloquy, "For who so firm that cannot be seduc'd?" (309) fully confirms the nature of the process we have been witnessing. Cassius's temptation of Brutus is a kind of rehearsal for that later scene of Shakespeare's in which Iago effects his conversion of Othello during a dialogue which can be played on the stage in little more than a quarter hour's time. What separates the two scenes is, of course, the larger historical perspective that stands behind *Julius Caesar*: as in the miracle plays, we are aware that all subsequent human history is at stake. In both scenes, however, temptation emerges essentially as a triumph of rhetoric, one in which the tempter employs all the means of persuasion at his command to realize those hidden potentialities in his victim that will achieve his own, clearly foreseen, end.

Julius Caesar could, in fact, be described as a play about the uses of rhetoric, for it is through rhetoric that all the central turns in the play's action are brought about—not only in Cassius's temptation of Brutus, but in Brutus's convincing himself and his fellow conspirators of both his own integrity and that of their common cause, and, even more memorably, in Brutus's rhetorical failure to hold the Roman crowd in the face of Antony's rhetorical success. It is as though historical changes are less a consequence of real issues than of the ability of leaders to manipulate others by means of language. History plays (and conspiracy plays in particular) tend to be notoriously rhetorical in nature. Persuasiveness, one could say, is a necessary complement to conspiracy: after all, one's prospective conspirators must be persuaded that a cause is worthy; the main conspirator, in soliloquy, has to keep reassuring himself, as well as the audience, that he is doing the right thing; potential opponents must be tricked into forestalling any attempt to prevent or undo the conspiracy; and (at least outside the classical tradition in drama) the crowds in the streets have to be persuaded to give their loyalty to one side or the other.

If *Julius Caesar* is preeminent among conspiracy plays for its exposure of the rhetorical basis of political action, it also stands at the head of a tradition which one might term the tragedy of the "tainted idealist." In a whole line of conspiracy plays which includes such works as *Venice Preserved*, Schiller's

34

Don Carlos, Byron's *Marino Faliero*, and Musset's *Lorenzaccio*, the idealism of the conspirator becomes questioned in the course of the play, with the result that those large abstractions which he voices — liberty, republicanism, justice, tyranny, and the like — are subjected to the audience's critical examination. In *Marino Faliero*, to take a rather bookish example, every conspirator who gains our sympathy is carefully endowed with some fatal flaw, that of the hero being described as a "quick sense of honour which becomes / . . . a vice / When overstrain'd."[3] It is noteworthy that Shakespeare, as though to achieve just the right balance of taintedness and idealism in his chief conspirator, portrayed Brutus somewhat less favorably than he found him in Plutarch.

But one might also note that as soon as a writer engages a character in a conspiracy, he is faced with the problem that conspiracy, by its very nature, is a dirty business. Shakespeare made the most of his opportunities with Henry IV, who, though not by any means an idealist, at least turned out to be a wise ruler, yet one whose reign was forever tainted by his usurpation of the throne. Shakespeare faced a special problem in treating the conspiracy of the Earl of Richmond against Richard III, for his larger historical framework (or at least the political authorities) would obviously not allow him to besmirch the character of the first Tudor king; though critics have been brooding about the problem ever since, Shakespeare at least was able to skirt it by surrounding Richmond with a maximum of ritual and giving him a minimum of characterization. A tainted conspirator retains at least a semblance of his dignity, though not necessarily his honor, when, like Brutus, he attempts to implement his ideals by outright physical violence rather than by petty intrigue.

A dramatist writing in the classical tradition, with its demands for temporal and spatial compression, often has to work hard to keep from compromising our image of a conspirator-hero whose only means of action is a clockwork plot executed within the constricting confines of the seat of power. Outwitting the monarch's private guard is scarcely an appropriate occupation for a noble mind. This, I suspect, is at the root of our problem with *Don Carlos*, whose chief conspirator, the Marquis Posa, though a lofty spokesman for the ideals of the Enlightenment, is constantly lowered in our eyes by the palace intrigues — deceptive letters, a planned abduction, and the like — to which he is forced in order to execute his (and the drama's) plot. Corneille and Racine, one might add, generally avoid confusing the role of conspirator with characters with whom we are meant to sympathize; in Corneille's *Cinna*, for example, both the title character and his antagonist, the Emperor Augustus, have sworn off plotting when we reach those points in the play where we are meant to take their ideals seriously.

Since conspiracy by its very nature works to degrade an otherwise worthy hero, dramatists (or at least their characters) have often found ingenious ways of ennobling conspiratorial actions. Shakespeare's Brutus does not rest

35

satisfied with assertions of his integrity but asks us to view his action as a ritual sacrifice. As one reads through various conspiracy plays from *Cinna* down to Strindberg's *Gustav III*, one notes, in turn, how regularly conspirators have cited Brutus's example as a means of ennobling themselves. Invoking Brutus, whether Shakespeare's or the real-life one, is almost an essential part of the rhetoric of a conspiracy play. In situations of abrupt and violent change, the invocation of earlier revolutionary acts which have already been assimilated — especially if the analogy is clothed in noble language — serves as a way of asserting the continuities of history, of giving a venerable cover to bloody actions. Revolution becomes a way of restoring an ideal past which was somehow disrupted. Corneille's Emilie helps Cinna work up his resolve with a lofty declamation:

> Regarde le malheur de Brute et de Cassie:
> La splendeur de leurs noms en est-elle obscurcie?
> Sont-ils morts tous entiers avec leurs grands desseins?
> Ne les compte-t-on plus pour les derniers Romains?
> Leur mémoire dans Rome est encor précieuse,
> Autant que de César la vie est odieuse.[4]

Shakespeare, in need of an appropriate analogy for Cassius to use in tempting his victim, invokes Brutus's ancestor Junius Brutus:

> O, you and I have heard our fathers say,
> There was a Brutus once that would have brook'd
> Th' eternal devil to keep his state in Rome
> As easily as a king.
>
> (I.ii.156-59)

Although dramatists who wish to stress the idealism of their conspirators normally invoke Brutus (whether the earlier or the later Roman one), those who stress their scoundrel-like qualities tend to liken them to Catiline. *Venice Preserved* carefully distinguishes between its two kinds of conspirators, the Brutus-like Pierre and the Catiline-like Renault. Analogy serves here above all as a form of rationalization:

> Pierre: Friends! was not Brutus,
> (I mean that Brutus, who in open Senate
> Stabbed the first Caesar that usurped the world)
> A gallant man?
> Renault: Yes, and Catiline too,
> Though story wrong his fame, for he conspired
> To prop the reeling glory of his country;
> His cause was good.[5]

From the standpoint of an audience's sympathies, the great conspiracy plays characteristically thrive on ambivalence. Whether about tainted idealists such as Brutus, or noble opportunists such as Bolingbroke or Wallenstein, they play on the spectator's ability to shift his attitude between the extremes of sympathy and condemnation, sometimes, in fact, to fuse both extremes in what modern critics have been wont to praise as a "complexity of response" to the action. There are, of course, simpler forms of the conspiracy play which demand a quite uncomplicated response: nobody could conceive of anything but loathing for the Herod of the mystery plays. But the conspiracy play, by and large, forces the audience to find a middle ground between the opposing sides. The major conspiracy plays do not inspire us to pursue either action or revolution but rather set us at something of a remove from the world of action; through our ambivalence of response we often feel we are experiencing not merely our own complexity of attitude but also the complexities of history itself. When commitment to the forces on either side of a conflict seems impossible, one's only recourse is to sit back and comment upon the difficulties of resolving the issues which divide men. The emotions one directs to the characters on stage are often a fusion of irreconcilable attitudes — admiration for a man's idealism, yet despair at his egotism; respect for a ruler's authority, yet impatience with the manner in which he exercises his authority. A similar ambivalence of attitude is directed toward the processes of history one is witnessing — regret and relief at the passing of an old order, exhilaration and terror at the coming of the new. Whatever the political affiliations of their authors, conspiracy plays, in the effect they exercise on the audience, have a way of directing the spectator toward a political middle ground — not because of any positive values in this middle ground, but because the extremes on both sides turn out to be sorely wanting.[6] In times of crisis, of course, no play can guarantee to be middle-of-the-road. Despite the web of ambiguities which qualify the actions of the opposing sides in *Richard II*, the play could scarcely have had a moderating effect when it was revived during the Essex uprising in 1601. The expectations a history play evokes often lie as much in what people feel about its essential subject matter as in what the text is actually saying.

Yet a dramatist can also use an audience's expectations about conspiracy plays to achieve insights which, in the long run, have little to do with conspiracies as such. In *Wallenstein* neither the worth of the established authority (that is, the emperor) nor the worth of the conspirators' cause is really the central issue; rather, Schiller uses the form of the conspiracy play as a means of questioning the control which men can exercise over their destinies. His aims, one might say, are ultimately metaphysical. In *Cinna* the conspiracy is stifled in the middle, the conspirators won over by the authority, and their energies transformed to higher uses; the audience is gradually led to view conspiracy as an unsatisfactory means of establishing a human community. In *Dantons Tod* the hero is executed for a conspiracy which he never organized at all and which he would have been too bored to lead even if he had believed in it; with characteristically modern insight, the play uses conspiracy to attack the public world for its oppressiveness and meaning-lessness.

Among conspiracy plays one can distinguish a particular form which might be called the pretender play, and whose most distinguished examples are Ford's *Perkin Warbeck* and the Demetrius-Boris Godounov dramas of Schiller and Pushkin. The fact that Schiller wavered for a while between writing about Warbeck or Demetrius suggests that he was not so much interested in presenting the history of a particular man, period, or nation as in exploiting the possibilities inherent in the situation of a pretender.[7] Every pretender play, in one way or another, exploits the uncertainties surrounding the pretender's real identity. Schiller's hero is certain of his legitimate right to the throne but later (at least from what we know about the author's plans to complete his fragment) learns he is simply an impersonator; Ford's remains heroically certain to the end, though many of his followers have their doubts. Pushkin's pretender is a conscious impersonator from the start, but his uprising, which his coconspirators cynically use for their own political ends, awakens the guilt of his antagonist, the usurper Boris Godounov, whose wavering sense of reality gives the play a magnificently tragic dimension. Ibsen contrasts the two rival kings in *The Pretenders* (a fine early play based on medieval Norwegian history) by virtue of their varying degrees of self-confidence: it is as though a healthy sense of self, he implies, can determine one's legitimacy to the throne.

From the standpoint of that most sophisticated of modern pretender plays, Pirandello's *Enrico IV*, one is easily tempted to read the problem of illusion and reality into all the earlier examples of the genre;[8] in *Enrico IV* the psychological and epistemological are at the center of our interest, while what little history the play is concerned with is something that has no substantial existence of its own but is only a fiction within the protagonist's crazed mind. Pretending to rule becomes a metaphor for the pretense involved in the very act of making theater; the "real" actions which earlier history plays could take for granted dissolve into that larger epistemological questioning which the literature of our century has assumed as a central burden. In an age when writers and audiences question the possibility of apprehending historical reality on the stage, pretense as a metaphor (whether the pretense of a man who claims the right to rule, or the pretense of imaginary conspiratorial plots in one's midst) offers a way of mediating between a private inner world whose primacy remains unquestioned and a public world which must be grasped with uncertainty if it is to be grasped at all.

TYRANT AND MARTYR PLAYS

Maximin: Go, bind her hand and foot beneath that Wheel:
Four of you turn the dreadful Engine round;

38

> Four others hold her fast'ned to the ground:
> That by degrees her tender breasts may feel,
> First the rough razings of the pointed steel:
> Her Paps then let the bearded Tenters stake,
> And on each hook a gory Gobbet take;
> Till th' upper flesh by piece-meal torn away,
> Her beating heart shall to the Sun display....
> Catharine: No streak of blood (the reliques of the Earth)
> Shall stain my Soul in her immortal birth;
> But she shall mount all pure, a white, and
> Virgin mind;
> And full of all that peace, which there she
> goes to find.

> Spoken by the tyrant and the martyr,
> respectively, in Dryden's *Tyrannick Love*

The roles of tyrant and martyr are natural accompaniments to conspiracy plays. A conspirator needs to feel that the force he is overthrowing is tyrannical, yet once the tyrant has been toppled the latter can all too easily assume the attributes of martyrdom. Shakespeare's Caesar is assigned a tyrant role for the first half of the play, but almost as soon as he is dead he emerges as something of a martyr. Roles are forced upon characters according to the circumstances surrounding them. Although Shakespeare goes to great lengths to provide "rounded" portraits of his two antagonists in *Richard II*, Richard's role inevitably shifts from tyrant to martyr as his power wanes, while Bolingbroke's goes in precisely the opposite direction. Tyrant and martyr, of course, are much too absolute terms for a work which cultivates the subtle shading of its characters; rather, Richard's conduct as tyrant shows itself to be the tyrannical behavior of a weak and passive man, while his martyrdom turns out to have a large component of what was once popularly called a martyr complex (it is significant, however, that those who oppose the House of Lancaster in Shakespeare's later historical plays invoke Richard's martyrdom whenever it suits their political purposes).

If conspiracy plays tend to push certain of their characters into tyrant and martyr roles, those plays that are centered around tyrants and martyrs often depend on conspiracies to bring about the necessary shifts in power relationships. Tyrant plays such as *Richard III* or Grillparzer's *König Ottokars Glück und Ende* are generally full of real or imagined conspiracies which their heroes need to put down to maintain their power. The heroes of martyr plays are usually unsuccessful conspirators, or the victims of conspiracy, or something in between, like Gryphius's Charles I or Schiller's Mary Stuart, who prepare themselves for martyrdom after the failure of the conspiracies which their admirers had hoped might set them free. Tyrants, moreover, need martyrs to demonstrate their total power—witness, for instance, the succession of innocent victims in a simpleminded tyrant play such as Preston's

Cambises. By the same token, martyrs need tyrants to justify, in fact to define their martyrdom; as a recent analyst of baroque martyr plays has put it, "A martyr is not someone who simply is executed, but one who dies for an idea and is sentenced to death by the tyrant who holds power."[9] What Freud said of nations in *Civilization and Its Discontents* can be said of the ideal audience for a martyr play, "It is always possible to bind together a considerable number of people in love, so long as there are other people left over to receive the manifestations of their aggressiveness."[10]

The differences between tyrant and martyr plays are essentially differences in the particular roles which the dramatist chooses to emphasize. Each type of play has its particular analogies and antecedents: the tyrant play looks back to the various medieval depictions of Herod, while the martyr play inevitably echoes the Passion story (though Walter Benjamin would trace its "origins" to the death of Socrates, which he sees as a parody of Greek tragedy).[11] Each form has its characteristic vices: the tyrant, to the extent that he characteristically moves toward rage, always risks going over the line to the comic, while the martyr, to the extent that he engages in self-lamentation, risks turning sentimental. Unlike the best conspiracy plays, tyrant and martyr plays tend to cultivate as little ambiguity as their audiences — or the writers' artistic consciences — will let them get away with: to qualify a figure's tyranny or martyrdom is at once to reduce the amount of terror or pity that an audience could be expected to grant him.

A tyrant play, by its very nature, is about the fall or the ultimate impotence of a tyrant. A play detailing his complete and unqualified triumph would not only violate an audience's moral sensibilities but would give the impression of a crude joke which has yet to be resolved. When a tyrant scores a triumph at the end, the dramatist has to find a way of denying him something he dearly desires. Writers in the French classical tradition had a ready-made device in the sense that they could undercut a tyrant's public triumph with his powerlessness in love. Thus, at the end of Voltaire's *Mahomet* the tyrant-hero is thwarted in love just as he captures Mecca, while Racine's Nero, in *Britannicus,* finds that his love-object Junie has escaped his grasp just as he has managed to set up one of the most absolute tyrannies in all drama. Although the medieval Herod plays depict the triumph of absolute tyranny over absolute innocence, the audience always remains aware of the ultimate triumph of Christ. Tyranny is most vividly demonstrated through its persecution of those who cannot fight back, above all children, like the innocents massacred in the Herod plays (who serve as surrogates for the Christ child), the murdered princes of *Richard III,* Macduff's children in *Macbeth,* or the boy from the top of whose head the famous apple is shot in Schiller's *Wilhelm Tell.* Herod's proverbial rage works theatrically to indicate both his power and his impotence — the former through its sheer volume and the attention it draws to itself, the latter through its implicit admission that he can no longer exercise his power with total efficiency.

As soon as we become aware of a tyrant's weakness, the awe which he arouses is threatened; thus, every tyrant play in a sense implies the ultimate bankruptcy of tyranny. In *Cinna* Corneille frustrates our expectations about tyrants by portraying Augustus, the play's true hero, as a ruler who has the power to be a tyrant but finds that he can exercise this power far more successfully through an act of generosity to his would-be assassins. The irony behind tyrant plays, Corneille implies, is that power can best be maintained by means of political manipulation, which of course no longer marks a ruler as a tyrant. And in a later play, *Nicomède*, Corneille ruthlessly exposes the tyrant couple Prusias and Arsinoé to the point where they are rendered ridiculous. Since the Enlightenment, serious dramatists have customarily tried to "psychologize" their tyrants, with the result that they are not only robbed of their awe but that we also grant them a degree of sympathy. In art, if not always in life, understanding is tantamount to forgiving. Schiller, in *Don Carlos,* through a brilliant act of psychological understanding, has created a Philip II wholly incapable of evoking tyrannical awe; to maintain the tyrannical element in the play, he is forced to introduce a "higher" authority, the Grand Inquisitor, whom he carefully fails to characterize in detail and who simply appears at the end as a kind of diabolus ex machina to help bring about the catastrophe. Although the capriciousness and cruelty of Camus's Caligula seem dramatically real, they are also shown up as absurd; when a character tells him, "I cannot hate you, because I don't think you are happy," we recognize our own need to look condescendingly at tyranny.[12]

If individual tyrants all too easily fall victim to psychological understanding, dramatists have often succeeded in transferring their potential tyranny from the individual personage to the political atmosphere as a whole. Few tyrannies, whether imaginary or real, are as frightening as that created by Büchner in *Dantons Tod*, yet Robespierre, the tyrant who presumably wields the power, is presented as a nervous and frightened being at the mercy of forces larger than himself. The figure of Sade in *Marat/Sade* serves to symbolize the particular psychological tyranny which the contemporary mind recognizes behind a tyrannical political atmosphere. "There are no villains in the piece," Shaw writes in his preface to *Saint Joan.* "Crime, like disease, is not interesting."[13] And although Shaw's imagination was too sanguine to conceive a political atmosphere comparable to Büchner's, the tyranny that makes possible Joan's martyrdom is one we are meant to recognize as peculiarly modern — the tyranny of small-minded officials who band together to withstand anyone who threatens the roles they are assigned within the social order.

If tyrant plays have in one way or another become problematic in the modern world, they flourished in periods such as the Renaissance and seventeenth century, in which a providential view of history could be taken seriously and the imagination could easily conceive that the awesome power in the newly centralized state might be exercised illegitimately (to the point, in

41

fact, that regicide became a central issue in politics and drama). In *Richard III, Macbeth,* and *Athalie,* perhaps the three greatest tyrant plays, we experience both the terror and the inner contradictions of evil when it is exercised from the seat of absolute political power; and we are also made to experience that sense of relief which accompanies the fall of the usurper together with the restoration (if ever so temporary) of divine order.

In *Athalie*, with its concise, classical structure, Racine creates what would seem to be the ideal form for the tyrant play, a form, moreover, in which everything is arranged so that the tyrant figure will move memorably from total power to the most abject possible fall. It is as though all the resources of language and theatrical spectacle were used to build the play toward Athalie's resounding cry of defeat, "Dieu des Juifs, tu l'emportes!" and her bloody offstage murder which quickly follows.[14] This at least is the outward shape of the play, and it is doubtless that aspect of the play which the young ladies of Saint-Cyr, for whom it was written, thought they were experiencing. What Racine has done is to create a kind of ideal form which we can experience at a relatively simpleminded level and then to complicate it by qualifying the absoluteness with which we are to interpret the representatives of good and evil in the play.

Let us look at Racine's "ideal" form, that outward aspect of *Athalie* which strives, as it were, to be a model tyrant play. To engage his audience to assent to his tyrant's fall, Racine had first of all to present her as a usurper—something by no means clear in his source, but an important point for a drama written at a time when kings ruled by divine right. The words "usurper" and "tyrant" remain conspicuously synonymous throughout the play. At the same time Racine had to give Athalie an adequate antagonist who would seem in every way her opposite—namely, the boy-king Joas who, as a descendant of David and a prefiguration of Christ, could provide the means for the restoration of the true line of kings. When he reveals himself before the defeated Athalie at the end, we are to experience his victory as the showing forth of a god. By using an obscure biblical theme (rather than a well-known historical theme as Shakespeare did in his histories), Racine had the advantage of being able to shape his characters and situations with a high degree of freedom; his source (a page or two in the Second Book of Kings, several pages in Josephus) was obscure enough, in fact, that he had to take some pains to fill in the historical background in his preface to the play. At the same time he had the authority of what could pass as universal history. Moreover, the providential view of history, with its black-and-white moral distinctions, made possible clear lines of dramatic development which could combine the most miserable possible fall with the most uplifting possible restoration.

Beyond the biblical theme, Racine also enjoyed certain advantages through the classical form within which he was working. The single, compressed action which the unities make possible is essentially all that the subject of a tyrant's fall will bear. (In this sense *Richard III* is only incidentally about a tyrant's fall, and more fundamentally a long, brilliantly sustained improvisation whose chief character places himself in collusion with the audience and asks it to marvel — with horror and fascination at once — at how much outrageous behavior he can get away with.) In *Athalie* one could even speak of a perfect consonance between the single-minded direction of the plot and the divinely inspired design which shapes its view of history. Given the sparseness of means and the decorum which we generally associate with classical form, the play's various elements of spectacle — the choral praying and praising, the ritualized coronation of the restored king Joas, the gathering of armed priests on stage just before the catastrophe — all work to create a more highly charged dramatic atmosphere than they would if imbedded in an Elizabethan play or a Spanish *comedia*, in which spectacle can be taken for granted; Racine's "classicism," one could say, serves to call attention to those very elements by means of which he transcends the classical style. By the same token the "sacred" element shows through all the more conspicuously in the light of our knowledge that in *Athalie*, as in Racine's other biblical play, *Esther* (these were among the few French plays on biblical themes in almost a century), it is attached to an essentially secular mode of drama.

Such at least is the "official" level of *Athalie*, a level which, however much it is tested by the actual text, remains a central part of our experience of the play. On another level of our awareness, however, we are made to question the seemingly unambiguous moral values which give the play its outer shape. This level manifests itself, for instance, in the brutal militancy with which Racine has his saints execute their conspiracy against Athalie. Voltaire, otherwise a great admirer of the play ("Le chef-d'oeuvre de l'esprit humain," he in fact called it),[15] was bothered by this militancy, though Racine himself, in his preface, had implied his own qualms about it through some fast rationalizing ("tout devait être saint dans une si sainte action").[16] In one sense, of course, Racine was forced into this action by the very form of a tyrant play: to bring down Athalie he needs a conspiracy, which, if it is to work with dramatic efficiency, has to be militant (needless to say, Shakespeare faced the same problem in *Richard III* and *Macbeth*).

A fundamental questioning of the play's moral absolutes occurs in Racine's treatment of Joas, who, despite the fact that he carries the symbolic weight of restoring the reign of God, is himself shown up as tainted. Although in his appearances in the play he remains a perfect embodiment of innocence and wisdom (to the extent that contemporary taste tends to find him priggish), we are reminded at several key points (above all in Athalie's final curses) that in adulthood he will follow in her tyrannical footsteps. Even Racine's reminder, in the preface, of Christ's eventual ascendancy is not enough to undo the undercurrent of coming doom which he injects into the play at crucial moments.[17]

The play's moral complexity manifests itself most notably in the figure of Athalie, who, despite the fact that she appears in only two of the five acts, emerges as one of the most fascinating creations in all drama. Throughout the play Racine is able to stress her power and her weakness at once. If the plot attempts above all to chart the tyrant's loss of power, it also dramatizes the stages of her psychological disintegration, which has been set in motion even before her first appearance. Both her power and her weakness are evident in such words as "colère," "rage," and "fureur," with which she is persistently associated. If words such as "audace" and "superbe" point to her outward shows of power, other terms such as "chancelant," "désordre," and "égaré" enact the process of disintegration. By making his tyrant-figure a woman, Racine is able to take dramatic advantage of the possibilities within both male and female characterization. Through her external power Athalie can exercise the tyranny of a man, while the emotional complexity which she shares with the great heroines of Racine's earlier dramas is at once a sign of her vulnerability: "Tu vois mon trouble et ma faiblesse," she says in her first line,[18] yet soon thereafter she reverts to her male role of boasting of imperial power, only to lapse a moment later into the celebrated dream narration which, revealing as it does her strange maternal fascination with the young boy who will later emerge as her oppressor, gives visible shape to her feminine "weakness." In the course of the play she moves from an omnipotence "unnatural" to her sex ("cette reine... / Elevée au-dessus de son sexe timide") to an impotence which, by its very nature, deprives her of the capacity to rule ("Elle flotte, elle hésite; en un mot, elle est femme").[19] The dramatic sympathy with which Racine treats his tyrant in no way prevents a conclusion in which we literally feel "joy at her blood":

> La fer a de sa vie expié les horreurs.
> Jérusalem, longtemps en proie à ses fureurs,
> De son joug odieux à la fin soulagée,
> Avec joie en son sang la regarde plongée.[20]

In the total effect achieved by his characterization of Athalie and by his historical vision, Racine contrives to have both his subtlety and his barbarism at once.

A degree of barbarism is, in fact, necessary to our experience of any tyrant play. Our joy at a tyrant's downfall lies, I think, in our sense of relief that a force threatening the normal order of things has been contained; a tyrant's barbarism, moreover, evokes a response in kind, one which, through our communal participation in the theater, provides an eminently safe outlet for our own barbaric impulses. Like the tyrant play, the martyr play moves toward a communal experience of joy, though whatever barbarism we feel is directed only to those who persecute the martyr; our joy comes through the sense of triumph we share with a martyr who has managed, in one way or another, to escape or transcend the barriers which the world has put in the way of his spiritual realization.

The martyr play, whether about a saint, a monarch, or simply some exemplary individual, can never completely escape being an imitation of Christ. Thus, both the suffering and the transcendence of the Passion story lend their shape to the martyr play, whose plot must find a way of accommodating these two seemingly contradictory movements. When we repeat the old notion that there is no such thing as a Christian tragedy, we are simply saying that Aristotle's conception of tragedy took no account of the Christian writer's (and audience's) need to turn suffering into transcendence.

If the plot of a tyrant play tends to limit itself to the circumstances surrounding the tyrant's rise and fall (the latter only in plays within the classical tradition), the plot of a martyr play has even more severe limitations, for it must center itself in the martyr's inward development; outward events, as a result, function largely as a prelude or accompaniment to the process by which the hero prepares himself to achieve his martyrdom. Many martyr plays in the classical tradition (from Gryphius's *Carolus Stuardus* to Eliot's *Murder in the Cathedral*) limit themselves, in fact, to the final stages of a martyr's preparation. Because of its essential inwardness, the process of achieving martyrdom is in itself untheatrical. Since the martyr expects to be acted upon, what action occurs comes largely from outside forces. For a martyr the only meaningful action consists in preserving his integrity against these forces, and if he acts in conventional theatrical ways it is usually to challenge the secular authority to tyrannize him and thus test the staying power of his integrity. A typical action of this type is the destruction of Roman idols which the early Christian martyrs in many baroque plays perpetrate to initiate the process of martyrdom. The purpose of this violent action is, of course, not simply to elicit a counteraction, but above all to create an outward show of heroism that will make martyrdom, or at least conversion to Christianity, as infectious as possible. In Corneille's *Polyeucte,* the greatest play about a Christian martyr, the heroic example is so infectious, in fact, that it draws in all the major characters—not only the hero's wife, but also the two potential tyrant-figures, her former lover and her father, both of whom represent the pagan Roman state.

Still, the limited plotting possible in a martyr play has forced dramatists to "internalize" the action. The typical internal action of a martyr play is a movement "upward" as the martyr rids himself of earthly things and readjusts his desires toward more spiritual endeavors. The inward action of *Polyeucte,* for instance, encompasses a series of steps in each of which the hero succeeds in transcending his preceding stage of development. If it is easy for us to read *Polyeucte* in political as well as religious terms, this is only to say that the major Corneillian heroes from the Cid onwards undergo a similar movement of self-transcendence; from the point of view of dramatic effect, it scarcely matters whether their actions are grounded in the political or the religious realm.[21] In one important respect, however, *Polyeucte* is more "social-minded" than most martyr plays, for its focus is not only on the titular hero but on those surrounding figures whose admiration for Polyeucte's actions causes them to imitate his process of transcendence.

Admiration and infectiousness are, of course, not limited to the relations between characters in martyr plays but are even more fundamentally a function of the relation of martyr to audience. Every martyr play, whether religious or secular, works rhetorically to excite the audience's admiration for the martyr and convince it of the rightness of his cause (though it usually stops short of asking the audience to join him in martyrdom). The greatest martyr plays—works such as *Polyeucte*, Calderón's *El príncipe constante*, and *Samson Agonistes*—succeed in presenting images of heroic possibility with a convincingness and lack of ironic qualification such as we rarely find elsewhere in drama. In such plays we often gain the illusion that we have experienced human greatness, a greatness analogous to that of the traditional epic hero: the physical feats which in epic narratives become a sign of the highest human attainments find their closest dramatic equivalent in the spiritual feats of the martyr-hero.

The inward development which is the central concern of a martyr play can be structured in dramatic terms through "stages" which the audience or reader can readily distinguish from one another and in which one can recognize a distinctly ascending movement. The delineation of easily discernible stages of development is, of course, natural to dramatic form; a play does not have the expansiveness to depict those "natural" processes of growth which have become a principal feature of the novel of the last two hundred years.[22] Polyeucte's growth is defined for us through his changing attitudes about his relation to the secular world: what starts out as hesitation at receiving baptism for fear of upsetting his wife becomes in the end a conscious decision to seek martyrdom. Fernando, the martyr-hero of *El príncipe constante*, moves by his own choice (and against the wishes of those he is defending) from the magnificence of a royal prince to the most abject slavery; yet his gradual physical and material degradation is counterbalanced at each point by a corresponding spiritual advancement. *Samson Agonistes* and *Murder in the Cathedral* are both shaped around a series of temptations in which the martyr is confronted with various earthly comforts and pleasures which he not only rejects one by one but which serve, in effect, as negative challenges to goad him into martyrdom.

The great age of the martyr play is also the age of the Counter-Reformation, which, through its otherworldly zeal and its contempt for earthly things, provided the ideal metaphorical framework for the "upward" movement essential to the genre. To the degree that a martyr enacts the process of

46

freeing himself from the shackles of the historical world, the martyr play is essentially antihistorical in nature. The lofty perspective toward which a martyr play moves knows nothing but contempt for the ordinary political give-and-take which forms the substance of most historical drama. The more a play stresses the fate of the individual martyr, the less it is likely to stress the fate of the community or the complexities of the historical process. Indeed, the martyr play is essentially opposed to any complexity which might detract the audience from participating imaginatively in its hero's martyrdom. If the martyr in one sense transcends historical process, in another sense he takes himself to be very much a part of history, for the memory of his acts will create an entirely different conception of his time from that held by his contemporaries; his task, one might say, is to free himself from history in order to create a new historical consciousness.

The characteristic "doctrine" which a martyr voices at the end of the play often takes some form of stoicism, and it is usually expressed in a rhetoric liberally sprinkled with the various *topoi* that have accumulated for centuries around the theme of *contemptus mundi*. The "insights" which a baroque martyr-hero achieves are nearly always the same. If these insights are often expressed at what we today take to be undue length, this is because a display of rhetorical power is a necessary part of a martyr's self-fulfillment. Muteness does not suffice to attain glory in drama. But a martyr's rhetorical power also serves as an extension of (or replacement for) the earthly power which he has had to abandon. Given the high degree of physical passivity which a martyr's role requires, a stoic stance, as though in compensation, allows him a maximum amount of verbal activity. If the heroes of baroque martyr plays often seem creatures with an uncommon drive and zeal, this is because they have transferred the ambitions associated with the worldly realm to a spiritual one. By the same token, one can say that abandonment of the world comes to have tremendous meaning in the seventeenth century only through the fact that the symbols of the world — throne, scepter, empire — were themselves able to exert an uncommonly high degree of power over an audience.

Baroque martyr plays indicate in an extreme form certain tendencies characteristic of martyr plays even in more secular periods. Thus, Schiller's two martyr plays, *Maria Stuart* and *Die Jungfrau von Orleans*, simply substitute a new form of stoicism — the achievement of "inner freedom" in the face of the world's buffets — for the more orthodox Christian stoicism of the seventeenth century. Martyr plays of all times attempt to elicit the most favorable possible response from the audience toward the martyr's ascent. T. S. Eliot places all of Thomas à Becket's temptations in the first act in order that he may appear in the second act with the "purity" of mind necessary for martyrdom; after his death the outrageous secular arguments of the four knights serve only to condemn these men in our eyes and to confirm our support of Thomas's martyrdom. If dramatists with Aristotelian scruples have sometimes given their martyrs some moral flaws, these flaws all seem readily forgivable from a worldly point of view. Although Schiller's Mary Stuart consents to Mortimer's conspiracy, it is this conspiracy, after all, which is meant to save her life; we are meant to be even more indulgent to his Joan of Arc, whose "flaw," though it gets in the way of her leadership in war, consists of falling in love! A martyr's "flaws" ultimately serve less to make him seem like a fellow human being than to provide a worldly temptation beyond which he can grow; although they may begin by showing common human weaknesses, martyrs by their very nature are heroes whom the audience must come to recognize as superhuman.

One does not need to be a practitioner of *Stoffgeschichte* to notice that the same figures have repeatedly had their martyrdom dramatized over the centuries. Indeed, the various plays, as well as operas, about Mary Stuart (Montchrétien, 1601; Vondel, 1646; Haugwitz, 1684; Schiller, 1800; Slowacki, 1835; Donizetti, 1835; Maxwell Anderson, 1933), Joan of Arc (Schiller, 1801; Verdi, 1845; Tschaikovsky, 1879; Shaw, 1924; Claudel, 1939; Anderson, 1947; Anouilh, 1953), and Becket (Tennyson, 1884; Eliot, 1935; Anouilh, 1959) virtually form subgenres in themselves. Despite many modern examples, Mary Stuart plays also had a heyday in the seventeenth century, at which time they served (besides their loftier purposes) as vehicles for anti-English and/or anti-protestant feelings on the Continent. Joan, perhaps because she is a relatively secular saint (Shakespeare, of course, knew her only as a witch) has doubtless been the most popular martyr figure of the nineteenth and twentieth centuries.

Anyone scanning through the names of martyr plays will note that women predominate unduly (at least considering their relative status in earlier times) among protagonists within the genre. A recent commentator has attributed this predominance to a natural affinity, first, between feminine passivity and martyrdom and, second, between sacrificial heroism and what he calls "the mysteries of fertility."[23] Although one's speculations could go on endlessly in an issue of this sort, I might add that women, like children, have traditionally provided natural symbols for dramatic situations which demand that the audience feel outraged by wronged innocence. Moreover, from the point of view of verisimilitude, at least in the images with which they have been presented throughout most of Western culture, women are more appropriate repositories of emotion than men — particularly to the extent that they can manifest their emotions more easily in the ostentatious manner which drama requires. One might add that tyrant plays, particularly in France, have often centered around women — for instance, *Athalie*, Corneille's *Rodogune*, and Voltaire's *Sémiramis*. Part of the fascination of such plays lies in the fact that our expectation of feminine passivity is jarred by the "unnaturalness" displayed in the very conception of a woman tyrant; part of our fascination

48

with *Macbeth,* for instance, stems from watching the "unsexed" Lady Macbeth play the tyrant role from behind the scenes.

Audiences rarely seem to tire of seeing the same figure undergo some new expression of martyrdom. Just as an ancient Greek audience or a medieval audience was familiar in advance with the tale it saw dramatized, the audience of a martyr play generally knows the main facts about its hero, who, whether a Christian saint or a more secular type of martyr, carries an automatic "halo-effect" for those about to witness his martyrdom. A martyr play perhaps needs to take such a challenge for granted more than other forms of drama, for its central effects depend upon its achieving the audience's unbounded enthusiasm for the action of its hero.

The aesthetic success of a martyr play is to a high degree dependent on a particular audience's receptivity to particular styles of martyrdom. Like much else, martyrdom exists largely in the eye of the beholder, and martyr plays, as a result, tend to "date" with the rapidity characteristic of the more ceremonial forms of drama.[24] To the extent that human beings in all ages can easily be tempted to feel wronged, all are capable of participating ceremonially in a character's martyrdom. What differs from age to age is the particular mode of idealism for which the martyr is sacrificed.[25] A successful martyr play works to flatter its audience by making the latter's particular style of idealism triumph. The audience, in effect, shares vicariously in the victim's sacrifice and enjoys the satisfactions of his triumph.

I have myself witnessed the immense satisfaction displayed by a crowd when Kipphardt's "documentary" martyr play, *In der Sache J. Robert Oppenheimer,* was performed in the midst of a campus sit-in in the late 1960s protesting the university's connection with the so-called military-industrial complex. The ceremonial character of the performance was especially evident when the name of the university president, who had himself been a witness against Oppenheimer (but who had not actually been named in the script by Kipphardt) was placed in the dialogue by the actors: immediately a lively and in many ways pleasing shudder went through the audience, for one of the tyrant figures who was persecuting the martyr on stage had turned out to be a man who intersected with the audience's own daily life. Like all but the few greatest martyr plays, *In der Sache J. Robert Oppenheimer* is relevant only to certain times and places, and, like most ceremonial dramas, martyr plays have considerably less impact in print than in actual performance, for the sense of community which the spectator shares with the audience is missing. I happen not to be much impressed by *The Crucible,* which I know only in its printed text, but I might very well have been overwhelmed by it in performance, especially if I had been able to see it during the McCarthy period or at some later period when the fear of repression was in the air. An audience, moreover, must be at least partway prepared to accept the basic ideological premises of a martyr play to have anything like the theatrical experience planned for it by the author. *Carolus Stuardus* would have seemed heinous in every respect to a Puritan audience of the 1650s, as would *The Crucible* to that majority of the American public which briefly supported McCarthy during the early 1950s.

Every modern martyr play must find some way of coping with the secular prejudices of its particular audience. Although Eliot designed *Murder in the Cathedral* for an audience of believers (at least to the extent that those who attend a modern religious festival are believers), he cunningly introduced the speeches of the four knights at the end to play upon and, through the unpleasant clichés which we come to recognize in their rhetoric, to undercut the secular prejudices of that larger literary public which has since come to accept his play as a minor modern classic. Shaw, whose status as a non-believer no one would question, was able to create a plausible Saint Joan for his nonbelieving audience by translating the traditional saintly virtues of purity and endurance into such characteristically modern virtues (at least as of 1920) as high-spiritedness and pluckiness, while the tyrant figures who bring about her martyrdom become bureaucratic types whose contemporary representatives anybody would recognize. When the fourth, and most dangerous, tempter in Eliot's play tempts Becket with these lines —

> What can compare with glory of Saints
> Dwelling forever in presence of God?
> What earthly glory, of king or emperor,
> What earthly pride, that is not poverty
> Compared with richness of heavenly grandeur?
> Seek the way of martyrdom, make yourself the lowest
> On earth, to be high in heaven.[26]

we recognize that what would be a most legitimate desire for any baroque hero has become an insupportable vanity for the modern mind.[27]

Any honest modern martyr play has to face up, as well, to the theatricality inherent in the very act of martyrdom. What would a real-life martyr be, after all, without the audience or the posterity for which he expects to set an example? When Schiller complained of the operatic quality of the last scene of Goethe's *Egmont*, he meant, of course, the music and the dream-vision with which Goethe embellished his martyr-hero's final speech, but the operatic element is inherent in the theatrical self-consciousness of the speech itself, which culminates in Egmont's command to his people to "fall joyfully, following the example I am setting for you."[28] The theatricality implicit in martyrdom is frankly acknowledged, as it were, in those plays about the martyrdom of a real actor — Lope de Vega's *Lo fingido verdadero* (*The Truthful Feigning*) and the French play based on it, Rotrou's *Saint-Genest*, in which the hero, with obviously fatal consequences, suddenly announces his newly adopted Christian faith while performing before the pagan Roman emperor. By a happy insight Sartre appropriated the title of Rotrou's play for his great study of Jean Genet, which, faithful to its subtitle, "Comédien et martyr," explores the authenticity both of its subject's theatricality and of his martyrdom.

Büchner, in the poignant prison scenes of *Dantons Tod*, was perhaps the first dramatist to face up to the problem of the authenticity of a martyr's stance. "My name will soon be in the Pantheon of history," Danton, with a defiance characteristic of impending martyrdom, had told the revolutionary tribunal at an earlier moment in the play. But as the execution of Danton and his friends approaches, they are hard put to find the appropriate stance to take: "Let's sit down together and scream," Hérault suggests, "Greeks and gods screamed. Romans and Stoics made heroic grimaces." To which Danton replies cynically, "The ones were as much Epicureans as the others. They managed to give themselves a very comfortable feeling about their own worth. It isn't at all bad to drape your toga around you and look around to see how long a shadow you're casting."[29] In Büchner the stoicism which in its various religious and secular forms had served as the stance of last resort for such diverse heroes as Calderón's steadfast prince, Addison's Cato, and Schiller's woman martyrs, has become nothing more than a pose. To put it another way, with the emergence of the antihero, martyrdom has come to lose that heroic quality which had once given it dignity or made it seem at least a worthwhile way of dying.[30]

Büchner's disciple Brecht, for whom not merely heroism but all theatrical illusion was suspect, did his utmost to keep us from experiencing the fate of his Galileo as martyrdom. Not only did he (like Shaw before him) reduce his tyrant figures to bureaucrats, he stressed the sensualism in his protagonist at the expense of his idealism and found his legacy to posterity to lie in his establishing an image of the scientist as the servile instrument of whatever ruling powers he happens to have over him. Yet however much Brecht intended to blacken Galileo in our eyes, audiences tend to experience *Leben des Galilei* as a genuine martyr play. Not only was Brecht unable fully to erase that conception of Galileo as a culture-hero with which we enter the theater, but the structure of a martyr play, which Brecht employs, arouses expectations in us which he was never wholly able to thwart. Nor should he have, for the forces that crush Galileo, however much they may lack the more traditional accoutrements of villainy, are in every way more reprehensible than their victim. One might add that the honesty which Brecht's Galileo displays toward himself, together with his refusal to assume heroic pretensions, is precisely what makes it possible for a modern audience to accept him as a martyr.

The most ambitious attempt to make the traditional martyr play workable in the contemporary theater is Jerzy Grotowski's famous production of *El príncipe constante*. "The producer believes that although he is not faithful to Calderón's text to the letter, he nevertheless retains the inner meaning of the play," we read in the play's program. "The performance is a transposition of the profound antinomies and most characteristic traits of the baroque era such as its visionary aspect, its music, its appreciation of the concrete and its spiritualism."[31] Whatever Grotowski meant by "inner meaning," the differences between Calderón's play and Grotowski's performance are sufficiently formidable to indicate the immense gulf which separates baroque from contemporary conceptions of a martyr play.[32] Grotowski has radically reduced Calderón's play in size and scope; not only has he cut the huge cast to six actors—encompassing only the prince and his persecutors—but he has narrowed down the plot from what in Calderón was still a chronicle about a Portuguese expedition in Morocco to a single, intense scene corresponding only to the final scenes of the original. If Calderón's prince dies asserting public values, namely, the preservation of his nation and its religion, Grotowski translates these values into their private equivalent—what the program note calls "preserving his independence and purity to the point of ecstasy."[33] Since the conflict between nations and religions is irrelevant to Grotowski's purposes, it is no wonder that one reviewer of the production thought the prince's persecutors were his own subjects![34] Calderón's prince, like all his heroes, is notable for the eloquence with which he voices both his suffering and his triumph, but Grotowski's expresses himself principally by means of his body. Indeed, for Grotowski all the public aspects of martyrdom are essentially peripheral to the relation of persecutor and martyr, which he portrays as a ritual game that provides its characteristic satisfactions for all the players. The audience, moreover, has its particular role within the game: seated as it is behind wooden barriers, as in an operating theater, it becomes the public for whom the martyrdom is performed. When the program note describes the relation of society toward the prince as "not uniformly hostile," but "an expression of a sense of difference and strangeness combined with a sort of fascination,"[35] we recognize ourselves in a late-twentieth-century world in which the fact of relationship has become primary to the outward circumstances surrounding and generating relationship; in fact, I suspect that my whole discussion of the nature of the martyr play is itself, like Grotowski's interpretation of Calderón, an expression of this world.

Although Grotowski at least recognized the ecstatic, triumphant aspect of martyrdom, the modern mind has generally been willing to extend the concept of martyr to the mute and ineloquent, to those who simply get crushed (without the possibility of ecstacy) by forces larger than themselves. With the democratization of tragedy since the late eighteenth century, the tragic figure comes to have increasingly less awareness of the nature and meaning of his fate. The progressive stages of growth which accompanied the martyrdom of earlier heroes are obviously impossible for those who can at most display a sense of shock at what has been done to them. The burden of growth falls instead upon the audience, which discovers the meaning of the

52

martyrdom that it witnesses enacted in, say, the oppression of a martyr by a social class higher than his own (for example, in the many German "bourgeois tragedies" from Lessing to Hebbel), or, if the play's orientation is more metaphysical than social, in his oppression by some "mysterious" higher force (as in Beckett).

Within this conception of martyrdom, Büchner's *Woyzeck* is perhaps the representative modern martyr play. The oppression which crushes its protagonist, an illiterate, half-mad soldier, can in fact be taken as either social or metaphysical or both, depending on the predilections of the interpreter. If Büchner, in his first play, *Dantons Tod*, allowed his hero to question the authenticity of a martyr's pose, in *Woyzeck* he created a hero quite incapable of the reflection necessary for any serious questioning. If Danton's antiheroism is the conscious choice of one whose heroism in actual history remains a central fact throughout the play, Woyzeck's antiheroic role is defined for him at the start. And if *Dantons Tod* retains the public perspective and theatrical conventions common to most historical drama since Shakespeare, *Woyzeck*, like most serious dramas since its time, is based on private history. The historical document from which the author drew his material was a case study about mental aberration in a medical journal, a study, moreover, which treated its subject with what today seems an astonishing lack of compassion.[36] The tragic framework within which Büchner placed his unpromising material (the word "unpromising" is applicable to most of the anecdotes and documents which have fed modern literature with the private histories of nonheroic personages) was precisely what makes it possible for us to experience Woyzeck's fate as a version of martyrdom.

Within those theories of tragedy — notably those of Gilbert Murray and Northrop Frye[37] — which stress the hero's role as victim rather than his moral character or the metaphysical makeup of the play's poetic world, the martyr play would not be readily distinguishable from other forms of tragedy. Just as conspiracy, in one way or another, finds its way into most dramatic plots, so the idea of martyrdom can easily attach itself to that multitude of dramatic situations in which we feel that larger forces have succeeded in rendering the hero a victim. In the broadest sense the martyr play encompasses a whole spectrum of works whose readers or audiences, according to their prevailing styles of feeling, seek to experience a victim's hurt — whether the hurt of the stoically lamenting heroines of learned closet dramas such as the Roman *Octavia* or Daniel's *Cleopatra,* or of titanic figures such as Prometheus or Lear wrestling against impossible odds, or of a contemporary antihero stunned into muteness by his (or simply our) recognition of the absurdity of existence.

THREE

HISTORY AS MAGNIFICATION

> Because the acts or events of true history have not that magnitude which satisfieth the mind of man, poesy feigneth acts and events greater and more heroical: because true history propoundeth the successes and issues of actions not so agreeable to the merits of virtue and vice, therefore poesy feigns them more just in retribution, and more according to revealed providence: because true history representeth actions and events more ordinary, and less interchanged; therefore poesy endueth them with more rareness, and more unexpected and alternative variations: so as it appeareth that poesy serveth and confereth to magnanimity, morality, and to delectation.
>
> Bacon, *Advancement of Learning*

> When beggars die, there are no comets seen;
> The heavens themselves blaze forth the death of princes.
>
> Calpurnia, in *Julius Caesar*

> Unglücklich das Land, das keine Helden hat!...
> Unglücklich das Land, das Helden nötig hat.
>
> Spoken, respectively, by the hero's disciple
> and by the hero of Brecht's *Leben des Galilei*
> after the hero's recantation

HISTORY AND HEROISM

The distinction which Bacon draws between history and poetry echoes an idea established in the critical tradition by Aristotle and continued by numerous critics in the Renaissance—that history, "being captived," as Sidney put it, "to the truth of a foolish world,"[1] does not enjoy the philosophical, or imaginative, or moral advantages of poetry. I propose to approach the problem with a different bias—not to defend the primacy of poetry over history (poetry, or "imaginative literature" as we call it today, has not been lacking in eloquent defenders on those innumerable occasions in which it has been attacked) or to offer still another distinction between the two modes of writing (we include such a diversity of genres within both history and poetry nowadays that the distinction could only be made on the highest possible level of abstraction). Indeed, I shall not be concerned with historical writing as

54

such, and I shall focus on drama among the literary genres — though I shall also introduce other genres and art forms to isolate those qualities that we perceive as "historical" and "dramatic" in art. My point is, simply, that the very presence of historical content serves, if I may cite Bacon's phrase once again, to give a work "that magnitude which satisfieth the mind of man." History, in short, magnifies, for it invests a subject within the eyes of its beholder with the illusion of its dignity, scope, and overriding importance.[2]

Whatever Aristotle may have intended with his statement about the high station of tragic heroes, his influence has helped insure that the goings-on of the characters in a play will strike an audience as matters of considerable significance. Whether or not we accept these goings-on as "true" history, the very fact that the personages on stage are capable of wielding great power lays a special claim on our attention. Shakespeare's tragedies, built as they are around kings and consuls, take place within a thoroughly historical atmosphere which is designed to convince us of the high import of the events we see enacted (although the personages of *Othello* are of reasonably high station, the domestic activities around which the play is centered have often cast a doubt on its relative status among the tragedies). History helps create the dimension through which a play such as Racine's *Mithridate,* with its plot about an aging man whose beloved is pursued by his two sons, is "raised" from the level of cuckold comedy to the dignity characteristic of tragedy. The confrontation scene between the Scottish and English queens in Schiller's *Maria Stuart* would sound like little more than a nasty quarrel between two middle-class women if we were not meant to be aware that the fate of nations was at stake (the fact that the two women never met in "actual" history is, of course, irrelevant to the way we experience the scene). The illicit passion of Don Rodrigue and Doña Prouhèze in Claudel's *Le Soulier de satin* reaches cosmic proportions through the colorful symbols of religion and imperialistic power that characterize the sixteenth-century Spanish world in which this passion defines itself. The author of a modern middle-brow play, *A Man for All Seasons,* has bluntly confessed to the advantages which a historical setting affords a writer: "In two previous plays . . . I had tried, but with fatal timidity, to handle contemporaries in a style that should make them larger than life. . . . For this one [*A Man for All Seasons*] I took a historical setting in the hope that the distance of years would give me Dutch courage, and enable me to treat my characters in a properly heroic, properly theatrical manner."[3]

If, as the saying goes, no man is a hero to his valet, it is equally hard for a man to be a hero to his contemporaries, unless, of course, he takes up the role of political martyr common within many recent documentary dramas. But martyrdom is a limited instance of heroism which provides only one of the satisfactions possible to those who can respond to the heroic impulse. Among the most potent conceptions of heroism in recent centuries is that of Hegel, who, in his philosophy of history, speaks of the greatness of spirit inherent in such "world-historical individuals" as Alexander, Caesar, and Napoleon. Hegel distinguishes sharply between the emotional objectives of his heroic figures and those of ordinary men. Whereas the former seek "satisfaction" ("Befriedigung"), the latter are content with "happiness" ("Glück"). Each of these objectives, moreover, exists within its separate realm. "History is not the ground for happiness," he writes, adding that "the world-historical individuals doubtless found satisfaction, but they did not want to be happy."[4] Using Hegel's distinction, one could divide the history of literature into those genres which allow the "satisfactions" of heroism (epic, tragedy, historical drama) and those which are willing—and even proud—to provide a "ground for happiness" (lyric, pastoral, comedy). Historical drama, insofar as it deals with issues of power and larger forces in conflict with one another, provides a natural arena in which the heroic impulse can manifest itself.

When embodied in a drama, the heroic impulse creates an image of reality at once more intense and overpowering than what we find in the more modest genres (or, for that matter, in "life" itself). As Dryden's spokesman Neander puts it in the "Essay of Dramatic Poesy" when comparing what he calls a "serious play" with a comedy, " 'Tis Nature wrought up to an higher pitch [than in comedy]. The plot, the characters, the wit, the passions, the descriptions, are all exalted above the level of common converse, as high as the imagination of the poet can carry them, with proportion to verisimility."[5] In this passage Dryden is defending the use of rhyme as a means of rendering that "wrought-up Nature" which a serious play is meant to convey to an audience. The "exalted" in contrast to the "common," "high" against "low"—such are the antitheses by means of which the heroic mode asserts its identity. In his own dramatic writing Dryden presents an extreme version of the heroic that doubtless goes beyond that of any dramatist whom we can still treat (if not necessarily take) seriously. In plays such as *The Conquest of Granada*, *The Indian Emperor* (about Cortez and Montezuma), and *Aureng-Zebe* (about political upheavals in the India of Dryden's time) the historical basis of the action is all but abandoned in order to achieve the maximum in heroic effect. Indeed, the historical setting of each play serves principally to create a sense of the faraway (in place more than time) in which men considerably larger than life can, with what Dryden calls "proportion to verisimility," engage in power struggles to excite our admiration and wonder. "None can enough admire, or praise too much"—these words, spoken by the aged emperor at his son Aureng-Zebe's military exploits,[6] are emblematic of the rhetorical effect at which Dryden's heroic plays unceasingly aim.[7]

Yet the very need to sustain the heroic illusion in a drama creates a paradoxical situation for a writer: to the extent that he must fill a space of several hours, he must constantly work to prevent the illusion from breaking down. Dryden attempted to meet this problem by keeping the action at a high pitch, with one peripety following another. Marlowe's *Tamburlaine* proceeds for ten acts with a series of constantly repeated actions: a new enemy appears and takes up battle with Tamburlaine, who emerges each time as conquerer —until his natural death at the end makes it possible to conclude the play with the heroic action unbroken. Often a play can establish and sustain a sense of the heroic by setting up analogies with various heroes (mythical or historic) of the past. Tamburlaine is compared (or compares himself) variously to such figures as Achilles, Hector, Alexander, and, for that matter, Jupiter himself.[8] Every hero of the past has certain special qualities which help color our image of those later heroes who invoke his ancestry: Achilles, for instance, has his wrath; Hercules (among other qualities), his endurance under trial; Alexander, his ability to transform the historical world with his heroism. After *Tamburlaine* the memory of Marlowe's hero, combined as it is with the earlier heroes who have created his image, made possible still another analogy which could be attached to heroes, as when a character in *Aureng-Zebe* refers to the two competitors as "Too truly *Tamerlain's* Successors they, / Each thinks a World too little for his sway."[9] Dryden, for that matter, consciously created his heroes out of epic tradition. "The first image I had of [Almanzor], was from the *Achilles* of Homer," he wrote of the hero of *The Conquest of Granada*,[10] while he described the characters of *Aureng-Zebe* as "nearest to those of an Heroick Poem."[11]

The writer of epic, of course, enjoys considerable advantages over the dramatist in sustaining the heroic. For one thing, he can keep his characters at a considerable distance, allowing them to sulk, for instance, or simply to be talked about by others throughout much of his poem. The dramatist must take his chances with an actor whose heroic gestures are always likely to risk absurdity (except for those brief moments in history—for instance, the early 1590s and 1670s in England and the 1770s in Germany—when audiences and readers have been willing to suspend their distrust in the heroic illusion). To the extent that epic relies on a rhetorically high style and allows the poet to speak in his own voice for much of the time, it can set up an automatic distance between hero and audience, whereas drama, no matter what artifices of language it may cultivate, must constantly sustain itself by means of dialogue between the hero and the members of his surrounding world.

Epic, moreover, can elevate its hero by means of long, elaborate, and painstakingly built-up descriptions of battle, while the nature, amount, and variety of fighting that a drama can support is limited by the physical conditions of the theater and an audience's ability to sit through repeated fencing matches (it is significant that Dryden, in contrast to his French contemporaries, strongly advocated the use of fighting on stage, and, in fact, employed it to a maximum degree).[12] The epic writer working in the mode of romance not only can extend the possibilities of heroism by means of supernatural action, but his hero's lapses from the heroic ideal can be excused by the magic spells cast upon him; if we are tempted to attach the term "romance" to such nonsupernatural works as the plays of Dryden and Victor Hugo, it is because their actions are rooted not in the historical world which they purport to depict, but in a romance world in which anything is imaginatively achievable (one might note that Dryden, though he cited Achilles as the initial inspiration for his Almanzor, added Tasso's Rinaldo and Calprenède's Artaban to his list of models).[13]

No literary genre, however, can sustain the heroic with the ease possible in painting and sculpture—if only because the visual artist does not face the problem of sustaining an action in time. Painting, for example, must arrest an action at what Lessing called "the most pregnant moment, out of which we are able to apprehend most fully what has gone before and what is to follow."[14] Lessing, voicing the distinctly theatrical bias that informs all his writing, in effect indicates the perfect theatrical situation, one in which a total action can be implied (if not quite enacted) without danger that the illusion might break down. In painting and sculpture the heroic moment is in a sense sustained forever, or at least until the observer chooses to glance somewhere else. The directness with which heroic effect can take place in the visual arts was suggested by Addison in a passage prescribing an antidote to the "low gratifications" of contemporary comedy; after first suggesting "the representation of noble characters drawn by Shakespeare and others" as a means of "amending" the bad effects of comedy, he turns to the example of historical painting: "How forcible an affect this would have on our minds, one needs no more than to observe how strongly we are touched by mere pictures. Who can see Le Brun's picture of the battle of Porus, without entering into the character of that fierce gallant man, and being accordingly spurred to an emulation of his constancy and courage?"[15] For immediacy of heroic effect, sculpture may well have an advantage over the "mere pictures" that Addison cites. Compared to a crowded battle scene, Michelangelo's David and the great equestrian statues of Donatello and Verrocchio work with a concentrated and a dramatic force which perhaps no other art form in our culture has achieved; indeed, the numerous progeny of Donatello's famous horse-and-rider to be found in public parks everywhere serve as an archaic (and, for that matter, absurd) reminder of heroic possibility in an otherwise prosaic modern world.

We often explain our contemporary discomfort with many visual representations of heroic action by complaining of their "theatrical" effect; in fact, for those to whom either the "heroic" or the "theatrical" are suspect, the two terms are virtually synonymous. An art historian, Michael Fried, has recently described the development of French painting in the late eighteenth and early nineteenth centuries as a "progressive theatricalization—the gradual usurpation of action by the theatrical and of expression by *grimace*."[16] The period of which he writes is also the great age of historical painting, an age, moreover, in which heroic action manifests itself far more successfully in painting than in the literary embodiments of the time. In one of the most original and influential paintings of the period, *The Oath of the Horatii* (1784), David invented an incident absent from Livy's narrative in order to condense within a single moment the drama of the three brothers who saved the small and ancient Roman kingdom.[17] The painting shows the brothers standing together in a single line, each with an arm raised solemnly toward his sword. As Fried describes David's achievement,

> The swearing of an oath provides a powerful, and perhaps unique, means of involving a multiplicity of figures in a single action *in the same way*. That is, the nature as action of swearing an oath is such as to have enabled David in the *Horatii* to represent the three brothers as participating in it equally and at the same time. And by that I mean not just simultaneously but so to speak *synchronically*: as if each of the participants is felt to belong to exactly the same *phase* of the action as every other. Furthermore, the nature as action of swearing an oath makes possible what in the *Horatii* is experienced as a perfect matching or fusion — a further, deeper synchrony — of the moral or spiritual and the physical or bodily: as though the inner meaning, even the private intensity, of swearing an oath were *entirely* manifest in its outward, public expression.[18]

The synchrony which Fried describes is a triumph possible only within a visual work: in a drama an oath, no matter how impressive in its immediate effect, takes up at best a single moment within a varied larger structure. In that great dramatic embodiment of the Horatio story, Corneille's *Horace*, the heroic moment of David's scene finds its theatrical equivalent with something of the same force we experience in the painting. What David accomplished by means of his synchrony Corneille accomplishes through a dialectical development in time. As Jean Starobinski, writing of Corneille in general, has put it, "Time, at first fragmented in separate acts, is transformed into massive duration, for such is the will of the hero."[19] Theatrical time in Corneille becomes the means by which the hero achieves his identity and asserts his place in history. Unlike *Tamburlaine,* a Corneillian drama does not need to keep repeating its hero's triumphs in order to sustain the heroic illusion. Rather, the play is so organized that the heroic ideal emerges *in the course of* and *through* the dramatic action. *Horace* develops through a testing of values, a testing that takes place not only within the characters of the play but above all within the consciousness of the audience. Such terms as "honneur" and "gloire," those positive values which, as everybody knows, Corneille constantly asserts, are actually attached to a variety of ideals, many of which do not survive the testing to which they are subjected in the course of the play. In *Horace,* for instance, we are temporarily allowed to sympathize with such traditional values as conjugal love ("Des frères ne sont rien à l'égal d'un époux"), family piety ("Pour aimer un mari, l'on ne hait pas ses frères: / La

59

nature en tout temps garde ses premiers droits"), and a sense of one's basic humanity ("J'ai le coeur aussi bon, mais enfin je suis homme").[20] Corneille's rhetoric is so persuasive that at the moment a character voices any particular value, we are willing to accept it as universally valid—only to find a moment later that it does not measure up to the test to which the dramatic situation subjects it. The patriotic ideal that we come to accept by the end of the play is at best a hard-earned value: when the hero's sister Camille at one point attacks his "brutale vertu,"[21] we are forced to acknowledge the essential inhumanity inherent in the demands that heroism makes. Admirable though David's painting may be as an affirmation of heroism, and successful though it may be in what Fried calls its "perfect matching" of spiritual and bodily, its need to confine itself to a single moment does not allow it to guide its viewers (as *Horace* is able to guide its audience) through the process by which heroic values are earned.

Yet the particular mode of heroism in which *Horace* culminates differs from the various forms the heroic ideal takes in Corneille's other plays. Like Ibsen much later, Corneille—at least in his major period—allowed each play to be an implicit answer to (and questioning of!) the values which the preceding play had seemed to affirm. Thus Serge Doubrovsky brilliantly describes Corneille's progress from *Le Cid* (1636) through *Polyeucte* (1641 or 1642) as a dialectical development from the heroism of conquest over others (*Le Cid*), through a heroism defined by conquest of self (*Horace*) and the exercise of total political power (*Cinna*), to the "conquest of God" which *Polyeucte* celebrates.[22] Yet what matters is not so much the particular forms of heroism in Corneille as the *process* by which the heroic ideal defines itself, both within a single play and from one play to the next.[23] The genius of the Corneillian theater consists in the constant "upward" movement by means of which one set of values is at first espoused and then absorbed by a new and "higher" set of values. The heroism we experience exists in the very act of transcendence. History and heroism work in a kind of reciprocal relation to one another: our knowledge that the hero lives within a particular historical context gives meaning to his acts, while his acts, in turn, endow history with its central meanings. History magnifies and is magnified in return.

As powerful and moving emanations of heroic action, Corneille's four major plays occupy a unique place in the history of drama. The only other dramatic form which sustains the heroic with comparable success is not, properly speaking, a literary form at all: I am referring to opera, which, especially in its nineteenth-century manifestations, provides the major vehicle by which theater audiences today are able to experience the heroic. The boundaries between "literary" and "musical" drama have of course never been absolute. Everybody knows that Greek drama managed to combine the various arts, but nobody knows enough about the nonverbal arts, especially music, to discuss the experience of the Greek audience with any precision. We often resort to an analogy with opera in describing "literary" dramas which are unable to communicate adequately to us on a verbal level alone. Schiller, as I indicated in the preceding chapter, complained of the "opera world" ending to Goethe's *Egmont,* which culminates in a dream vision (accompanied by music) of "freedom in celestial garb"; [24] Goethe must have recognized that words alone (or at least the dramatic method he employed throughout the play) would be unable to create the powerful heroic effect he needed at the end. Nearly every recent study of Dryden's heroic plays mentions, in one way or another, the peculiarly "operatic" character of these works. Like most opera libretti they always hover at the edge of absurdity; they present us with characters who seem larger than, or at least different from, life; and they are concerned not so much with the analysis of human conduct as with the assertion of heroic action.

In their attempt to overwhelm the audience with heroic rhetoric, Dryden's plays find their perfect realization for us today not in the baroque operas with which they were contemporary, nor in the *opera seria* of the eighteenth century, but in nineteenth-century opera, which, with its massiveness of effect and the lavishly varied means which it exploits—solos, ensembles, choruses, ballets—has become our principal means of apprehending heroic action in the theater. In *opera seria* and above all in Handel and Mozart, its greatest practitioners,[25] the heroic exists in the musical style itself; but with its strict economy of means—its dependence on solo arias and its paucity of choruses and ensembles—*opera seria's* ability to strike a modern audience with heroic effect pales in comparison, say, with French "grand opera" or Italian "tragic opera" from Meyerbeer and Donizetti onwards. Music can provide theater with a rhetoric of the sublime which words can only rarely achieve. Such a rhetoric can be found in the dominantly florid style of singing of *opera seria* and of French and Italian opera during the early nineteenth century: it is as though the effort of negotiating an apparently impossible passage of music with grace and precision comes to seem an heroic achievement in itself. One could speculate, moreover, that the greater flexibility of the female voice in florid singing may well have something to do with the fact that women (or men played by castrati) assume the burden of the heroic action in *opera seria*: if the most heroic passages of an opera often take the form of revenge arias, this is because women by tradition did not initiate action but could at least react with vigor when acted upon. (Giving the leading role to a woman such as Cleopatra or Semiramide of course enables a composer to allow a female singer ample heroic opportunity.)

The heroic effect of nineteenth-century opera is closely linked to its ceremonial character, by means of which we are meant to feel ourselves overwhelmed by forces larger than ourselves. Nineteenth-century operas are full of ceremonial scenes such as oaths (*Les Huguenots, Un Ballo in Maschera, Die Götterdämmerung*), curses (*Rigoletto, Das Rheingold, Tristan und Isolde*), prayers (*Der Freischütz, La Forza del Destino, Cavalleria*

Rusticana), waltz interludes (*Faust, Die Meistersinger, Eugene Onegin*), marches (*Tannhäuser, Le Prophète, Aida*) friendship-vow duets (*Norma, Don Carlos, Otello*), and ensembles of varying sizes (the *Faust* trio, *Rigoletto* quartet, *Meistersinger* quintet, *Lucia* sextet) in which diverse, often warring personages fuse their individual contemplations into musical statements of rare magnificence. *Don Carlos* embellishes the original Schiller play with a huge auto-da-fé plus a fantastic final scene in which the long-dead Charles V emerges from his tomb to carry the doomed hero back with him. In opera even the love duets have a public, ceremonial character. Berlioz's *Les Troyens* is essentially a five-hour succession of ceremonial scenes—with designations such as "Marche et Hymne," "Prière," "Imprécation," "Pantomime," and "Chasse Royal et Orage." In the opera's final moments, as we witness a vision of the future Roman Capitol over Dido's funeral pyre, the conflict of Troy and Carthage is magnified so that we are allowed to feel the whole weight of historical process as only a nineteenth-century imagination could have conceived it.

As history, the great nineteenth-century operas retain only the most tenuous possible relationship to what our common sense considers historical truth. *Rigoletto* is at least vaguely about the capers of Francis I (though for political reasons Verdi shifted the scene from France to a minor Italian court), and *Un Ballo in Maschera*—though with the grossest inaccuracy—is centered around the assassination of Sweden's Gustav III (here Verdi, again for political reasons, shifted the scene to Puritan Boston); *Les Huguenots* attempts to render the feel of St. Bartholomew's Day by liberally mixing the sounds of gunfire with the music. Like the dramas of Victor Hugo, which inspired such famous works as Donizetti's *Lucrezia Borgia* and Verdi's *Ernani* and *Rigoletto*, operas cultivate history as a means of creating a picturesque and often exotic setting; yet unlike these plays, the music is able to give them a heroic dimension which the plays are unable to achieve by words alone.

The history we experience in operas such as these has nothing to do with what we generally mean by the term, and yet it remains a history of sorts. What we experience through the driving force of the music is the illusion of huge and fateful events and larger-than-life characters engaged in some mysterious struggle with these events—history not in its subtlety or its richness but history as sheer power. It is true, though also quite irrelevant, that the libretto of *La Forza del Destino* (not to speak of the Spanish "historical" play on which it is based) is utterly absurd. Yet the difference between the libretto and its total musical realization is at least as great as that between melodrama and tragedy—between, for instance, *King Leir* and *King Lear*. If even the most serious operagoer has difficulty remembering the intricacies of the plot he is witnessing, this is because the plot structure, with its complicated tangle of human relationships, does not assume the same importance for the viewer that it does in verbal drama; rather, he experiences every passage—be it

revenge aria, choral rejoicing, or an aria pleading for mercy—in its ele-
mentalness, as though he were participating in a ceremony. And as with
other, more institutionalized ceremonies such as the mass, the participant
does not seek novelty, nor does he care about being kept in suspense, as in a
verbal drama; instead, he comes to welcome repeated performances and in
fact often does not even begin to "enjoy" his participation until after he has
become thoroughly familiar with the opera.

The illusion of power which music can create, or, more precisely, our
feeling that we are experiencing a powerful force as we listen to music, is by
no means limited to opera. It is a feeling we experience, for instance, in
Beethoven's *Eroica,* which, even without its label (or the reference to
Napoleon that the composer temporarily attached to it), would strike us
immediately—especially in relation to the history of the symphony up to its
time—as an attempt to express heroic action in musical terms. However well
such earlier composers as Monteverdi and Handel may have seemed to their
contemporaries to have embodied the heroic in their work, it is Beethoven,
above all other composers, whom we have come to associate with the heroic.
It does not seem accidental that the literary settings for which he produced
overtures or incidental music included Goethe's *Egmont, Prometheus* (a
ballet score) and *Coriolanus* (not Shakespeare's version, but one by a
contemporary Viennese playwright). His one opera, *Fidelio,* built on a
libretto suffused with French revolutionary ideology, uses music to render love
as a heroic force which can overcome the most brutal authoritarian oppression. The symphonic style he created in the *Eroica,* with its solemnity and its
unrelenting drive toward its climaxes, established the heroic mode as the
central tradition of nineteenth-century music—with such success that it has
become the burden of every twentieth-century composer to discover a style
which would advertise its refusal to be heroic.[26] (When Stravinsky, like many
in our time, declared his preference for Beethoven's quite "unheroic"
even-numbered symphonies, he was simply voicing the characteristic modern
suspicion of heroism.)[27]

The sense of power we experience in nineteenth-century music can remind
us that heroic action does not need to be embodied in individual heroes, or in
a form of action which achieves its autonomy regardless of its agents. It
scarcely matters whether the name of Napoleon was attached to the *Eroica,*
whose action moves at its own momentum regardless of what particular figure
inspired the work. When Hegel defined "world-historical individuals" as those
"who grasp . . . a higher universal, make it their own purpose, and who realize
this purpose in accordance with the higher law of the spirit,"[28] he suggested a
world of action that moves awesomely above (note his repeated use of the
word "higher") and virtually independent of its agents. By the nineteenth
century the historical process rather than the individual had become the chief
carrier of heroic action. When the writer can no longer conceive of a properly

heroic hero, the historical process can assume the magnitude appropriate to heroism. "Je suis une force qui va," the famous tag line of Hugo's Hernani, expresses the author's desire to portray the heroic impulse at the same time that it demonstrates the absurdity of locating heroism in a single individual.[29]

Yet even in earlier periods the difficulty of realizing or sustaining the heroic within an individual could often make a writer postulate some impersonal force which would give his work a heroic dimension. In Racine, for instance, no trace is left of the heroic individualism around which Corneille's major plays had centered, yet his plays contain a heroic dimension through the oppressive force which we feel overpowering his characters — "une cour qui l'accable," as one person describes the political world victimizing Bérénice, or the irrational powers which destroy Phèdre ("C'est Vénus tout entière à sa proie attachée"); [30] character and audience come to recognize the irresistibleness of these powers with something of the awe which was traditionally granted the feats of great heroes.

If *Henry IV, Part 1,* with its balancing of Hotspur's and Falstaff's attitudes to heroism and its vindication of Prince Hal on the battlefield at Shrewsbury, is essentially concerned with the nature of heroic action, the play's second part noticeably lacks a serious interest in heroism — unless one locates its heroic impulse in the conception of history which emerges from the solemn conversation which the king and Warwick conduct midway in the play. After the king's outcry about man's inability to understand the workings of history,

> O God, that one might read the book of fate,
> And see the revolution of the times
> Make mountains level,

(III.i.45-47)

Warwick attempts to comfort him by asserting the presence of discernible patterns in history:

> There is a history in all men's lives
> Figuring the nature of the times deceas'd;
> The which observ'd, a man may prophesy,
> With a near aim, of the main chance of things
> As yet not come to life, who in their seeds
> And weak beginnings lie intreasured.
> Such things become the hatch and brood of time. . . .

(80-86)

If patterns exist, they still maintain their mystery for us, as we feel in that rich phrase "the hatch and brood of time." Whether or not they take a specifically Hegelian form, the processes of history become the cause and object of awe when individual heroic action is no longer possible. One could perhaps speak of a principle of compensation in great drama whereby the historical process assumes a heroic role to compensate for the loss, or impossibility, of

64

conventional heroism; it is as though the human imagination demands a sense of greatness whether this greatness is located in the individual will or in processes beyond human grasp.

Whatever the compensations we are offered, the declining role of the hero remains a central fact within our consciousness whenever we look at literary history diachronically. Northrop Frye, in an influential and attractive theory, has used the progressive decline of the hero as a means of charting the history of fictional forms in the various Western literatures since the Middle Ages. According to Frye's scheme, the hero moves from a "mythical" mode (in which he is "superior in *kind* both to other men and to the environment of other men") through a series of stages — the "romance" hero, superior only "in *degree*"; the "high-mimetic" hero of Renaissance literature, "superior in degree to other men but not to his natural environment"; the "low-mimetic" hero of comedy and realistic fiction, "superior neither to other men nor to his environment"; and, finally, the hero of the modern "ironic" mode, "inferior in power or intelligence to ourselves."[31] As though testing his theory by extending its range, Frye goes on to claim "something of the same progression" in ancient literature from Homeric epic to Roman satire.[32] Like all ambitious and far-ranging theories, Frye's tends to work much better if we treat it as a general image of history than if we look too hard for specific applications. And like all good theories, it was designed to support its maker's fundamental beliefs, in this instance Frye's notion that imaginative literature exists as a coherent and autonomous body of knowledge.

Since I do not view literature as "autonomous" but rather as a mode of discourse which is constantly reshaping itself according to the challenges we perceive to be imposed by the "outside" world, I shall improvise on Frye's theory by proposing the principle that heroes tend to diminish not only within a literary tradition as a whole, but also in a genre, in a period, in the writings of a particular author, and, indeed, in the course of a single work. Within historical drama, for instance, one can cite the diminution of the hero from *Tamburlaine* to Ben Jonson's various rogues, who, whether in his comedies or tragedies, derive considerable ironic sustenance from their implicit commentary on the unreality of Marlowe's heroes. A striking loss of heroic power takes place as one looks from Corneille's heroes of the 1630s and 1640s to Racine's heroes of the 1670s, not to speak of Corneille's own sharply diminished later heroes. German drama moves from such assertive *Sturm und Drang* heroes as Goethe's Götz and Egmont to the circumscribed heroes of the post-Napoleonic period — Grabbe's titanically willed figures who find themselves compromised within a prosaic world (his play on Napoleon, significantly, is set during the Hundred Days); Grillparzer's various protagonists who serve virtually as object lessons about the dangers inherent in action; Büchner's Danton and Woyzeck, each of whom, in varying ways, we recognize as direct ancestors of the contemporary antihero.

Shakespeare's most uncompromised and "traditional" hero is Talbot, who appears in what is perhaps his first play, *Henry VI, Part 1.* The heroes of the "major" tragedies are all compromised, in one way or another, by the particular flaws — vacillation, jealousy, imprudence, ambition — which we variously assign to them. Although the last two tragedies, *Coriolanus* and *Antony and Cleopatra*, are very much concerned with the nature of heroism, these plays are also concerned, respectively, with the difficulty and meaninglessness of heroic action in the existing public world. As Reuben A. Brower has pointed out, the Coriolanus we observe fighting in Corioli early in the play and his deeds which we hear recounted in Cominius's great panegyric (II.ii.80-128) reflect images of traditional heroes that Shakespeare would have encountered in Virgil and in Chapman's translation of the *Iliad*;[33] yet the heroic ideals which the play voices so eloquently at the beginning are subjected to the most merciless questioning in the course of the play.

Dryden's heroes decline from the high-spirited Almanzor of *The Conquest of Granada* (1670-71) to Aureng-Zebe (1675), whose heroic actions within an intriguing Indian court were neatly described by Dr. Johnson when he wrote of the play, "The personages are imperial; but the dialogue is often domestick";[34] and thence to Don Sebastian (1689), a captive king who is depicted as enduring rather than acting. (Once the more assertive forms of action have come to seem impossible, endurance — passive though it may be — defines itself as a mode of heroism.) When Dryden, in the preface to *Don Sebastian,* described "Love and Honour" not only as "the mistaken Topicks of Tragedy" but also as "quite worn out,"[35] he hinted at what we might take to be a general principle — that heroic actions have less staying power than most other literary themes and conventions.

Even with the sustaining power of music, the universal history which Wagner mythologizes in the cycle of works comprising *Der Ring des Nibelungen* takes the form of progressive diminution: thus between *Das Rheingold* and *Die Götterdämmerung* we witness the decline of the characters from gods to heroes and thence to something only little above ordinary men. Wotan moves from the commanding deity of *Das Rheingold* to the lonely wanderer of *Siegfried*; the heroic, short-lived Siegmund of *Die Walküre* is replaced in the cycle by his son Siegfried, who declines from dragon-killer to the unwitting tool of mere plotting mortals; Brünnhilde, undeified by the magic fire at the end of *Die Walküre,* ends up a ranting, deceived wife in the final work. (When George Bernard Shaw disparagingly labeled *Die Götterdämmerung* an "opera" in contrast to the more lofty designation "music-drama" which he allowed the earlier three works of the cycle, he was in effect commenting on the commonplace operatic doings — jealousy, treachery and the like — in which its characters engage.)[36]

Audiences and readers, one suspects, can bear only a limited amount of heroism before tedium or, for that matter, laughter sets in. Mock-epic is an old and hallowed genre but nobody writes mock-comedy, if only because it could not easily be distinguished from the object of its parody. The more solemn an action, or the higher the style in which it is described, the more easily it invites parody. *The Conquest of Granada* was parodied within a year after its production by the Duke of Buckingham in *The Rehearsal,* a play which, like all good parodies, retains a certain charm independent of one's knowledge of the work it attacks.[37] The parody of Hebbel's *Judith* by the Austrian comic writer Nestroy is in every way a more satisfying work than its unrelentingly solemn model. Shaw's history plays, for instance *The Man of Destiny, Caesar and Cleopatra,* and *Saint Joan,* are at once parodies of fancy-dress Victorian heroic-historical dramas and attempts to beat their models at their own game; indeed, Shaw was so successful in the latter purpose that we scarcely remember the parodistic side of these plays today.[38]

The most serious plays often contain passages parodying a high-flown earlier style as a means of establishing the validity of their own, much more sober-minded styles. When we note the outmoded rhetoric of the Player's Speech in *Hamlet* (II.ii.454-522)[39] or Falstaff's excursion into "King Cambyses' vein" (Part I.II.iv.381-89),[40] Shakespeare is telling us, in effect, that his own stylistic norm comes closer than those of his predecessors to establishing a real and believable world. Near the beginning of *Dantons Tod* Büchner presents the absurd ranting of the drunken stage-prompter Simon, who, unable to distinguish the language of the theater from that of the world around him, lapses into what Büchner's readers would have recognized as the elevated rhetoric of Schiller and his imitators;[41] Büchner's parody of a dead theatrical language makes it possible for him to establish his personal style (which, as it turns out, has its own florid moments) as the norm of the play.

The precariousness of heroism is in one sense a precariousness of language. Language in the "high" style demands a tacit assent from the listener that he is willing to listen with a straight face. If the middle and lower levels of style become boring to us once a particular writer's manner has worn itself out, the higher levels are constantly risking our laughter; indeed, one could speculate that the "higher" the style the more quickly a linguistic convention is apt to wear itself out. As long as the classical rhetorical tradition prevailed, the writer could count on an audience's willingness to accept the appropriateness of certain set phrases for specific heroic occasions. Cominius's speech of praise for Coriolanus — with its traditional locutions such as "valour is the chiefest virtue and / Most dignifies the haver" (II.ii.82-83) — is in one sense a tissue of clichés, yet we find it moving, partly because it acknowledges deeds we have just seen enacted, but also because we accept its words and phrases as a time-honored (rather than time-tarnished) mode of description. Without such linguistic conventions which can claim our assent, a writer would be forced to create a style of his own for every purpose; parody thus becomes easier to achieve than "straight" language, dispraise prevails over praise, the antihero is born out of the writer's inability to forge a language for heroes.

If heroic energy tends to decline within the course of a drama, it also succeeds in reasserting itself at moments when it would seem to have been wholly dissipated. One could speak of "heroism remembered," a phenomenon which occurs in *Coriolanus*, for instance, when, just before he is killed by Aufidius's conspirators, the hero challenges his antagonists with a reminder of his past great deeds:

> If you have writ your annals true, 'tis there,
> That, like an eagle in a dove-cote, I
> Fluttered your Volscians in Corioli.
> Alone I did it.

> (V.vi.114-17)

Coriolanus's heroic assertion comes at the most absurd possible moment — when he is about to assume the role of tragic victim. One can go through the final scenes of innumerable plays for comparable examples — Egmont's dream-vision, Antony's eulogy to the dead Brutus, Horatio's to Hamlet, and so on. Greatness always has its locus in some irretrievable past. (Through Wagner's Leitmotiv technique, the past heroism which the dying and degraded Siegfried remembers in the final act of *Die Götterdämmerung* can be recaptured, if only briefly, with all its earlier sublimity — and with an intensity impossible in a purely verbal drama.) Büchner's Danton, who presents nothing but the most unheroic images throughout the play — to the point, in fact, where he proclaims the meaninglessness of all heroic endeavor — reminds the tribunal which is about to order his execution of the feats he had once (long before the opening of the play) performed to create and preserve the Republic: "I declared war on the monarchy on the Champs de Mars, on the tenth of August I defeated it, on the twenty-first of January I killed it, in front of the kings [of Europe] I threw down as a gauntlet the head of a king."[42] (If Danton's heroic assertion comes in the next-to-last rather than last act, this is still another sign of the anticlimactic and ironic tone which dominates the play.)

Such last-minute reminders of heroism within a form which tends to undermine heroic action are a way of satisfying our cravings for the heroic at the same time that the very basis of these cravings is questioned. In one sense these reminders are part of the paraphernalia of tragedy — attempts to show us how far a mighty hero has fallen, or to reestablish our sympathy with him after we have watched him weaken, or to demonstrate the magnitude of "tragic waste" — all depending on the particular theory of tragedy that happens to structure our thinking. But in another sense these reminders suggest something basic to drama as a genre — its ingrained difficulty in sustaining the higher ranges of style and action, and, at least in the noncomic forms, its tendency to move from a heroic to a more prosaic world. When Goethe has the dying Götz von Berlichingen lament the coming of "an age of deceit,"[43] he is articulating a notion about the death of heroism that can be found in numerous dramas of all times.

The process of diminution which I have described in drama—both within individual plays and in the course of a period as a whole—is central to our image of the novel as a genre. In its origins the novel reveals its antiheroic impulse in the most obvious possible ways—in Cervantes' parody of heroic romance, in Fielding's constant reminders in *Tom Jones* of the discrepancies between his own characters and the more lofty personages of the traditional genres. It seems natural, in retrospect, that Fielding moved from *Tom Thumb,* an antiheroic parody in the tradition of *The Rehearsal,* to the writing of novels. The use of prose in itself makes possible the introduction of lowly matter which poetry could not accommodate. If the epic writer kept his hero at a distance through the loftiness of his style and a narrative technique that concentrated on external actions, the novelist can all too easily give his hero an intimacy of exposure which removes whatever heroic aura he might be tempted to surround him with. The history of verse epic since the Renaissance has of course been one of an increasingly diminishing heroism: *Paradise Lost* makes a big point of locating its "heroic argument" not in the battles traditional to the genre, but in a spiritual revolt within the Garden, while *The Prelude,* in turn, moves its own heroic argument from what in Milton was at least an external drama to the private spiritual experiences of its author (if both poets claim to offer more rather than less heroic argument than their predecessors, they are simply admitting that earlier modes of heroism have lost their power to persuade). Although the long poem has persisted by turning the scene of action inward,[44] the novel, through its ability to render private experience in all its intimacy, has assumed the major burden during the last two centuries of undoing older attitudes toward heroism. Whenever we proclaim the commonplace that the novel is the characteristic genre of the modern world, we are saying, in effect, that the world we live in is a very prosaic place and that the more poetic genres that the novel replaced could emerge only in times that were less imaginatively impoverished than our own; we are at once lamenting the loss of heroic values and congratulating ourselves on our ability to accommodate to a less noble and satisfying mode of reality.

Just as the novel has been conspicuously anti- or at least unheroic since its origins, so it has claimed to speak as history (though history of a deliberately prosaic sort). The word "history" that forms an essential part of Fielding's titles; the complicated ruses about editors and manuscripts in Richardson and his various epistolary successors such as Rousseau and Goethe; the introspective personal-memoir form of *Tristram Shandy*—all are attempts to assert the historical truth of a fiction which each author has ingeniously fabricated. In one sense such a claim was an extension of the demand for verisimilitude which played so decisive a role in dramatic theory from the

Renaissance until the eighteenth century; more fundamentally, perhaps, it was a way of distinguishing the new genre of the novel from those romances which had been the major form of prose narrative during the preceding century or two.[45] But the notion of the novel as history also worked to endow the intimate details of private life with something of the significance that had hitherto belonged only to public history. As a recent writer on eighteenth-century historical narrative has put it, "Fielding attempts to liberate men from the public history that dealt in deductive political and social exempla subsuming the individual in its search for generalization."[46] As a result of the early novelists' extension of the idea of history from the public to the private domain, the sexual indiscretions of such diverse fictional creations as Moll Flanders, Jenny Jones, and Clarissa Harlowe come to achieve an importance, even a public status of sorts, which would have been inconceivable for characters of such lowly background in earlier literature.

As with drama, the presence of a historical perspective is a means of magnifying the characters and events of fiction. Yet the magnifying effect does not function in the same way in fiction as it does in drama. Historical drama, after all, deals with persons who wield power and who thus carry an aura of fascination about themselves from the start; the men and events about which a historical play centers have a public status independent of their role in the play. The magnifying effect of fiction is more modest, if only because the novelist starts with the most "unpromising" matter and is satisfied if he has made the insignificant seem significant. Even when he is writing an overtly historical novel, public characters never achieve quite that sense of significance which we find in historical drama. To some degree this is a difference in media: as Schiller expressed it in one of his typically pithy theoretical statements, "All narrative forms turn the present into past; all *dramatic* forms turn the past into present."[47] A Tamburlaine or a Richard III in a novel could never radiate the same degree of wonder which they can in drama. Narrative works to create a distance, both temporal and physical, between us and the personages it depicts, while drama seeks an immediacy of effect which succeeds in giving its personages a direct power over us. In his great study of the historical novel, Georg Lukács has observed that while historical dramatists make central characters out of kings and heroic figures, historical novelists keep their public personages on the sidelines.[48] The Rob Roy of Scott's novel and the Napoleon of *War and Peace* remain peripheral to the main action while the central events of these novels—as of virtually all the great historical novels of the nineteenth century—remain in the hands of the invented and less "powerful" characters.

It is as though the historical novelist, recognizing the essentially unheroic nature of the novel as a genre, instinctively knows enough to keep his heroes in their place. When Tolstoy, in the second epilogue to *War and Peace,* provides a theory of history to account for Napoleon's impotence in shaping events, he is, in effect, telling us about the inability of heroic figures in novels to convince us of their power. Long before people started talking about antiheroes, the central characters of novels were unformed young men who, even if they became fully "formed" by the end of the book, never turned out to be very heroic. The novel has always tended to define itself by the distance it sets up from heroic ideals. Fabrice's failure, in *La Chartreuse de Parme*, to recognize what was going on at Waterloo, is emblematic of the attitude toward heroism and public events which has prevailed in fiction. Novelists have found a multitude of ways of reminding us of the genre's antiheroic intent. After announcing, in one of the prefatory chapters to *Tom Jones,* that "the hero [in our tragic poets] is always introduced with a flourish of drums and trumpets, in order to rouse a martial spirit in the audience,"[49] Fielding gives us a first glimpse of Sophia Western by parodying a heroic introduction. *Vanity Fair* advertises its ability to do without a hero in its famous subtitle. The Homeric parallel in *Ulysses* serves to remind us of the unheroic nature of modern life throughout the book.

Despite their essentially antiheroic bias, many novels, like many historical dramas, move from "relative" heroism toward the disintegration of whatever heroic assertions they were able to make at the start. The heroic figures in Scott's novels of eighteenth-century Scotland—Rob Roy, for instance, or Fergus MacIvor in *Waverley*—are shown up as noble anachronisms who must inevitably make way for the unheroic new world of commerce. *Crime and Punishment* proceeds from Raskolnikov's "heroic" act in the pawnbroker's apartment (an act which is later rendered absurd through our recognition of its explicitly Napoleonic model) to the introspective process which we watch going on in the hero's mind. *War and Peace*, after the heroic actions of the war (for Tolstoy, of course, heroism emanates from a people rather than from its leaders), culminates in the domestic peace of Pierre and Natasha at home. The sublime mountain world which Thomas Mann, in *Der Zauberberg*, contrasts with the prosaic world of the plains, gradually "declines" in stature in the course of the book (its decline symbolized, for instance, by modish experiments in hypnotism on the mountain); not only does Hans Castorp, at the end, return to the plains, but the war he participates in lacks all traditional heroic meaning. Beckett's trilogy records the progressive deterioration of what, already at the start of the book, seems an uncommonly extreme version of the antihero.

Yet memories of past or possible heroism, or new internal forms of heroism, can provide a compensation of sorts for the antiheroic tendency that prevails in fiction. Scott's doomed heroes are meant to "inspire" the unformed young men who will have to make their way in the new and prosaic commercial world. The "time recaptured" which triumphs within the mind of the hero at the end of *A la recherche du temps perdu* is Proust's version of the internalized heroic argument which Wordsworth celebrates in *The Prelude,* but it is only

71

partial compensation for the fact that the vulgar Madame Verdurin (in her new guise as the Princesse de Guermantes) has come to reign over Paris society. Although Julien Sorel and Raskolnikov have given up all heroic ambition by the end of their novels, the self-knowledge and "authenticity" they achieve represent a new heroism — the only kind, in fact, which can function in the world as it is. In the novel, as in drama, we engage in constant imaginative gestures to compensate for a steadily depleting heroism.

FORMS OF MAGNIFICATION
History as tragedy

And tell sad stories of the death of kings.

Richard II

To conceive of history as tragedy is to view reality through a special lens. The alliance that history and tragedy have, for one reason or another, maintained since the Renaissance has all too easily made us see tragedy as an action in historical dress and history as an unending movement toward catastrophe.[50] We rarely think of history as comedy, despite occasional attempts to join the two. When Scribe, in *Le Verre d'eau*, tried to attribute a major change of policy during Queen Anne's reign to the glass of water mentioned in the title, the play that resulted was as trivial as the historical situation around which it was built. Shaw's *Caesar and Cleopatra*, a work of considerably higher stature, achieves much of its comic effect by constantly reminding us of its historical anachronisms. If Shakespeare set his comedies in faraway places to remove them from the everyday world of the audience, the distancing was strictly geographical rather than historical; and although *The Merry Wives of Windsor* is relatively local (and "unromantic") by Shakespearean standards, the historical dimension within which Falstaff operates in *Henry IV* is conspicuously missing in the comedy. Most comedies from antiquity to the present have been set not only in the historical present but in the very cities in which their audiences are assembled; the Athens of Aristophanes, the Florence of Machiavelli, the London of Ben Jonson and Congreve, the Paris of Molière — all remain central to our experience of their particular comedies. Indeed, through their presentness and their localness, comedies often provide later generations with historical "records" of a period in a far more obvious way than tragedies: thus, we are more likely to turn to *The Shoemaker's Holiday* than to *Hamlet* for information about life in Elizabethan London, or to *Tartuffe* than to *Phèdre* about life in the Paris of Louis XIV. If tragedy cultivated earlier history as a means of achieving verisimilitude and grandeur, comedy could claim that, despite its fictive base, it might later be taken for history itself.[51]

A "domestic" tragedy such as *Arden of Feversham*, despite the essentially private matters which it reports, retains at least a historical base in a once-famous scandal which its unknown author drew from the same chronicle on which Shakespeare's histories are based. Although tragedy after the Enlightenment was often "democratized" to the point that it made no pretense to be either historical or of public import, the most influential modern bourgeois tragedy, Lillo's *London Merchant*, retains a sixteenth-century historical setting appropriate to the old ballad from which it is derived. Even the major bourgeois tragedies of the last two centuries — plays such as Schiller's *Kabale und Liebe* (*Intrigue and Love*), Hebbel's *Maria Magdalene*, Miller's *Death of a Salesman*, not to speak of the great plays of Ibsen's "realistic" period — though not historical in any temporal sense, are concerned with some of the issues traditional to historical drama, for example the conflict of classes within society and the pressures of the public order upon the individual will.

The reciprocal relation traditional to history and tragedy makes it difficult for us wholly to separate one from the other in our consciousness. History magnifies an action to create a properly "tragic" effect, while it also provides the verisimilitude necessary for us to take a play seriously. Tragedy, in turn, gives history a way of making "sense" out of what might otherwise be a chaos of events; or the catastrophe whose inevitability it demonstrates works to confirm our worst fears about the nature of events and, by one of those apparent paradoxes that we often find when we examine the effects of art, it ends up helping us to cope with an otherwise unbearable reality. The special prestige which tragedy has enjoyed among the poetic genres until recently gave a correspondingly special status to those public historical actions out of which great tragedies could conceivably be built. Corneille's statement in his First Discourse, "The dignity [of tragedy] demands some great state interest or passion nobler and more virile than love, . . . [one] which causes us to fear misfortunes greater than the loss of a mistress,"[52] gives some indication of the dependence upon history that tragic dramatists since the Renaissance have felt. The relationship of history and tragedy was, of course, especially fruitful in Corneille's own dramatic writing: if his use of tragic form allowed him to give historical events an inevitable connection to one another, the authority and dignity which tragedy confers allowed him, in turn, to extend the possibilities of tragedy beyond what his many critics thought permissible within the genre, for instance his vindication of an unpunished murderer in *Horace*, or his celebration of a quite un-Aristotelian martyr-hero in *Polyeucte*.[53]

Seeing history as tragedy has at certain times seemed a natural act for the imagination. "They thought they could seize tragedy itself directly within the historical process," Walter Benjamin wrote of the way that German baroque dramatists such as Gryphius and Lohenstein conceived of their historical sources.[54] The "tragical-historical" in Polonius's famous list of genres (II.ii. 401-5) indicates an affinity which must have come naturally to many writers. In describing the background for the Elizabethan history play, F. P. Wilson pointed to the poems in *The Mirror for Magistrates* as examples of how historical action naturally assumes a tragic shape: "The authors of *The Mirror for Magistrates*...saw that there are some historical actions which can be composed into a unity more easily than others, and none more easily than those which lead up to the death of a king or counsellor of state. Then History becomes almost indistinguishable from Tragedy."[55]

Despite such natural affinities between history and tragedy, almost every commentator on Shakespeare's English history plays has been at pains to distinguish them from the tragedies. Not only was the history play a recognizable genre in the 1590s, but the editors of the First Folio confirmed the distinction in 1623 by printing the histories separately from the tragedies and comedies. Moreover, since the histories (except for the late *Henry VIII*) were written before the major tragedies, they achieve a separate status, if only as a means of talking about Shakespeare's development. "In the purely historical plays, the history *informs* the plot," Coleridge theorized; "in the mixt [such as *Henry IV*], it *directs* it; in the rest, as *Macbeth, Hamlet, Cymbeline, Lear,* it subserves it."[56] If Coleridge stressed the relation of history and plot to distinguish between the histories and tragedies, a recent critic, A. C. Hamilton, stresses the differences in content: "While the history play remains social and communal, tragedy becomes impersonal and remote."[57]

In searching for keys to Shakespeare's development, one can multiply distinctions such as these to the point of making countless insights into individual plays. If one looks at the endings of, say, *Richard II* and *Hamlet,* one notes that, whereas the former stresses continuity and accommodation, the latter leaves us with unresolvable ironies and a sense of total disruption. Between Shakespeare's two great plays about tyrants, *Richard III* and *Macbeth,* the emphasis has shifted markedly from the historical and political order to something we are likely to label "cosmic" or "universal"; but this is largely a matter of emphasis, for Margaret's prophecies and the providence that guides the Earl of Richmond at the end find their fulfillment in the supernatural machinery which plays such a crucial (and also perplexing) role in the later work. Indeed, in my present context I am less concerned with differences than with the fact that the tragedies build upon and intensify certain themes and attitudes developed in the histories.[58] In the face of the "ultimate" questions which the tragedies raise it is easy to forget such typically "historical" matters as the rottenness that afflicts Hamlet's Denmark, the folly of Lear's dividing his kingdom, the breach of order in Macbeth's act of regicide — above all, the symbols and ceremonies of state that magnify the dramatic action of the tragedies and convince us of its world-shaking importance. It is significant, moreover, that Shakespeare's pervasive influence on the great German historical dramas from the early Goethe through Büchner (not to speak of the historical "closet" dramas of the nineteenth-century English poets) stems at least as much from the tragedies as from the histories.

A play can look at history as tragedy in several quite distinct ways. At one extreme it can assume the essentially tragic nature of history from the start, as in most of the German baroque plays whose attitude toward history Walter Benjamin describes so incisively in the above quotation. For instance, the opening lines of Andreas Gryphius's martyr play *Catharina von Georgien* —

> O die ihr auf der kummerreichen welt
> Verschrenckt mit weh und ach und dürren todten-beinen
> Mich sucht, wo alles bricht und fält. . . . [59]

quickly establish a tragic perspective which leaves little room for intensification. In *Dantons Tod* Büchner goes to great lengths to prevent us from raising our hopes about the world he depicts: when Danton, shortly before the end, voices the insight "The world is chaos. Nothingness is the world-god yet to be born,"[60] he is simply articulating a notion that the play has been demonstrating all along. Whether we attribute the gloom of such works to a Counter-Reformation interest in the art of dying or to modern existential despair, the central vision is that no real choices are possible and, as a result, whatever "plot" the play offers is finally irrelevant. The interest of such plays centers not in the plot but in the attitudes (fear, indifference, defiance, lament, good humor) which the characters take toward their common doom. The relative unimportance of plot in plays of this type invariably creates difficulties for critics who habitually think about drama in Aristotelian terms, as when they refer to *The Trojan Women* as "lyrical" tragedy.[61] Needless to say, through their relative lack of plot, very few of these plays have been able to maintain their hold on us over the ages, for they depend to a high degree on the audience's ability to share the ideological assumptions which stand behind their various visions of doom.

In some plays a single character or segment of the play's action may represent a "tragic" view of life, only to be set into a larger, nontragic perspective by the play as a whole. Thus, although Richard II conceives of history as tragedy, his opponent Bolingbroke, finding he can wield history to suit his purposes, forces us to see Richard's plight as a limited approach to reality. In Corneille's *Cinna* Emilie and her conspirator friends, though they trick us at first into accepting their tragic premises, end up as only a part of a larger "truth" which the Emperor Augustus (as well as the audience) creates to resolve the problems of the play. If the tragic characters had the final word in these plays, *Richard II* would be a single, long, lyrical lament and *Cinna* an unmitigated cry for vengeance. The title character in Kleist's *Prinz Friedrich von Homburg* gradually comes to will his own execution, only to find himself pardoned through the "maturity" he demonstrates in learning how to judge himself: in the course of this play the same person thus "grows" from a tragic into a distinctly nontragic character, from being at the mercy of events to being their master. Although Brecht's Mother Courage and Galileo become the victims of history, the author's constant reminders that their failings were unnecessary is meant to goad the audience to do better in the face of history. The happy ending that was conventional within most Spanish Golden Age plays automatically forces a writer to plot his way out of potentially tragic dilemmas. In each of these instances history emerges at the end as not so utterly tragic after all. Indeed, history becomes the arena for those who wish to shape it to their will. Whether we call such plays histories, tragicomedies, or simply dramas — the Spanish term *comedia* conveniently covers drama in general — much of their vitality comes from the confrontation of tragic and nontragic perspectives.

If history is unrelievedly tragic at one extreme, and if its tragic quality is questioned or transformed at the other, one can also point to a type of play in which the tragic perspective emerges only in the course of the action. This is of course tragedy within the central Aristotelian tradition, where plot is primary to character and catharsis is a major means of artistic persuasion. History provides a temporal succession of events which the dramatist manipulates to create the maximum tragic effect at the end. Yet for most of the play the workings of history must maintain a certain "mystery" which the tragic character, if he comes to understand them at all, understands too late. Consider the kinds of problems which Schiller faced (and largely solved) in the writing of *Wallenstein*. On the one hand he was working with what, on the surface, would seem the most inappropriate material for a historical tragedy: a none-too-appealing hero; an event of the Thirty Years' War sufficiently remote from his audience that he would need to supply a goodly amount of background information; subject matter that had no obvious or immediate relevance to the revolutionary decade — the 1790s — in which it was written.[62] But since Schiller's central purpose was to build toward an overwhelming tragic effect, the distance he could count on between the audience and his material allowed him the opportunity to mold this material to suit his needs. "Some [of the material] is hard to fit into the narrow confines of a tragedy-economy," he wrote to Goethe at one point during the composition, although a year later he could pronounce triumphantly, "The whole is poetically organized, and I venture to say the material has been transformed into a purely tragic fable."[63]

The intricate mechanism which Schiller created in his trilogy seems in many ways the perfect union of history and tragedy; to put it more precisely, although the historical matter has been thoroughly molded into the pattern of classical tragedy, it succeeds at the same time in making us feel that real history — with its ruthless political pressuring, its suppression of idealistic endeavor, its questioning into the cause and nature of great events — is being enacted before us. One could even say that many of its historical insights are revealed to us directly *through* the plot. The plot, like that of any Aristotelian tragedy, demands the hero's progressive isolation and decline of fortune; but the *poetic* need for Wallenstein's isolation is accompanied by a *historical* insight into the psychological and social consequences of the hero's breaking the bond which had tied him to the Hapsburg cause. The plot demands as well a series of concrete actions which work to diminish the hero's fortunes; yet these actions are inextricably connected with the intrigues and power games we recognize as central to the historical process — as when the hero's assassin is recruited from among his most loyal followers through the revelation that Wallenstein had once recommended against the man's promotion. The plot demands a hero in whose fate we can feel some concern but with whom we do not identify too closely; yet the character who best suits the author's needs also allows him to analyze the thirst for power in political men — a thirst which in *Wallenstein* ranges from a petty ambition that distances the hero from us to dreams of imperial glory that excite our wonder.

The plot demands a certain mystery as to whether men can will their fate: on the one hand events must achieve their own inexorable momentum, yet on the other hand Wallenstein must be capable of bringing about his own catastrophe without being explicitly responsible for it. Contemplating a deed becomes ultimately inseparable from performing it; thus, though he thinks his secretly sending an intermediary to bargain with the Swedes does not commit him to a break with the Hapsburgs, the fortuitous capture of the intermediary in effect creates the break. The plot mechanism in turn suggests the great historical question that reverberates throughout the play: to what degree can men exercise control over events? (The question is answered not with facts but with the awe we come to feel about the workings of history.) When Goethe, writing of the trilogy's last play, complimented Schiller for moving from the "political" to the "human," he was saying, in effect, that the dramatic mechanism Schiller had created had fully absorbed its historical materials by the end of the work.[64]

In *Wallenstein* Schiller, whose essay *Ueber naive und sentimentalische Dichtung* reveals him as the first modern writer thoroughly self-conscious about the problem of artistic self-consciousness, succeeded in writing perhaps the last great tragedy in the classical tradition. (Though its stature has not been acknowledged outside the German-speaking countries, one might remember that Coleridge, who translated the last two plays of the trilogy soon after they were written, fully understood its distinction.)[65] Through his very self-consciousness Schiller, unlike most great dramatists who came after him, was able to recognize that tragedy has its own conventions independent of any notions which one might have about the tragic nature of history. As one reads through the play with the whole tradition in mind, one notes the various elements he drew together from earlier works — the dramatic irony by which the audience is aware of each stage in the hero's decline before he himself is; the *hybris* he displays as he demands a royal match for his daughter at a time we recognize as much too late; the "cosmic" level of awareness introduced into the play by Wallenstein's faith in his astrologer; the analogies to such

77

earlier examples of greatness (and ultimate failure) as Caesar, Pyrrhus, and Attila;[66] our sense that something sacred is being violated when Wallenstein's assassin is warned, "O mordet nicht den heilgen Schlaf"[67] (it does not seem coincidental that Schiller translated *Macbeth* soon after completing *Wallenstein*); the terror that is unleashed at the catastrophe, with its panic, screams, and lament at the collapse of past greatness ("Dies Haus des Glanzes und der Herrlichkeit / Steht nun verödet").[68] But thinking in "tragic" terms such as these came as naturally to Schiller in his role as a professional historian as it did when he was writing a play: if one glances through his *Geschichte des Dreissigjährigen Kriegs* (*History of the Thirty Years' War*), which he had completed before starting the trilogy, one finds Wallenstein described in such characteristically "tragic" language as this: "durch Ehrgeiz emporgehoben, durch Ehrsucht gestürzt, bei allen seinen Mängeln noch gross und bewundernswert, unübertrefflich, wenn er Mass gehalten hätte."[69] If Schiller was the greatest of narrative historians among the major tragic dramatists, in his historical writings as much as in his dramas he has succeeded in making the union of history and tragedy seem complete.

History as ceremony

> . . . with rough and all-unable pen,
> Our bending author hath pursu'd the story;
> In little room confining mighty men,
> Mangling by starts the full course of their glory.
> Small time, but in that small most greatly liv'd
> This star of England.
>
> *Henry V*, Epilogue

When Shakespeare awkwardly excuses himself in these lines for his "rough and all-unable pen," we recognize those quite familiar *topoi* of "affected modesty" and the "inexpressibility" of language which most of the best writers since antiquity have invoked. But Shakespeare's protest is something more than affectation: in the contrast he sets up here between the smallness of the stage and the greatness of the men depicted on it, between the fragmentariness of the narrative and the magnitude of the events, he implies that *Henry V* is not a self-contained drama, that the modest theatrical piece he has created can at best supply a few hints about the glory it purports to depict. The self-deprecation voiced in these lines can be matched in the relatively low evaluations to which one Shakespeare critic after another has subjected the play and its chief character. For Dr. Johnson "the poet's matter failed him in the fifth act, and he was glad to fill it up with whatever he could get"; Hazlitt, who would scarcely have felt sympathy with the play's ideology, dismissed it as "but one of Shakespeare's second-rate plays"; Tillyard, who could not complain about the political message, still noted a "great falling off in quality" from the earlier plays of the tetralogy; Mark Van Doren's indictment both of the play and its hero is so scathing and detailed that I merely note it as an extreme instance; Derek Traversi, whose analysis of the play's imagery and organization allows him to find under-the-surface subtleties which no other critic has mentioned, still complains that "the concessions made to human feeling in some of the most individual parts of the play are too few, their presiding spirit too rigid, to compel enthusiasm"; A. P. Rossiter, whose high praise for the earlier plays of the tetralogy comes from the "ambivalence" he so brilliantly demonstrates in them, blatantly calls *Henry V* a "propaganda-play on National Unity: heavily orchestrated for the brass."[70] Critics hoping to isolate the play's redeeming qualities often end up damning with faint praise, for example Sigurd Burckhardt, who, after attributing the play to Shakespeare's "epic" rather than his "dramatic" voice, writes, "Shakespeare [in *Henry V*] takes a rest from the labor of discovering the unifying model and knowingly chooses a partial and partisan clarity."[71] Among contemporary critics, M. M. Reese comes closest to facing the real issue when he writes, "The proof is in the theatre; and critics who dislike the play may fairly be asked to give an honest answer to the question of what their response has been when—if they ever have—they have seen it acted on the stage."[72]

The problem we have with *Henry V* is, of course, that it is a different kind of play both from the histories and comedies that immediately preceded it and from the great tragedies that Shakespeare wrote soon after. It is not simply that it manages to reveal its real quality in the theater more than on the printed page, but, above all, that it depends on its ability to establish a communal experience with its audience. Indeed, the difficulty that critics have had understanding its essentially ceremonial character should remind us of the limitations of the specifically literary modes of analysis we apply to dramas of all kinds; great tragedies, for instance, can be read successfully as "poems" even when we remind ourselves how much is "lost" in the reading of a play.

Ceremonial drama eschews the kind of unity which the literary mind is accustomed to seek in most forms of drama. Indeed, the unity of a ceremonial play exists less in its text than in the consciousness the audience has (*independent* of the text) of a unity in the events and in their traditional meaning; when Shakespeare, in the above quotation, excuses his text for "Mangling by starts the full course of their glory," he is playing the role of *literary* critic, one who recognizes the scenario-like quality of the text, but who hopes to count on the unity within "the full course of their glory" which the text at least tries to suggest. The "unity" which Schiller achieved through the closely linked chain of events in *Wallenstein* does not exist, for instance, in his ceremonial play *Wilhelm Tell*, whose audience is expected to be aware even before it attends the play of the unity inherent in such disparate events as the oath of the Swiss confederates on the Rütli, Tell's shooting the apple off his son's head, and the killing of the villain Gessler.

In our own century literary criticism has stressed the value of complexity over simplicity, of the private over the public modes of experience. But ceremonial drama is overwhelmingly public in character (those who find Prince Hal a prig can only think worse of him as Henry V), and the communal experience toward which it aims can support little if any of the complexity of language or character we rightly seek in what Northrop Frye has called the "mimetic" forms of drama.[73] If *Henry V* has not received full critical justice, the attention it receives from critics is a sign that its text is something more than the mere scenario that forms the texts of most ceremonial plays. It is remarkable, indeed, how complexly Shakespeare has worked the simpleminded idea around which the play is built: if Henry is merely a public person, he at least stresses the agony of his public role in his great speech (IV.i.263–90) before the battle of Agincourt; if ceremony is the chief aim of the play, the disdain he expresses for ceremony ("And what art thou, thou idol ceremony?") in this speech at least questions the values which the play as a whole affirms; if England must be thoroughly triumphant in this play, her enemies at least receive a degree of sympathy uncommon in national ceremonial dramas; and if the play defends the justice of Henry's war, it also provides some of the most eloquent arguments about the evils of war to be found between the antiwar plays of the Greeks and those of our conscience-stricken twentieth century. Yet the play's skepticism about itself is one that works less to undermine than to strengthen the essential values it expresses, and as a result we remember its simple-mindedness more than we do its skepticism.

The verbal aspect of a ceremonial play is so much less important than that of the more mimetic forms of drama that one could imagine many famous incidents from history done with powerful theatrical effect even without the mediation of words. A Swiss or even a German audience could easily follow the story of William Tell in pantomime, just as anybody who has been exposed to Christian culture could follow (if not necessarily "experience") the Oberammergau Passion play without knowing German. Musical and visual effects carry a proportionately higher role in ceremonial than in mimetic drama, as one quickly notes when reading the bare text of a great national ceremonial "music-drama" such as *Die Meistersinger*. It is not simply that Wagner wrote bad poetry: indeed, we are quite willing to forgive the pretentiousness of his verse when the words are discernible (which is none too often) through the thick orchestral texture. But the ceremonial ending, with its homage to Hans Sachs and, through him, to German art and culture, is a profoundly moving spectacle in performance. Those who know *Die Meister-singer* only through recordings (or through a study of the score), though they gain something different both in quality and kind from the mere reading of the libretto, still miss an essential part of the ceremonial experience which the opera offers. I suspect that even a televised performance would be unable to render the experience with anything approaching the communal effect it has in the theater. Although it would doubtless take a social psychologist to describe and account for the experience in adequate conceptual terms, I should speculate that it has something to do with the mutual awareness that the members of an audience have of one another in the theater; if I may attempt to be more precise on matters which I have no way of measuring, I should also guess that the members of the audience are not simply aware of the *presence* of others, but of the fact that the others are *sharing* the same experience. A work such as *Die Meistersinger*, which is capable of inducing a communal experience far outside the bounds of its natural German habitat, will, of course, elicit somewhat different responses among different audiences: a non-German audience will direct its celebratory impulse to the figure of Sachs and perhaps also to his advocacy of art; a German audience, especially during the Wilhelmine and Nazi periods, would celebrate as well the apotheosis of German tradition, expressed as it is not only by Sachs's final lines but by the visual effect of the Nuremberg setting and the medieval guilds that we watch trooping across the stage in all their regalia.

The visual effects of ceremonial drama can be so powerful that even an essentially literary text may depend on them for its climactic moments. Although Grillparzer's *König Ottokars Glück und Ende* contains some of the loveliest poetry among verse dramas in German, for an Austrian audience much of the play's power comes from such scenes as the one in which a tent is suddenly torn open to reveal the defeated tyrant-king Ottokar kneeling in vassalage before the Austrian emperor whom he has defied.[74] Medieval settings are especially effective in ceremonial drama, if only because the pageantry they can utilize speaks a powerfully communicative visual language to a postmedieval audience (the visual trappings of life in modern industrial society have little ceremonious potential).

A play such as Cervantes' *El cerco de Numancia* (*The Siege of Numantia*), which commemorates the collective martyrdom of an ancient Spanish town besieged and finally defeated by the Romans, thrives on its symbolic, ritualized scenes. Thus, one encounters stage directions such as these:

> Spain enters, crowned with towers and bearing in her hand a castle which signifies Spain.
> Enter the river Duero, with three other tributaries represented by three boys.
> The corpse comes out in its shroud...and goes on gradually emerging until in the end, when it has finally come out, it collapses on the stage.
> A woman personifying War enters with a spear in her hand and a shield, and brings with her Pestilence and Hunger.[75]

If *Numancia* is more overtly allegorical than most ceremonial plays, it also helps illustrate the tendency of ceremonial drama as a whole to rely on "generalized" and "exemplary" characters and scenes—in Cervantes's play, for instance, unnamed mothers (each with a child in her arms) lamenting their hunger, or the boy Bariato, whose plunge from the tower in which he had sought refuge is designed to illustrate the movement from fear to the heroism of self-immolation.

Within ceremonial drama the actions of rulers rarely deviate from a "generalized" level. The horseplay in which the soldiers engage in *Henry V* is of course impossible for the king (as it was not in his princely days), whose courtship of the French princess, charming though it is, totally lacks the significant and memorable details which we associate with the courtship scenes in Shakespeare's comedies. Those who complain of the "lack of characterization" of Malcolm in *Macbeth* (a tragedy with strong ceremonial overtones), or of the Earl of Richmond in *Richard III*, or of Rudolf of Hapsburg in *König Ottokar,* forget the largely ceremonial roles their respective audiences expected them to play; if by medieval tradition the king possessed two bodies — his mortal body and the deathless one that adheres to his office — ceremonial drama emphatically ignores his physical one (it is significant that in each of these plays the *defeated* kings — Macbeth, Richard III, and Ottokar — are viewed in their mortal roles and that they impose their physical presence on us to an overwhelmingly high degree). The problem of sustaining the heroic in drama is scarcely a problem at all in plays such as *Henry V* and *Wilhelm Tell*, which focus on their heroes' public selves.

The general and representative quality of characters and scenes in ceremonial drama naturally extends to the language. Despite the fact that the verbal aspect of a ceremonial play is often subordinated to the visual, the greatest ceremonial dramas show a brilliance of language whose quality we are often hard put to appreciate adequately. The "general" images that prevail in a play such as *Henry V* — "the widow's tears, the orphans' cries, / The dead men's blood" (II.iv.106-7) — have none of that Shakespearean density of language which we have come to value in our century and which, in fact, has helped define the very standard of what poetic language in drama should be. The brilliance of *Henry V*'s language, like much else in the play, is perhaps most evident in actual performance, for the great set speeches are dependent on oral delivery to achieve their peculiarly dazzling and often quite moving effect. With its vast variety of types of discourse — the condemnation speech addressed to the conspirators (II.ii.79-181); Henry's exhortation to his troops ("Once more unto the breach" — III.i.1-34); the two defiance speeches, one of the French dauphin (I.ii. 259-97), the second of the citizens of Harfleur (III.iii.1-43); the two commemorative speeches, the one before Agincourt (IV.iii.20-67), the second after the battle (IV.viii.82-128) — the play could virtually serve as a handbook of traditional rhetoric. For the play is nothing if not rhetorical; it could only have been written as long as the conventions of classical rhetoric were still honored and before the word "rhetorical" had become as suspect as it has today.

Although ceremonial drama elevates the general over the particular, to the extent that it celebrates a single nation or a national tradition it cultivates one type of particular, namely, that of place. The allegorized figure of Spain in *Numancia* lavishly praises the river Duero along which the doomed town is situated — after which the river and three tributaries take their own allegorized form and prophesy Spain's future greatness.[76] The most frequently quoted passage of *Richard II* is one which, though only peripherally related to the dramatic "plot," is closely tied to the national idea which stands behind the plot; I refer, of course, to John of Gaunt's speech in praise of England, which, with its biblical overtones and its saber-rattling implications —

> This royal throne of kings, this scept'red isle,
> This earth of majesty, this seat of Mars,
> This other Eden, demi-paradise

(II.i.40-42)

has long had functions analogous to those of a national anthem. In *König Ottokars Glück und Ende,* a play whose dramatic structure has much in common with *Richard II,* Horneck, an otherwise unimportant character, launches into a lyrical apostrophe to the scenery surrounding the Danube —

> Schaut rings umher, wohin der Blick sich wendet,
> Lachts wie dem Bräutigam die Braut entgegen!
> Mit hellem Wiesengrün und Saatengold,
> Von Lein und Safran gelb und blau gestickt,
> Von Blumen süss durchwürzt und edlem Kraut
> Schweift es in breitgestreckten Tälern hin [77]

which has a meaning for Austrians similar to that of John of Gaunt's speech for Englishmen.

National-ceremonial plays often go to great lengths to praise the local particularities of ethnic groups which have been absorbed into the larger nation. The presence of the charming Fluellen in *Henry V*, with his leek, his celebration of St. David's day, his conspicuous accent, and his reminder of the king's own Welsh background, helps the play celebrate, among the many things it celebrates, the union of England and Wales. Spanish plays on Portuguese history during the period of union between the two nations (1580-1640) implicitly treated this history as part of their own national tradition. Grillparzer's *Libussa,* a mythical play about the foundation of Prague, similarly serves to affirm the Hapsburg hegemony over Bohemia.

The celebration of national place, moreover, is usually designed to carry the authority of prophecy. "Methinks I am a prophet new inspir'd," John of Gaunt begins his great speech, which, after all its gorgeous imagery of "scept'red isles" and "silver seas," ends with a dire prediction of the evil days about to plague the island through Richard's mismanagement of his royal office (II.i.40-60). Moments of temporary defeat are accompanied by prophecies of future national greatness. In *Wilhelm Tell* the patriot Attinghausen, though he dies before the victory at the end, with his dying breath (and with what Schiller calls a "prophet's tone") predicts the coming triumph of Swiss freedom.[78] Although *Numancia* above all commemorates the total destruction of a Spanish town, the solemn prediction of future Spanish greatness in the first act creates an undercurrent of celebration beneath the predominantly elegiac tone. The great German dramatists of the age of Goethe had a special problem in writing national-ceremonial dramas, if only because their nation did not yet exist as a political entity. Kleist in *Die Hermannsschlacht*, as I pointed out earlier, had to go back to the Teutonic defeat of the occupying Roman army in A.D. 9 as a means of rousing his compatriots to a national uprising during the Napoleonic occupation. Schiller, who was less interested in nationhood than in the idea of freedom, wrote his ceremonial play about a nation he had not even visited, but with which he at least shared a language.

If we tend to associate ceremonial drama with the national interests which it advocates, this is because the examples which immediately come to mind were written since the idea of nation-states began to dominate the political (as well as spiritual) life of Europe. Although medieval drama is ceremonial to the core, its object of celebration is not the nation but the city of God. And as with all ceremonial drama, the texts of medieval plays which have come down to us give little sense of the powerful effect these plays must have had in performance.[79] The contemporary playgoer can perhaps recapture something of this effect in the annual performances of Hofmannsthal's adaptation of *Everyman*, which was designed for presentation in a festival atmosphere before the Salzburg Cathedral. The presence of a real cathedral instead of simply a scenic background suggests the importance of place in ceremonial drama. *The Lost Colony,* by that inveterate writer of American ceremonial plays, Paul Green, was performed in North Carolina at the exact spot where the historical events it depicts took place.[80] It is as though a special sacredness adheres to the spot where events were originally enacted. It is known, for instance, that a Palm Sunday procession following the path of Jesus' footsteps took place between Jerusalem and the Mount of Olives as far back as early Christian times.[81] Time is as important as place: just as the Palm Sunday procession attempted to recapture both the time and place of Christ's journey, so the various medieval plays and cycles were performed at particular times in the Christian calendar.[82] Even secular national dramas have their appropriate times of performance: the effect that *Numancia* must have had when it was performed under siege in Zaragoza during the Peninsular War, or a century later in various cities during the Spanish Civil War, could never be repeated in normal times. Those who saw Sir Laurence Olivier's film of *Henry V* when it was first shown at the end of World War II will never experience it again in quite the same way—unless of course England is engaged in some future invasion of France.

Not only does time play a central role in the performance of ceremonial dramas, but the internal time-scheme of these dramas is directed toward seeing the historical moments depicted as great turning points. History at any given moment is shown moving from good to bad times, or vice versa; individual incidents, moreover, serve as preparation for a turn to better or worse times. The ceremonial mode works most effectively with a time-scheme that views reality in apocalyptic terms. The providential temporal framework of the medieval cycles remains essentially the same in Shakespeare's history plays, however much Shakespeare may have secularized and subtilized his individual characters and the ideas he has them voice. Racine's *Athalie,* which preserves a Christian time-scheme in a relatively secular age, celebrates the change of ages from an evil to a good time; the whole course of the play is carefully prophesied for us at Athalie's first entrance when she describes her dream of the mysterious child ("Un jeune enfant couvert d'une robe éclatant") who disturbs her peace.[83] The most memorable thing in Shelley's ceremonial play *Hellas,* in which the poet's national sympathies are characteristically not with his native England but with the revolutionary Greeks, is the powerful apocalyptic lyric that begins "The world's great age begins anew, / The golden years return."[84]

With their prophetic, apocalyptic forward thrust, ceremonial dramas easily lend themselves to cyclical development. Given their teleological direction, the various plays in a cycle achieve a unity through their anticipation of a common "ending"—the restoration of the kingdom of God in the medieval cycles, the restoration of good rule through the establishment of the Tudor monarchy in Shakespeare's histories. The "idea" of a cycle is a ceremonial idea, whether or not the individual plays within the cycle take specifically ceremonial forms. Doubtless because of Shakespeare's example, writers in various countries have conceived of and sometimes even completed cycles based on some national "idea"—for instance, Strindberg's idea of a conscious will that manifests itself in one great man after another through history, or Eugene O'Neill's idea of the "dispossessing" of America in his late and uncompleted cycle.[85]

Just as the times in ceremonial drama tend to be either "good" or "bad," so the opposing forces are characterized in absolute terms—namely, those who act to carry out the divine or national will, and those who attempt to thwart it (in the process of thwarting, the latter often goad the former into "positive" action).[86] The black-and-white characterization toward which ceremonial drama aims creates obvious problems in sustaining our interest—especially if we know a drama only from the printed page. The Herods and devils of medieval drama gain considerable interest through the aggressions which an audience can exercise on them communally (the Herods were known to have run off the platform into the audience) and the triumph it can feel in their defeat. Schiller, who was able to give a high degree of sympathy to his tyrant-figure King Philip in *Don Carlos*, in *Wilhelm Tell* allows his villain to perform all the nasty acts that characterize evil in a ceremonial drama — among other things, violating women and gouging out children's eyes. If the courtly, gallant, and somewhat effeminate French in *Henry V* are not the kind of villainous force we find in the Romans of *Numancia* or the Austrians of *Wilhelm Tell,* their characterization must have posed a special problem in view of Shakespeare's larger historical scheme: they could not be dastardly enough to keep the king from marrying their princess, nor so weak that victory over them would prove too easy. In that earliest of extant historical dramas, *The Persians* of Aeschylus, the enemy is not only treated with a high measure of compassion, but the whole action is seen (though not evaluated) from the enemy's point of view. With its playing on recent Greek patriotic feeling, together with its implicit warning of the dangers of national *hybris*, *The Persians* must have demanded a complexity of response from its original audience that reveals it to be a very different kind of play from the ceremonial dramas of the postclassical world — many of which go out of their way, in fact, to advocate national *hybris*. Within the canon of a single writer (even within a single cycle, as one notes when setting *Henry V* next to the plays that preceded it), ceremonial dramas seek a separate identity from those that refuse to let us think in black-and-white terms. To the extent that they let our analytical faculties go on holiday, ceremonial plays provide an ideal outlet for those aggressions which the more "refined" types of drama allow us to exercise at best in muted or sublimated form.

History as panorama
Wie gross ist alles angelegt!
Goethe on Marlowe's *Doctor Faustus*

If ceremonial drama is essentially "unliterary" and suffers when judged by literary standards, the panoramic dramas of the nineteenth century — works such as Ibsen's *Emperor and Galilean,* Hardy's *The Dynasts*, and Karl Kraus's *Die letzten Tage der Menschheit (The Last Days of Mankind)* — are so literary that they suffer when judged by theatrical standards. A play such as *The Dynasts* has all the makings of a ceremonal play except for performability: like *Henry V*, it supports the English national cause against the French, and, like all ceremonial plays, it depends on spectacle for much of its effect — though it is a spectacle which the reader views through his imagination rather than in the theater. Again, like most ceremonial plays, it depends on the audience's knowledge of history to create what unity it has; as Hardy himself put it in his preface, "The subject is familiar to all; and foreknowledge is assumed to fill in the junctions required to combine the scenes into an artistic

86

unity."[87] When one talks about the audience of panoramic plays, one means, of course, the *reading* audience, for these plays—aside from all the production difficulties that would preclude performance—are often several hundred pages long. Karl Kraus opens his preface to *Die letzten Tage* with a snub at the theater as we know it: "The staging of the play, which according to earthly time would encompass about ten evenings, is intended for a theater on Mars."[88] Almost every author of a panoramic play makes clear from the start that he does not even intend to be writing for the theater. "Readers will readily discern," Hardy writes, "that *The Dynasts* is intended simply for mental performance, and not for the stage."[89] In a few instances, notably in Kraus's play, individual scenes are so theatrical by their very nature that segments of the play have been performed successfully; indeed, the very refusal of panoramic plays to achieve "unity" or to practice any ordinary sort of theatrical economy enables a director to cut and arrange scenes at will.

The sense of vastness and wonder which characterizes the attitude toward history in panoramic drama is characteristic of nineteenth-century ways of looking at history. Note, for instance, the huge visual panorama in these lines from Hegel's *Philosophy of History*: "When we cast a glance at world history as a whole, we see a tremendous picture of transformations and actions, of infinitely varied configurations of peoples, states, individuals in restless succession. Everything that can enter and interest the spirit of man, every sentiment of goodness, beauty, greatness comes into play."[90] Hegel's idea of a will that guides the seemingly chaotic "transformations and actions" within the panoramas he describes finds its embodiment in panoramic drama through the teleological purpose which works to hold together and give a forward impetus to the vast and varied array of scenes within the play. Ibsen could say simply of *Emperor and Galilean* that "it puts forward the world-historic idea as I have understood it."[91] Although Ibsen had already written a number of history plays, and in *Peer Gynt* had even attempted a kind of panoramic drama, all these plays, except for his first play, *Catilina*, had been distinctly national in character. *Emperor and Galilean*, as Ibsen later reported, was the first play he wrote "under the influence of German cultural life. . . . My view of world history and of human life had hitherto been a national one. Now it widened to become an ethnic one, and then I was able to write *Emperor and Galilean*."[92] The resulting play, encompassing ten acts and some three hundred pages, portrays the late Roman world of Julian's apostasy—not with the antiquarian purpose of capturing some precious moment of the past, but to dramatize a tragic conflict between Julian's individual will and the inscrutable world-will, and, perhaps even more fundamental to Ibsen's intent, to prophesy (through Julian's idealism) a "third empire," a new Dionysianism which was to transcend the old dispensation of the classical world and Christianity. The notes that Strindberg left toward a cycle of "world-historical" plays to dramatize the workings of the "conscious will" in history reveal a project far more ambitious in scope than Ibsen's.[93] As it turned out, however, Strindberg completed only a national cycle, one which illuminated what he saw as the pregnant psychological moments of Swedish history; indeed, Strindberg's closest approximation to the panoramic tradition was the trilogy *To Damascus*, which transfers the historical vision of most earlier panoramic plays to a wholly psychological realm while at the same time retaining their vastness and their imaginative grandeur. Despite its frankly national point of view, *The Dynasts* uses its various choruses of spirits that guide and comment upon the action to set up a characteristically nineteenth-century world-historical perspective.

The vastness of scope which panoramic drama seeks can take the form of a long span of time, or multiple areas of physical space, or several levels of society — indeed, sometimes all of these at once. Goethe's comment (quoted at the head of this section) about the grandeur of conception in *Doctor Faustus*, is typical of the way a nineteenth-century, but not a contemporary, mind would look at Marlowe's play.[94] If one can speak of panoramic drama as a genre, Goethe's own version of the Faust story doubtless created this genre. Spatially, Goethe's vast drama (whose label "tragedy" is misleading for the work's final version) shifts from heaven through the world to hell and ultimately back to heaven; temporally, though it remains rooted largely in a medieval Gothic atmosphere, it encompasses the classical world of Helen of Troy and the emerging world of modern technology; socially, it moves from the small-town world of Gretchen to the "large" world of Holy Roman emperors ("Wir sehn die kleine, dann die grosse Welt," Mephistopheles informs his master as they start their journey);[95] stylistically, it mixes realism with fantasy, the low style with the sublime, and it also manages to include virtually every metrical form possible within German.

Inclusiveness, in one form or another, is the essential aim of every panoramic drama. The Hungarian poet Imré Madách, in his Faustian *History of Mankind*, moves down the centuries from the Garden of Eden to capitalist London. Grabbe's *Napoleon oder die hundert Tage* (*Napoleon, or the Hundred Days*), though considerably shorter and more constricted in time (as its subtitle indicates) than most panoramic dramas, attempts to "cover" various areas of society, from the crowds on the streets of Paris to the generals and the contenders for political power. *The Dynasts,* moving as it does from the events of 1805 to Waterloo, not only includes a far greater segment of the Napoleonic war than Grabbe's play, but in its choruses and stage directions it is constantly breaking through conventional categories of time and space. Note the following stage direction: "A view now nocturnal, now diurnal, from on high over the Straits of Dover, and stretching from city to city. By night Paris and London seem each as a little swarm of lights surrounded by a halo; by day as a confused glitter of white and grey. The Channel between

88

them is as a mirror reflecting the sky, brightly or faintly, as the hour may be."[96] In passages such as this, the earthly historical events upon which Hardy's play is centered are absorbed, as it were, within a larger cosmic vision. Temporal and spatial contraries — day and night, Paris and London — can be fused in a single image. Above all, Hardy is able to suggest a realm of permanence against which the transiency of temporal events may be viewed.

However chaotic the flux of images and events they present, panoramic dramas usually end with a universal overview that sets this flux in its proper and "lower" perspective. As Goethe's Faust ascends toward heaven at the end, the various personages along the way — Pater Ecstaticus, Pater Seraphicus, and the different degrees of angels — declare his increasing distance from the impurities of earthly things until the Chorus Mysticus in the final passage is able to exclaim that "Alles Vergängliche/Ist nur ein Gleichnis."[97] *The Dynasts* culminates in the various choruses expressing their wonder at the inscrutable workings of the universal will. In one way or another every writer of a panoramic drama seeks a means of putting an end once and for all to the temporal doings he has been describing. Karl Kraus expresses the apocalyptic urge that stands behind panoramic drama with an uncommonly down-to-earth frankness in these lines spoken near the end by his alter ego the Grumbler ("Nörgler"): "I am preserving documents for a time which will no longer understand them or which lives so far in the future that it will say that I am a liar. But no, the time that says that will not come. For it will not take place."[98]

The sense of impending cataclysm which we feel in lines such as these can often be tied directly to upheavals which the writers of panoramic drama experienced. *Die letzten Tage der Menschheit*, whose apocalyptic bias is evident in its very title, was written during and immediately after World War I — at the very time of the dire events it sought to depict. Grabbe wrote *Napoleon* just before the revolution of 1830, but he made a point of the fact that his readers would think him prophetic of what he called "the world-historic events of July."[99] Among the central influences on *Emperor and Galilean,* Ibsen mentioned the fact that he was writing the play while living in Germany during the Franco-Prussian War.[100] And it is probably not accidental that the first version of Flaubert's *Tentation de Saint-Antoine* was begun directly after the revolution of 1848 and the final version written during the Commune.´

The visionary element that plays so prominent a role in panoramic drama often manifests itself in deliberately fantastic forms that are mixed in varying ways with realistic detail. George Sand, trying to define the genre in 1839 on the basis of *Faust,* Byron's *Manfred,* and Mickiewicz's *Forefathers Eve,* in fact referred to it as "le drame fantastique."[101] In Flaubert's *Tentation* the fantastic looms so strong that it virtually swallows up the historical vision. Since Grabbe's *Napoleon* omits the fantastic altogether, anybody with a narrow conception of genres will wonder why I even discuss it among these other works. Ibsen rigorously separates the realistic from the fantastic by limiting the latter to Julian's private visions, while Kraus remains scrupulously realistic for some seven hundred pages until he lets the visionary take over in the monstrously grotesque forms of his final scenes.

Given all the supernatural machinery of most panoramic dramas, it is no wonder that the actions of individuals have little effect on the resolutions of these plays. The debate between God and Mephistopheles in Goethe's "Prologue in Heaven" loads the dice from the start as to whether Faust will go to heaven or hell. Hardy's presiding spirits reduce his human actors to the role of puppets. Although Kraus saves the supernatural until the end, the pessimism he voices throughout, as well as the grossness of human stupidity that he portrays with such relish in one scene after another, makes it clear very early that the only possible resolution is a cataclysmic one. Perhaps I should state it the other way around and say that the writers of panoramic drama sought out this form to render a vision of life that leaves little or no room for human agency. Despite the struggles for power that we witness in plays such as *The Dynasts* and *Emperor and Galilean,* we always remain aware that political action is ultimately irrelevant. In Shakespeare's history plays, despite the providential framework, we feel that men are working out their destinies by means of politics. Panoramic drama, by contrast, seems conspicuously apolitical in its essential orientation; its focus, one might say, is less on politics than on prophecy, less on the workings of the individual human mind than on the world-will.

Yet despite their cultivation of largeness, panoramic dramas tend to stress the significance of local detail. If the world-will ultimately sweeps up all before it, it gains what awe it has for us through the power it displays over the individual forms of human life. As the Grumbler reminds his opponent, the Optimist, in *Die letzten Tage,* "small events led to the grand appearances of the real tragedy" which Kraus's play is enacting for us,[102] and it thus becomes the task of the play to present these small events in all their intimacy. Panoramic plays like *Die letzten Tage* are often built out of a vast succession of short scenes, each of which sketches out a single detail within the panorama and all of which together add up to what seems a huge and frightening vision of life. Since panoramic drama does not need to practice the economy of other dramatic forms, it can allow itself to luxuriate in detail to an extent that only the novel among literary genres has done. And like the nineteenth-century novel, it has taken a particular interest in stressing the role of "little" people within the historical process. Ibsen scrupulously finds a place for "representative" characters such as the dyer Phocian and the goldsmith Potamon, who are posed within his large canvas like the carefully costumed figures crowding an early nineteenth-century historical painting. Hardy includes a few scenes in *The Dynasts* centered around the little people of his native Wessex; as one might expect from one's knowledge of Hardy the novelist and lyric poet, the dialogue of these scenes has an authenticity that is all too often lacking in the scenes devoted to the great.

The difference between Hardy's achievement in *The Dynasts* and in his best poems or novels points to a critical problem relevant to any discussion of panoramic drama. By twentieth-century critical standards every panoramic drama can be seriously faulted for the unevenness and lack of "unity" which are a natural consequence of its attempt to be inclusive and to achieve a maximum degree of imaginative grandeur; aside from such stylistic considerations, modern audiences can scarcely be expected to respond easily to any work which suggests or expounds a doctrine about the world-will. With the exception of *Faust,* the various panoramic plays of the nineteenth century today seem to stand distinctly outside the critical mainstream — and despite the fact that their writers often preferred them to those more modest, yet "fully realized" works which have become central to their critical reputation. Flaubert made a point of how he preferred the process of writing the *Tentation* to the tedious labors of composing *Madame Bovary.* [103] Ibsen would much rather have been known as the author of *Emperor and Galilean* than of *Hedda Gabler.* [104] At the very time that they were effecting a literary revolution which was to give the depiction of everyday events a status which it never knew before, these writers could still view their major task in those traditional terms which set the ultimate literary value on the composition of a work of epic proportions on a universal theme. The aesthetic paganism which supplies much of the "doctrinal" content of *Emperor and Galilean* is never wholly lost in Ibsen's "realistic" plays, though it is surrounded and virtually overwhelmed by the domestic detail of these plays. Note, for instance, the awesome praise of Dionysus voiced by Julian in *Emperor and Galilean*: "Far be it from me to dictate to anyone. But am I to be blamed for wanting others to share in the ecstatic joy which pervades my being when I feel myself cradled in the company of the immortals? Praise, praise be to thee, vine-wreathed Dionysus! For it is first and foremost thou who dost perform such great mysteries."[105] The vine-wreathed Dionysus who officiates over an elaborate pagan pageant in *Emperor and Galilean* is reduced to a fatal whim within the bored consciousness of Hedda Gabler, who works the destruction of those around her by encouraging her former lover, Lövborg, to live aesthetically "with vine-leaves in his hair."[106]

The domestic and contemporary context which makes *Hedda Gabler* so much more accessible to us than *Emperor and Galilean* is precisely what makes such an early twentieth-century panoramic drama as *Die letzten Tage der Menschheit* seem "modern" to us in a way that its predecessors do not. I might add that readers with characteristically modern prejudices often forget that the Night-town episode of *Ulysses* (which covers fully a quarter of Joyce's book), as well as the whole idea behind *Finnegans Wake,* is thoroughly within the panoramic tradition. Like *Ulysses, Die letzten Tage* is notable for its pervasive irony, which specifically takes the form of satire and which owes

91

much of its success to Kraus's fabulous eye and ear for local detail. As the historical vision of a writer whose primary talent is satirical, *Die letzten Tage* depends on Kraus's virtuosity in subjecting virtually every facet of Viennese life during the First World War to what often seems the cruelest sort of mimicry. The greatest satire operates under the assumption that nothing should be spared, and Kraus displays his whole panorama of local life — the imbecile nobility, the social-climbing Jews (portrayed with a malice and a precision only possible for a writer who, like Kraus, was himself a Jew), the sensation-hungry "liberal" press, the bumbling, morally obtuse military leaders — with a completeness and a conviction that show he had no desire to spare anyone.

And as in all great satire the outrage that the reader comes to feel is directed not only against a particular group at a particular time and place (in this instance the citizens of Vienna in the early twentieth century), but at the human race in general. Indeed, it is the only work in my own experience which, through the power and precision of its language, as well as in its total vision of life, makes one feel that literature can possibly do justice to the horrors of our own century. Yet the universality which Kraus's play achieves can only be appreciated by those who are able to understand the local accents and allusions in which it is so thoroughly rooted; although a translator of genius may some day prove me wrong, it seems to me much less conducive to successful translation than *Ulysses*, a work with which it deserves to be ranked in stature. And as with *Ulysses*, the massive accumulation of local detail ultimately creates a sense that a vital, if also grotesque, energy has been unleashed, as though the heroic has been achieved through the intense concentration of the most unheroic imaginable matter.

The difficulties we encounter in accepting most panoramic dramas either as literature or theater to a great degree arise from their relative foreignness to our usual conceptions of each of these media. As John Wain has pointed out in his introduction to a recent edition of *The Dynasts*, there is another medium, namely film, within which the panoramic impulse can realize itself far more comfortably than in any of the traditional ones. Wain analyzes a scene from Hardy's drama in the following cinematic terms:

> First, we see a long-distance, wide-angle shot of the whole terrain, showing the fog lying over the lower part of the scene like a still, white sea; then the camera tracks forward until it picks out the great-coated figures of the Emperor and his staff on their stumbling horses amid the silence. . . . Then, with one of those broad symbolic effects which the cinema has made so very much its own, their heads emerge into clear air, and at that moment the sun of their good fortune comes up and shines dramatically on them. Close-up: Napoleon's face, which Hardy thoughtfully describes as "ash-hued," thus indicating how it is to be set off from the ruddier faces

around it. They all instinctively look first towards the sun—a pure piece of cinematic directing—and then towards what were, last night, the enemy positions. They see what they have longed to see, and the silence is broken by their jubilant voices.[107]

What Wain describes as the ability of film to move readily between close-up and wide-angle range and to derive "broad symbolic effect" from concrete objects recalls that propensity of panoramic drama to connect local detail with the largest possible context of meaning. Through our awareness that film provides a photographic representation of actual things, the medium is able to retain its contact with the local and the "real"; yet through its montage techniques it can detach us from our ordinary sense of reality and suggest new structures of consciousness. Like panoramic drama, it is not tied to "plot" and "unity" as theatrical drama is. As an enactment of history, film is able to do things that other representations of history cannot. If it is not as well suited as theatrical drama for rendering the everyday give-and-take of politics, its visual orientation provides its own unique way of giving significance to a historical situation. In *Ivan the Terrible,* Part 1, for instance, Sergei Eisenstein achieves a memorable image of grandeur as we watch Ivan, posed on a hillside against a background of moving clouds at the battle of Kazan, and then hear a voice comment, "Look, the Czar of all the Russias!" The use of close-ups, moreover, allows film to make its political points with a conciseness impossible in the more verbally oriented forms of drama. One remembers, for instance, the close-ups of the bowl of coins poured over Ivan's head at his coronation, or of the faces of the conspirators already plotting his overthrow during this very ceremony; indeed, the conspiracy of the boyars does not have to be developed with the mass of verbal detail necessary in stage drama, for the conspirators' facial expressions, their whispering, and Ivan's violent gestures of denunciation tell us all we need to know. Eisenstein makes perhaps his most powerful comments in this film through the obsessive interior imagery—an infinity of vaulted rooms with grotesque eyes painted on the walls.

In one of his theoretical writings Eisenstein describes a sophisticated technique he developed in his film *October* to comment on political events:

> Kornilov's march on Petrograd was under the banner of "In the Name of God and Country". Here we attempted to reveal the religious significance of this episode in a rationalistic way. A number of religious images, from a magnificent Baroque Christ to an Eskimo idol, were cut together. The conflict in this case was between the concept and the symbolization of God. While idea and image appear to accord completely in the first statue shown, the two elements move further from each other with each successive image.... Maintaining the denotation of "God," the images increasingly disagree with our concept of God.[108]

If the above analysis shows Eisenstein's attempt to achieve intellectual meaning through montage techniques, his later description of the famous battle-on-the-ice sequence in *Alexander Nevsky* stresses what he calls the "audio-visual impressions" he was trying to create.[109] In this sequence Eisenstein was able to capture precisely those elements of history — the movement of massive forces against one another, the conflict of men and nature — which theatrical drama, if it sought to capture them at all, was forced to do in a far less direct and powerful way. Through its ability to use eye and ear to suggest the largeness of great events, film provides a means of magnification unavailable within theatrical representation. Even the purely visual effects of the silent film *Potemkin* (though enhanced, of course, by the original background music of Edmund Meissel which Eisenstein intended to be used) are models for a kind of heroic action which film has made possible during an otherwise unheroic age. Feats impossible on the stage, such as the death of Vakulinchuk, the leader of the mutiny on the *Potemkin* — with his body shown floating on the sea and the daredevil actions of the rebels on the ship's rigging as they attempt to rescue him — have become a convention within the medium. Similarly, the incident of the white-winged boats welcoming the *Potemkin* with their grace and pageantry, and above all the Odessa steps episode (which incidentally has no basis in history, but which uses space and movement to suggest the horror of repressive violence as no stage work could ever do) create images of magnification which remain permanently within the viewer's consciousness.[110] One could even say that Eisenstein's use of montage in this film — for example the quick, percussive alternations of the ship's pistons with the revolutionary actions going on in other parts of the ship — provides a language for sustaining the heroic at a time when all the older languages had worn themselves out. If we no longer seek that universal vision of history which nineteenth-century panoramic drama strove for, film can at least enact certain individual moments of largeness — revolutionary struggle, communal triumph, cataclysms often of the most stupendous sort — which constitute some of the traditional thrills and satisfactions of history.

FOUR

THE HISTORICAL WORLD AS IMAGINATIVE PLACE

History as Middle Ground

"...tragedy, comedy, history, pastoral, pastoral-comical, historical-pastoral, tragical-historical, tragical-comical-historical-pastoral..."

Polonius, in the players' scene

Polonius's absurd recital reminds us that for the Elizabethans each genre suggested its own appropriate world, that even when a play belonged to four genres at once—as in that exotic hybrid he dubs "tragical-comical-historical-pastoral" (II. ii. 403-4)—each genre maintained a discernible identity among the diverse components which the dramatist chose to bring together. Although it would doubtless prove difficult, in practical terms, to separate the "tragical" from the "historical" in the *Henry VI* plays, Shakespeare at one point introduces a pastoral passage which, by sharply opposing two styles of life, sets up a dichotomy between the worlds of history and pastoral so that each defines itself unmistakably through its antithesis to the other. In the succession of bloody events that make up *Henry VI*, the audience is diverted for a brief interval during the third play while the harried and helpless king soliloquizes about the virtues of the pastoral life:

> O God! methinks it were a happy life
> To be no better than a homely swain;
> To sit upon a hill, as I do now,
> To carve out dials quaintly, point by point,
> Thereby to see the minutes how they run.
> (II. v. 21-25)

Although these lines are in every way a set speech, highly rhetorical, in fact ritualistic in nature, they call particular attention to themselves in the way they contrast with the prevailing mode of Shakespeare's early historical plays, for the lines provide a kind of pastoral relief from the bitter realities of the historical world in which the plays are rooted. Throughout the preceding acts, as the Yorkists and Lancastrians have alternately defeated one another, the passive king has watched his fortunes alternately rise and fall. As he gets ready to speak his pastoral lines, he sits down on a molehill like the one on which his opponent Richard, Duke of York, had been forced to stand several scenes earlier when he was taunted and stabbed by Henry's fierce queen, Margaret. Yet this molehill, which in one sense recalls the historical world in its most grotesque form, also serves to remind us of the king's isolation from this very world, at least to the extent that it places him in the role of outsider rather than actor. A total failure according to the demands of this world, he voices his despair in a guileless couplet —

> Would I were dead, if God's good will were so!
> For what is in this world but grief and woe?
>
> (19-20)

Henry's speech could well have ended at this point, before the introduction of his pastoral dream: within the context of the historical world which Shakespeare has depicted, defeat can lead only to death or humiliation. But almost as soon as the king voices his despair, he utters those lines I quoted earlier about his desire to assume the shepherd's life. It is as though he has initiated a new movement of the mind, as though a new order of reality could be posited as an alternative to the world which has rejected him. He starts out modestly enough in the subjunctive mood — "methinks it were a happy life / To be no better than a homely swain." The molehill now expands imaginatively to a "hill," a place from which he can watch the battle and at the same time isolate himself from it. Gradually, what had started in the subjunctive mood assumes a reality of its own:

> So many hours must I tend my flock;
> So many hours must I take my rest;
> So many hours must I contemplate;
> So many hours must I sport myself. . . .
>
> (31-34)

The very monotony of the anaphora, together with the movement from the subjunctive to "must" and finally to the indicative, works to establish a new world, one which, for a moment at least, seems to transcend the limitations of the historical world. But only for a moment: Henry has hardly succeeded in creating his little fantasy before he sets up a specific comparison of shepherd and king and, in the process, reminds himself — and us — of the perilous political world from which he sought to remove himself:

> And to conclude, the shepherd's homely curds,
> His cold thin drink out of his leather bottle,
> His wonted sleep under a fresh tree's shade,
> All which secure and sweetly he enjoys,
> Is far beyond a prince's delicates —
> His viands sparkling in a golden cup,
> His body couched in a curious bed,
> When Care, Mistrust, and Treason waits on him.
>
> (47-54)

As though it were not enough to remind us of the dangers to which a king is subject, Shakespeare follows Henry's speech with two highly ritualized tableaux illustrating the effects of civil war. Still sitting on the molehill on which his pastoral reverie has taken place, Henry witnesses first "a Son that hath kill'd his Father, with the body in his arms," and then, with perfect symmetry, "a Father that hath kill'd his Son, with the body in his arms" (after 1. 54 and 1. 78 respectively). With their morality-play formality, these tableaux serve as an intensification of the horrors which Shakespeare has been depicting all along: it is as though the pastoral soliloquy, through the very rigor with which it voices its longing for simplicity, demanded a new, theatrically more potent image of the historical world than we have seen before.

The contrast that Shakespeare has created between pastoral and historical worlds is stated with an absoluteness which we do not find in his more mature work, but which in its very lack of subtlety allows us to generalize with a minimum of qualification. It is a contrast, on the most obvious level, between two orders of time — the slow, predictable, regular time of the shepherd who devotes "so many hours," as Henry all too persistently puts it, to every one of his daily tasks, and the racing, unpredictable time processes which govern the historical world. In "carving out" his dials, the shepherd is asserting, if not precisely his control over nature, at least the harmony he can achieve with it. In the historical world, by contrast, events take their own course, to the point where Henry must sit as a helpless witness to the unnaturalness of a situation in which fathers and sons routinely kill one another; in Hall's chronicle, which suggested the father-son tableaux, Shakespeare would, in fact, have seen the comment "This conflict was in manner unnaturall, for in it the sonne fought against the father, the brother against the brother, the nephew against the uncle."[1] The unnaturalness described by Hall may have "called forth" a contrasting image with the absolute simplicity and regularity implicit in pastoral, while Henry's lines, in turn, called forth the ceremonial technique with which the father–son scenes were then presented. Each world, pastoral and historical, helps define the other: each, in fact, works dialectically to create the other with continually increasing intensity.

We easily recognize the pastoral world as an imaginative construct, not simply because of the make-believe quality which it retains throughout Henry's speech, but because Shakespeare calls upon an ancient literary convention to give it its particular embodiment. But the historical world in which the *Henry VI* plays are centered is an equally "imaginative" construct, though to the extent that it purports to be "history" we do not easily recognize it as such. In the later parts of Henry's speech, where Shakespeare resorts to the morality tradition for the father-son tableaux and the image of the prince attended by Care, Mistrust, and Treason, we become aware of the conventional nature of this world. But as Shakespeare develops his image of the historical world in subsequent plays, it assumes less distinctly "literary" or "theatrical" attributes and achieves the illusion that it is essentially an extension of the world of everyday events. "The province of the history play," Harold E. Tolliver has written of the *Henry IV* plays, "is not the inner world or the world of fable, but a historical world like the one outside the theater, engrossed in politics and asking that taxes be paid."[2]

As an imaginative construct, the historical world which Shakespeare created has attributes that separate it distinctly from other Shakespearean worlds. For one thing, it is a public world built out of recognizable public personages and events; private values and private experience achieve what meaning they have only within a public perspective, yet the latter, in turn, is constantly put to the test by the claims of the private. In one sense Henry's pastoral fantasy serves to contrast the private with the public world, or, more precisely, to contrast the private Henry, who could admirably step into a shepherd's role, with the public office whose demands Henry (through the very nature of his character) is unable to fulfill. Indeed, within the historical world that Shakespeare creates, the public roles which individuals find themselves called upon to play are often badly at odds with their particular propensities. By the same token, certain individuals, for example the various "opportunist" characters such as Richard III and Henry IV, have the private propensity to remake the public roles they so actively seek. The historical world as it develops in one play after the other becomes the natural arena for role-making as well as for its logical accompaniment, role-playing.

Furthermore, the roles which individual characters make and play (or are forced into) create multiple points of view through which we come to see the historical actions which are being enacted. Thus, the oppressive historical world that we see through the eyes of Henry VI does not provide the only bias through which we are expected to view the action of the play; the newly emerging Duke of Gloucester, after all, presents us with a quite different view. The multiplicity of points of view through which we come to experience the historical world, moreover, creates an image of fluidity in which time and change are perhaps the only constants. When Henry VI, near the beginning of his pastoral soliloquy, compares the battle he is witnessing to a sea—

> a mighty sea
> Forc'd by the tide to combat with the wind;
> Now sways it that way, like the self-same sea
> Forc'd to retire by fury of the wind.
> Sometime the flood prevails, and then the wind
>
> (5-9)

he creates an appropriate image for the constant changes of fortune that have marked not only his own reign, but also those of all the other kings Shakespeare was to write about. Indeed, the twin buckets in the well which

Richard II invokes in his deposition scene to symbolize the rise and fall of kings —

> That bucket down and full of tears am I,
> Drinking my griefs, whilst you mount up on high
>
> (IV. i. 188-89)

are a traditional symbol of the medieval figure of Fortune.[3]

The fluctuating quality of royal fortunes makes it impossible to isolate a typical historical "structure" in Shakespeare as one can a tragic or a comic structure. Unlike tragedy or comedy (structural patterns into which it is occasionally shaped) historical drama, whether that of Shakespeare or of later writers, does not in itself move towards a single, clearly foreseen end. Rather than speak of a genre, I prefer to use the term "historical world," which implies not so much a particular structure or type of language as a body of materials which a writer approaches with certain recognizable attitudes. Whether in formal or thematic terms, the historical world tends to take a kind of middle ground between extremes. For example, although a historical drama may, on one level, assert a larger pattern in history such as the providential pattern which governs Shakespeare's English cycle, from moment to moment it manages to leave us in doubt about the inevitability of such a pattern. The historical dramatist, one might say, is always walking a tightrope between a determinism which he needs to give his play its central momentum and a commitment to the individuality of particular moments and events. Within the realm of historical writing, historical drama would stand somewhere between micro- and macro-history, between the concrete details of specific historical situations and the larger processes, forces, and meanings to which they can be related. Although historical drama reminds us that change is normal and inevitable, it often goes to great lengths to leave us in mystery about the precise origins and agents, sometimes even the directions, of change. Its public locus is in itself a middle ground, for the public events it depicts are qualified by their reverberations within the private realm at one extreme and, at the other, within whatever metaphysical or religious realm it may choose to project around itself.

Despite the sense of dread or of exaltation which we are made to feel at individual moments, the historical world by its nature eschews absolutes. The predictable and static quality of pastoral, at least as Henry VI defines it in his speech, suggests an absolute world which, quite unlike the historical world in which the play is centrally located, is incapable of further development. The multiple marriages and other wish-fulfillments in which Shakespeare's romantic comedies culminate likewise suggest an absolute totally foreign to the historical world. Although the historical world has its tragic situations, indeed even its tragic heroes, these are never absolute but are "contained" within what we come to recognize as a larger framework. Thus, the tragic

99

resolutions of the lives of kings such as Richard II and Richard III are sharply qualified by the historical continuities which their victorious opponents guarantee. Richard II, as I indicated in the preceding chapter, plays the tragic hero within an essentially untragic play. The seemingly "episodic" Aumerle section in the closing act of this play is a thoroughly characteristic incident within the historical world: as a result of young Aumerle's unbending absoluteness in opposing the newly crowned Henry IV, we witness a conflict between the "public" and "private" biases voiced, respectively, by his father and mother, after which the king makes us question our own—as well as Aumerle's—loyalty to the dethroned Richard II through the political wisdom he shows in pardoning the young conspirator. Accommodation and continuity are to the historical world what absoluteness and finality are to tragedy. Thus, Claudius and his Danish court are distinctly characters out of the historical world who are placed in and evaluated from a tragic perspective; in the suaveness with which he maintains the appearance of normal political relationships, Claudius is more closely akin to Henry IV than he is to the more "absolute" villains of Shakespeare's other tragedies.

If the historical world often seems to hold compromise as an ultimate value, it also cultivates situations in which public pretensions are mercilessly unmasked. L. C. Knights, writing specifically of *Henry IV, Part 1*, points at this analytic tendency when he describes the play as "a realistic portrayal of the ways of the world and an insistent questioning of the values by which its great men live—with a consequent ironic contrast between public profession and the actuality."[4] Knights's statement is from a thoughtful essay which attempts to trace Shakespeare's increasingly analytical approach to political realities from *Henry VI* to *Henry IV*. As Shakespeare's image of the historical world develops in the course of his English history plays, it assumes characteristics which in recent decades have been described with such terms of high critical compliment as "complexity," "ambivalence," "irony," and "paradox."[5] The virtually universal use of *Henry IV, Part 1*, in introductory literature courses in American colleges during this period is a testimony to the harmony which many literary intellectuals must have felt between their own values and what they took to be Shakespeare's values in the play: one thinks of the much-repeated rhetorical exercises designed to show how Shakespeare mediates in the play between three diverse concepts of honor—Hotspur's and Falstaff's concepts at the extreme ends of the spectrum, with Prince Hal's gradually developing concept somewhere in the "healthy" middle.[6] Indeed, to the extent that Shakespeare seems to take a "mediating" role in this play, the historical world could be said to occupy an ethical middle ground between tempting but ultimately "dangerous" extremes. Although future critics may well move back and forth in their judgment of how much sympathy Shakespeare gave (and by implication the reader is to give) Falstaff, the very fact that the issue has been controversial for almost two centuries is a sign of the "complexity" with which he created the historical world of *Henry IV*. It is significant, for instance, that nobody seriously debates how we should react to Falstaff in *The Merry Wives of Windsor*, where the role he plays is determined by comic convention.

As a form of representation, drama — in comparison, say, with painting, lyric, even with prose fiction and narrative history — is ideally suited to the depiction of the kind of complexity we have come to value in *Henry IV*: through the confrontation of characters representing sharply divergent points of view, drama can expose the pretensions of public personalities, uncover the relationship between political acts and the motives that govern them, and portray a person's role in intricate ways in which the private self becomes a part of the roles it is forced to play in public situations. In contrast to other literary forms such as the lyric and the novel, which utilize point of view to guide us, directly or indirectly, toward a discernible set of meanings, drama can (even if it does not often do so) present a group of characters each of whom competes with the others to convince us to view the play as a whole from his own angle of vision. This tendency of drama to "expose" and "uncover," though it has often created difficulties in sustaining heroic assertions within a play, has also made the genre an ideal medium for the understanding of politics. (If *Henry IV* is one of the most thoroughgoing critiques of heroism in literature, it is also — through Prince Hal's behavior at Shrewsbury — a vindication of at least one politically viable form of heriosm.)

Thus far I have attempted to describe a particular mode of writing which Shakespeare developed in his cycle on English history and which, both in the experiences he focused on and the attitudes which he brought to bear on them, is among his distinctly original contributions to world literature. Although scholars with an evolutionary bent can doubtless find "anticipations" of Shakespeare's historical world in earlier chronicle plays, in the moralities and even in humanist historical writing, the peculiar form he achieved — with its secular focus on a discernibly "real" world, its cultivation of multiple points of view, its balance of public and private perspectives, not to speak of its artistic persuasiveness — is very much his own creation. My purpose here is not to indicate the nature of Shakespeare's achievement (modern Shakespeare scholarship, for all its controversies, has given ample enough accounts of it), but to use his image of the historical world as a kind of model to discuss historical drama as an ongoing tradition. If I were more of a critical monist than I care to be, I should, in the fashion of F. R. Leavis, distinguish those plays that fit this model as the "great tradition" of historical drama (though I shall not hide my partiality toward plays of this type). Even within Shakespeare's English cycle a primarily ceremonial play such as *Henry V* — weighted as it is in favor of public over private experience, of patriotic assertion over any serious self-questioning — scarcely fits the model I have set up.[7] The Roman plays, on the other hand, extend perspectives which

Shakespeare opened in *Richard II* and *Henry IV*; indeed, the sharp critique to which Shakespeare subjects the political realm in *Coriolanus* and *Antony and Cleopatra* gains particular significance if viewed against the historical world he created in the English plays of a decade before.[8]

If the model I am suggesting at once describes and evaluates a certain type of play, I might add that the plays which fit this model are themselves both descriptive and evaluative in their approach to the materials of history. In fact, it is through their very self-consciousness that they seem to take a middle ground politically, with the result that they cannot easily be classified according to the more extreme ideological terms such as "reactionary" or "radical." Note, for instance, the distinction the critic is forced to draw between the ideologies of "radical" dramatists such as Büchner and Brecht and the actual statements which their major historical dramas seem to be making. Although Brecht's *Mutter Courage* and *Galileo* are doubtless radical in their larger intent, from moment to moment they are full of ironic qualifications. It is significant, for instance, that the title characters of these two plays are intended as "negative examples," yet that Brecht has managed (more, apparently, than he intended) to endow them with a high degree of sympathy: the historical world, even for one who has mastered Marxist dialectic, is a very complicated thing.[9]

Although the biographical critic might trace the political disillusionment in *Dantons Tod* to Büchner's own disillusionment after the failure of the uprising he attempted to provoke at Giessen in 1834, one could also argue that disillusionment — or at least self-questioning — is one of the two options built into the kind of play he was writing: given the materials he chose to work, he could have written a panegyric to Robespierre (the "radical" approach) or he could, as he in fact did, subject Robespierre's rhetoric to critical analysis while at the same time lamenting the impossibility of successful revolution (the approach of the "middle ground," though a more radical-minded reader than I might simply call any deviation towards the middle "counter-revolutionary").[10] The "tainted idealist" whom I described in an earlier chapter as the typical protagonist of conspiracy plays is by his very nature a figure of the middle ground: unless a dramatist is prepared to celebrate (or denounce) conspiracy uncritically, his only recourse is to analyze his plot as he keeps it moving. The three characteristic types of dramatic structure I discussed earlier — conspiracy, tyrant, and martyr — all lose their clear outlines and, in effect, "compromise" themselves whenever they are subjected to the critical intelligence. *Athalie* is a different kind of experience from a tyrant play such as Preston's *Cambises* because of the complex attitude we take to the character Athalie and our recognition that the "innocent" successor in whose victory we rejoice will repeat her crimes. Historical complexity becomes an extension of human complexity.

Besides the human and political middle ground characteristic of the historical world, one could speak of a generic middle ground in many plays which we classify as tragedies. For example, most of the great historical tragedies have a way of avoiding cataclysmic extremes. If *Coriolanus* and *Wallenstein* exemplify a fine accommodation of history and tragedy, theirs is emphatically not the cosmos-shattering tragedy of *King Lear* and *Penthesilea*, two uncompromisingly tragic works each written within a decade of the former plays. In fact, one need only set the last-named play next to Kleist's *Prinz Friedrich von Homburg* to note the difference between a confrontation of catastrophe and an accommodation which leads to a happy resolution. If the ultimate avoidance of tragedy is sufficient grounds for reviving the controversial old term "tragicomedy," it can surely be attached to *Prinz Friedrich* (Kleist himself called the play simply "Ein Schauspiel" — "A Drama"). Although *Dantons Tod* projects a tragic world characterized by constant talk about ultimates, the point of view from which it approaches this world establishes a high degree of ironic distance. For all the claims that Corneille made to be writing within an Aristotelian tragic framework, such works of his major period as *Le Cid, Horace*, and *Cinna* are each master exemplars of the movement from tragedy to accommodation. Corneille, who, unlike the German writers, did not experience the influence of Shakespeare, is in every way a dramatist of what I have called the historical world (the many readers who have noted a peculiarly secular quality to his Christian martyr-play, *Polyeucte*, have rightly sensed the locus of his interests).[11] If in our time certain great tragedies have come to seem embodiments of some ultimate experience, it is significant that we accord a kind of mythical status to *Lear* and not to *Coriolanus*, to *Phèdre* and not to *Bérénice*: accommodation, though often satisfying to the critical intelligence, does not easily make for awe. And if we also tend to accord such status to *Macbeth*, it is because this, the last of Shakespeare's "major" tragedies, for all its historical details out of Holinshed and its relevance to the politics of James's court, makes all-out claims on our imagination which remove it emphatically from the historical world.

Boundaries of the Historical World

> Du leugnest die Tugend?
>> Robespierre to Danton at their
>> single confrontation in
>> *Dantons Tod*

> O, couldst thou speak,
> That I might hear thee call great Caesar ass,
> Unpolicied!
>> Cleopatra to the asp

Among plays rooted in the historical world, those we have come to recognize as indisputably great are small in number — after Shakespeare, a few from the seventeenth-century French theater, from the German theater of Goethe's time, perhaps a few from our own century. The great plays of the Spanish Golden Age are too far removed from the Shakespearean model on which I have based my definition to discuss in those terms.[12] Although the vast majority of noncomic plays within European drama before the late nineteenth century at least pretend to have some historical basis (if merely in setting or through the introduction of royal personages), only the smallest number display any serious concern for history. Indeed, many of the fundamental "literary" impulses — toward pastoral simplicity, toward a total tragic or comic resolution, toward satirical denunciation of existing reality — are distinctly at odds with the characteristic ways of the historical world. The complexities within history which the great historical dramas demonstrate create too much clutter to fit easily within the customary forms of the literary imagination. Literature seeks to impose patterns to which history, with its indifference to human desire and its penchant for unexpectedly shifting our perspective on events, often proves recalcitrant. Among the "antihistorical" literary modes, pastoral can embody itself within sufficiently brief segments to serve as a comment on the historical world against which it is imposed. Thus, when Henry VI dreams of becoming a shepherd, or when Kleist's Prince Friedrich, after learning he has been condemned to death, begs to retire to the life of working a farm, we recognize that each of these pastoral reveries is merely an island in time, momentarily appealing yet ultimately precarious, for each of these characters must return to make what accommodations he can amid the uncertainties of the historical world. For William Empson, who extended the notion of pastoral from shepherding and farming to other assertions of simplicity, the whole Falstaff action within *Henry IV* functions as a pastoral commentary on the historical world of the plays.[13]

Among the more extended literary modes, romance has traditionally had a special antagonism to history. A quick look at the dramatis personae of *Cymbeline* might suggest a historical play about Roman England — yet nothing could be further from the case. With its stolen babies (later restored to their rightful position as princes), wicked stepmother, and plot complications involving drugs and all manner of disguise, it has the obvious trappings of romance; it is significant, for instance, that Shakespeare borrowed little more than the setting from Holinshed, but went to Boccaccio and other writers of romance for his plot. Although Shakespeare reminds us throughout the play of the presence of a historical world, this world exists only to be disdained and rejected. In depicting this world, romance takes a necessarily simpleminded attitude, as we note in Belarius's narrative (III. iii. 55-73), to his adopted sons, about the political cruelties to which he has been subjected (a narrative which was to be paralleled, as though by convention, in Prospero's narrative to Miranda of his banishment [I. ii] in Shakespeare's last

104

and greatest romance — his only play, by a strange irony, to be based on an event from contemporary history).

Although recent scholarship has uncovered a multitude of political allusions in Dryden's heroic plays, it is very difficult for any reader today to experience these plays as serious historical drama, for the allusions (on local matters such as rebellion and the succession) are not genuinely integrated within the plays, which take the form of heroic romance. If Restoration audiences doubtless recognized a relevance to recent English history in Almanzor's political advice to Boabdelin —

> . . . or better thou wouldst know,
> Than to let factions in thy kingdom grow.
> Divided interests, while thou think'st to sway,
> Draw, like two brooks, thy middle stream away[14]

his didacticism is quickly forgotten during his more amorous or swashbuckling moments.[15] When history functions primarily to magnify, whatever political thought gets into the play must remain peripheral to the play's primary movement, which seeks to maintain and intensify our admiration for the hero. (Corneille, who was also concerned with establishing the primacy of his heroes, was considerably more willing than Dryden to put them through a series of dramatic tests, above all to portray them in the *process* of growth.) Moreover, when Dryden, in the preface to *The Indian Emperor*, writes, "I have . . . traced the Native simplicity and ignorance of the *Indians,* in relation to *European* Customes: The Shipping, Armour, Horses, Swords and Guns of the *Spaniards*, being as new to them as their Habits and their Language were to the Christians,"[16] we recognize that history has become a fascination with the exotic; to the extent that "local color" was to assume an increasingly prominent role in historical plays during the succeeding two centuries, the role of serious historical concern in drama was to be threatened. Like other aspects of romance, local color stresses the distance between the life of the audience and the life enacted on stage — while at the same time arranging for the audience's temporary escape into this new and distant life; if, on the other hand, the audience is to experience the full impact of a historical situation, it must remain aware of the parallels and continuities that connect the historical past enacted on stage with its own present.

Local color can achieve such relevance only when, as in Goethe's *Götz von Berlichingen*, the essential values of a distant culture (whether distant historically, or geographically, or both) become values whose adoption the writer is seriously recommending to his audience. The great age of local color (both in drama and fiction) was of course the nineteenth century, which, to echo a phrase used by Bulwer-Lytton in the preface to that old war-horse of a play, *Richelieu,* looked upon the task of historical drama "to place upon the stage the picture of an era."[17] In their attempts to be colorful, dramatists were often more intent to *evoke* a past world than to come to grips with its particular tensions. In Musset's *Lorenzaccio* an unnamed passerby at a fair points at a wildly gesticulating man and tells his companion, "Si je ne me trompe, c'est ce hâbleur de Cellini."[18] Cellini, one might note, has no further role in the play, and the very familiarity of the word "hâbleur" is meant to make the audience think itself privileged to be transported back to the Renaissance. Whenever the evocation of local color becomes a central aim, a play is likely to become burdened with a trivial antiquarianism: in the scene with the Cellini allusion Musset even provided a footnote to identify Monte Oliveto, the scene of the fair he was depicting — "People went to Monte Oliveto every Friday during certain months; it was to Florence what Longchamp used to be to Paris. The merchants found it suitable to a fair and took their merchandise there."[19] (One suspects that the local analogy — "It was to Florence what Longchamp used to be to Paris" — was meant to ease the audience's — or, more precisely, the reader's — journey toward a still unfamiliar time and place.) The willful and blatant anachronisms in Shaw's historical plays — one thinks of such parody characters in *Caesar and Cleopatra* as the precise and proper Englishman Britannus and the fin-de-siècle aesthete Apollodorus — remind us that the evocation of a historical atmosphere does not in itself create a historical world; indeed, to the extent that *Caesar and Cleopatra* shows a serious concern for how men are ruled, it succeeds in creating a genuinely historical world far better than its more self-consciously "accurate" predecessors.[20]

Besides the lure of local color, historical romance provides still another diversion from history in the heightened theatrical effects that constitute the climactic moments of innumerable plays. In watching plays such as those of Dryden or Victor Hugo, audiences must have accustomed themselves to suspend thought while awaiting some overwhelming theatrical gesture — whether in the form of a great speech, elaborate sword-play, or the abduction (or rescue) of a helpless heroine.[21] The history of theater is in a certain sense a history of sensational effects whereby an audience is stunned, titillated, or drawn together in some sort of communal experience; it is only at the rarest of intervals that writers have been able to use theatrical effect as a means of stimulating serious thinking. Among the characteristic forms of historical drama, the conspiracy play, to the extent that intrigue and plotting (both for the conspirators and the dramatist) become ends in their own right, runs a special risk of lapsing into automatic, if also "entertaining," theatrical actions. The play which succeeds in subordinating its conspiracies to exploring the rise and fall of political fortunes (for instance, *Richard II* and *Wallenstein*) or charting a man's personal and political growth (*Henry IV* and Corneille's major plays) is able to immerse itself in the flux and uncertainties of a genuinely historical world.

But an immersion of this sort becomes difficult when the object of the play is the sensationalism which can be achieved, as conspiracy plays all too often do through their rapid peripeties, their exploitation of secrecy, and violent actions which follow one after the other. A work such as Schiller's early play, *Die Verschwörung des Fiesko zu Genua* (*The Conspiracy of Fiesco in Genoa*), though it employs the conventions of the genre with brilliant theatrical effect, only rarely allows a breathing space for any serious thought to express itself. When Shaw's Caesar reprimands the politically immature Cleopatra for having the conspirator Pothinus killed,[22] he is not simply making a point about the art of ruling, but he is also, in effect, commenting on the automatic gestures that all too easily limit the impact of a historical play to an unthinking theatricality. The essential plotlessness of *Dantons Tod*, manifesting itself, as it does, both in its hero's refusal to conspire to save his life and in its author's refusal to grant us the suspense we expect, is at once a comment on the overemphasis of plot in earlier history plays and on the meaninglessness of plotting within an actual historical situation; one might note that the play's second act, in which Danton makes his decision not to plot, also includes a dialogue attacking the contemporary theater for being essentially false to nature.[23]

Yet there is a more fundamental form of theatricality which can serve the most serious historical purpose: I refer to the notion of theater as metaphor for the workings of history. In its most obvious instances, this metaphor, as I indicated in the first chapter, functions to remind us that the doings of the great — whether the histrionics of Richard II or the consciousness of Brutus and his fellow conspirators of the universal stage on which the assassination of Caesar is being enacted — can at once be defined, ennobled, and disparaged by their essential theatricality. As metaphor, theater provides an angle of vision which displays the historical world in all its complexity: it enlightens in the very act of providing the "entertainment" which we traditionally associate with it. No part of *Henry IV* is more "entertaining" than the scene in the Boar's Head in which Falstaff play-acts the king chastising his son and then shifts roles to play the prince while the latter plays Falstaff. Note the conclusion of Falstaff's last speech in the role of the king: "If that man [Falstaff] should be lewdly given, he deceiveth me; for, Harry, I see virtue in his looks. If then the tree may be known by the fruit, as the fruit by the tree, then peremptorily I speak it, there is virtue in that Falstaff; him keep with, the rest banish. And tell me now, thou naughty varlet, tell me where hast thou been this month?" (Pt. 1. II. iv. 420-26). By means of the play-making in which Falstaff and the prince engage, the central concerns of the drama as a whole are condensed into a single short scene and are evident to a high degree even within these few quoted lines. Take, for instance, the various public themes of the *Henry IV* plays (the suppression of rebellion, the establishment of legitimacy, the preparation of the prince for his future role as king). When Falstaff-as-king chides the prince for his loose ways ("tell me where hast thou been this month?") he is simply repeating the complaints which Hal's real father voiced in the preceding act (I. i. 77-89) and which he is to address to the prince directly in the succeeding act (III. ii. 4-161). But in the present scene these admonitions come from Falstaff, himself a major threat to order within the total scheme of the plays. We know from the start that Falstaff is also a surrogate-father to Hal, that in one sense the plays are centered around the question of who (the real or the surrogate father) will ultimately wield the greater authority over the man who is preparing to wield authority over the kingdom as a whole.

If we feel outraged (and amused) at Falstaff's whitewashing of himself ("there is virtue in that Falstaff"), we also remember that the king's authority is itself compromised, that in his earlier role of Bolingbroke he was himself a rebel against the authority of Richard II, and that throughout the plays that bear his new royal name he displays both guilt about his earlier acts and uneasiness about his own legitimacy; indeed, his concern about his son's proper education has to do with his need to insure the legitimacy of his line through a ruler whose authority will be untainted. We know that Falstaff is manifestly wrong in his contention that appearances tell the truth ("I see virtue in his looks.... If then the tree may be known by the fruit..."), though of course others will read Falstaff's physical appearance quite differently from the way he himself does, and they may, in fact, come very close to the truth about him. In a sense, however, Falstaff is quite right about the truth of appearances, for Bolingbroke's assumption of royal authority actually did make a real king of him in more than simply name. Men can all too easily become the roles they are playing, as Hal admits when, recognizing how close Falstaff comes to assuming his real father's role, he brings the make-believe to an end: "Dost thou speak like a king?" he asks, as though to remind Falstaff of the usurpation of authority which their play-making has allowed him, at which point Hal (as though desperate to reassert his own authority) decides to change to a new game entirely: "Do thou stand for me," he tells Falstaff, "and I'll play my father" (427-28). The possibilities for achieving complexity of meaning through the theatrical metaphor are endless, if only because it allows every phenomenon to be viewed in a double aspect — art as life (and vice versa), appearance as reality (and vice versa) — and to place these within an apparently infinite number of combinations; doubtless it would take an Empson to untangle the complexities of the above passage properly.

Henry IV surely provides the supreme example of a complex and serious approach to history that diverts in the very act of instructing; not the least of its achievements is its ability to unite these two functions which in most dramas move in separate directions. If the creation of a fully embodied historical world is threatened, on the one hand, by the more "sensational" possibilities — romance or the reliance on the unthinking sorts of theatrical effect—open to a dramatist, it is equally threatened by the application of too earnest or too rigid a moral perspective. Although one can cite innumerable reasons why Jonson's *Catiline* went wrong, certainly a major factor is the unrelenting moral voice we hear behind the play, above all in Cicero's speeches of condemnation, which at times virtually stifle the dramatic action. Like the Roman historians from whom he drew his material, Jonson in his plays was writing a predominantly ethical mode of history. The various controversies as to precisely what ideas Shakespeare was trying to propagate in his history plays testify to the relatively high degree of autonomy of the historical world he created. If we think we hear Shakespeare's "own" voice in the speeches of the bastard Falconbridge in *King John* (and to a degree that we are unable to hear it in any single character in the other history plays), it is a voice which does not violate this autonomy: even while railing against the ways of the political world in the Commodity speech (II. i. 561-98), he is willing to recognize them for what they are. The great historical dramas, whether they advocate or attack Realpolitik, at least demonstrate its pervasiveness (and fascination) in history. To the extent that drama seeks to uncover the realities of human behavior, to separate rationalization from its underlying motives, to expose the will to power that stands behind official moral rhetoric, Machiavelli obviously provides a more effective model than, say, Tacitus or any of the more "ethically" oriented commentators on the past.

Like romance, the ethical perspective seeks to transcend history, to thumb its nose at the political actions in which the historical world is rooted; and, like romance, it rejects the historical world in favor of some "higher" reality, though the latter is likely to take more colorful theatrical forms in romance than in a morally oriented history play, which usually depends on noble rhetoric to achieve its higher reality. When Schiller's Mary Stuart (like innumerable other martyr-figures) refuses to encourage the conspiracy which might save her life, or when she allows herself a gratuitous personal insult at her oppressor, she is asserting her disdain for the historical world as such. For a character in search of higher realities, participation in history serves as something to be left behind—often, in fact, something to feel guilty about. If conspiracy plays tend to overcomplicate the intrigues within history in the interest of theatrical effect, tyrant and martyr plays often simplify these intrigues in order to reject them with maximum dispatch. Contempt for the world can easily take the form of contempt for history. In historical dramatists otherwise as diverse as Chapman, Gryphius, and Schiller, stoicism (whether in Christian or secular form) provides the language and the ideas by which a character can transcend untenable historical situations in a way that creates the greatest possible distance between the nobility of his stance and the inevitable corruptions of the historical world. Although *Octavia* is the only extant Roman play based on an "actual" historical event, it looks down on the world of events with the same unbending moral perspective as the mythological plays of Seneca on which it is modeled. Present evil is contrasted in absolute terms with past virtue ("vera . . . virtus Romana");[24] as in the many high-minded Renaissance closet tragedies which also derive from Seneca, history is easily interchangeable with mythology, both of which function primarily to provide moral examples. *Octavia*, like many recent documentary dramas, deals with events that took place shortly before the writing of the play; and, as with documentary plays such as *In der Sache J. Robert Oppenheimer* and *Viet Nam Diskurs*, its lack of historical perspective is proportional to the intensity of its moral perspective. Moral assertions, to the extent that the fervor with which they are expressed depends on an illusion of their eternal validity, thrive best in a timeless, not a historical, world.

In that mode of drama which in its day was called the "moral play" the princes and potentates of the secular world display their greatness only as a means of asserting the paltriness of this world. An early seventeenth-century account of a morality play witnessed many years before indicates the timeless and unhistorical flavor of this mode with a vividness not readily evident in the texts we possess of such plays:

> The play was called (the Cradle of security,) wherin was personated a King or some great Prince with his Courtiers of severall kinds. . . .

The indefiniteness of *"a* King" and *"some* great Prince" is characteristic of the lack of specificity in a timeless and essentially unhistorical world. The exemplary and eternal character of the dramatic action in a morality is especially evident in the description of the end of the play:

> all the court was in greatest jollity, and then the foremost old man with his Mace stroke a fearfull blow upon the Cradle; whereat all the Courtiers with the three Ladies and the vizard all vanished; and the desolate prince starting up bare faced, and finding him-selfe thus sent for to judgement, made a lamentable complaint of his miserable case, and so was carried away by wicked spirits. This Prince did personate in the morall, the wicked of the world; the three Ladies, Pride, Covetousnesse, and Luxury, the two old men, the end of the world, and the last judgement.[25]

The prose easily reveals the spectator's relish at the abjectness of the prince's fall: note the adjectives "desolate," "lamentable," and "miserable" and the suddenness and absoluteness in the gesture of recognition "and the desolate Prince starting up bare faced." The timelessness within the secular world is of course that of a traditional Christian time scheme in which the persons and events of human history are not unique but exemplary, and in which human actions achieve meaning only through their relation to those temporal ultimates which the two old men (literally "the end of the world, and the last judgement") represent.

Although morality and history represent antithetical tendencies within drama, the idealizing imagination which imposes a timeless morality pattern upon the events it depicts is also quite capable of accommodating topical allusions (often with a sharp political bite) within such patterns. In sixteenth-century plays such as Bale's *King Johan* and Preston's *Cambises*, as David M. Bevington has shown, elements of morality and history exist side by side within the same work; even in Skelton's much more traditional *Magnificence,* the audience was expected to penetrate behind the timeless forms to recognize specific allusions to a time-bound Tudor world.[26] Indeed, the figures and forms of morality are still very much present within Shakespeare's early history plays, as we may remember from that image of the morality-play king —

> His body couched in a curious bed,
> When Care, Mistrust, and Treason waits on him.

which Henry VI conjures up at the end of his soliloquy to describe the historical as against the pastoral world. Henry's resorting to a "timeless" image — one which might have come out of a play similar to *The Cradle of Security* — could in fact serve as a comment on the naiveté with which the king, in contrast to his Yorkist opponents, apprehends the historical world.

Shakespeare's originality in his first tetralogy might be described as his ability to dramatize the interaction of incompatible views of historical reality. Thus, in *Richard III* the Senecan ghosts, curses, and lamentations (all of them conventional expressions of a fixed and timeless view of morality) are pitted against the cynicism and the political opportunism of Richard III; the historical world of the play cannot be defined simply by the "Machiavellian" one which the title character embodies but by the larger political drama which we perceive through the confrontation of two modes of reality. What I have called Shakespeare's historical world is not a static, but a shifting, form, one which develops from play to play and which defines itself anew through its confrontations with and absorption of other worlds, be they the pastoral worlds of Henry VI's soliloquy or the Boar's Head Tavern, or the traditional "moral" world which speaks through Margaret's curse in *Richard III*. (If *Henry VIII* seems a less rich play to us than Shakespeare's history plays of the 1590s, this is because it distinctly lacks that "confrontation" of worlds characteristic of the earlier plays: organized as a succession of falls from royal grace, it takes the form, to use Frank Kermode's words, of a "late morality," one which creates not so much a historical world as a series of laments that culminate happily in the birth of Elizabeth.)[27]

The confrontation between worlds manifests itself at its most conspicuous as

111

a confrontation between different modes of language. Throughout most of the first scene of *Henry VI, Part 1*, we hear nothing but ceremonial language, whether in the form of eulogy to the recently deceased Henry V —

> England ne'er had a king until his time.
> Virtue he had, deserving to command...
>
> (8-9)
>
> Henry the Fifth, thy ghost I invocate:
> Prosper this realm, keep it from civil broils,
>
> (52-53)

or of resolution to undo the recent defeat in France —

> Awake, awake, English nobility!
> Let not sloth dim your honours new-begot.
>
> (78-79)

At the end of the scene, with a single character (the bishop of Winchester) left alone on stage, a new, quite unceremonial voice is heard —

> Each hath his place and function to attend:
> I am left out; for me nothing remains;
> But long I will not be Jack out of office.
> The King from Eltham I intend to steal,
> And sit at chiefest stern of public weal.
>
> (173-77)

With the sudden intrusion of the voice of policy to undercut the high cere-mony which preceded it, Shakespeare has been able — within the first scene of his first history play (and perhaps also the first play he ever wrote) — to establish that interaction of voices which constitutes his historical world. Sigurd Burckhardt, in a brilliant essay on *Henry VI*, has described the dominant ceremonial tone of the play as "one of vaunt and taunt, of 'high terms' ceremonially put forward and ceremonially responded to," and has pointed to the scene between the Countess of Auvergne and Talbot as an example of "a ceremony...startlingly interrupted" as Talbot, "with ironic urbanity," refuses to play the ceremonial game which she expects of him.[28]

One could cite innumerable later confrontations, for instance those between Richard III and the various women (Anne, Margaret, Elizabeth) who attempt to confront him ceremonially with their outrage, or between the ceremonial Richard II and the plainer-speaking Bolingbroke. Much of the vitality of Shakespeare's English histories derives from the confrontations between those who know they live in historical time and those who speak a deliberately ahistorical, timeless language. The confrontations within *Richard III*, for instance, achieve their peculiar quality through the flair with which the title character, with his special talent for utilizing the individual historical moment, is able to manipulate the ceremonial characters (as in his wooing of Anne in return for the curses she directs at him) or to deflate their rhetorical pretensions. Note the following interchange in the midst of the lengthy and elaborate curse voiced by the aged Queen Margaret:

> Margaret: Thou elvish-marked, abortive, rooting hog!
> Thou that wast sealed in thy nativity
> The slave of nature and the son of hell!
> Thou slander of thy heavy mother's womb!
> Thou loathèd issue of thy father's loins!
> Thou rag of honour! thou detested —
> Gloucester: Margaret.
> Margaret: Richard!
> Gloucester: Ha?
> Margaret: I call thee not.
> Gloucester: I cry thee mercy then, for I did think
> That thou hadst called me all these bitter names.
> Margaret: Why, so I did, but looked for no reply.
> O, let me make the period to my curse!
> Gloucester: 'Tis done by me, and ends in 'Margaret'.
>
>   (I. iii. 228-39)

The opening passage of this quotation is representative of the high and exuberant rhetoric with which Margaret, quite oblivious to the fact that the man whom she curses can beat her at her own rhetorical game, has already carried on for most of a hundred lines.[29] If Richard belonged to her ceremonial world, his appropriate reaction would be to cringe in horror or to denounce her in language similar to her own. Like Talbot in the passage mentioned above, he simply refuses to play her ceremonial game. When he interrupts her to insert her own name in place of his within the curse (pronounced as a trochee, "Margaret" fits the same metrical slot as "Richard"), he is still in a sense continuing her game, for he is returning one curse for another. Yet she is so fully concerned with her own ceremony that she solemnly inserts his name as though he had never interrupted her. His quick reply, "Ha?" works to shift the action from her timeless ceremonial realm to that of everyday domesticity (it is as though he has translated her intention in voicing his name to mean simply, "Where are you, cousin?"). The irritability of her reply, "I call thee not," is an acknowledgment that he has succeeded in destroying her ceremony. The feigned innocence of his next two lines confirms the uselessness of her quite considerable rhetorical efforts, and the best she can do is remind him helplessly that she "looked for no reply," that in other words he had failed to abide by the rules of her game. She resorts to the technical language of rhetoric ("let me make the period to my curse!") in a last attempt to continue her ceremony: through a return to her earlier rhetoric perhaps she could make everybody who has been listening to her curse forget the breakdown that has occurred. But Richard quickly reminds her that by inserting her own name into the curse he has already brought it to its technical conclusion: he has reworked her game and destroyed it at once. The whole course of the play could be described as a similar conflict between the techniques of ceremony and those of Realpolitik, with the latter generally victorious until, at the end, it is undone by a new, more potent ceremonial force in the person of Richmond.

For Shakespeare the possibilities of history could be renewed in one play after another through the confrontation of a temporal view of things with views which, in one way or another, assert their timeless nature; it is as though a historical world could define itself only through a constant exploration of the boundaries which separate the temporal from the timeless — for instance, Bolingbroke's challenging the timeless old order of Richard II (and his subsequent adoption of some of its ceremonies and symbols); Antony's testing of Brutus's idealism; the continuing redefinitions of the nature of temporality and timelessness, of public and private, of history and romance, in the confrontations between Octavius's Rome and Cleopatra's Egypt.

Through his ability to renew and redefine his historical world from one play to the next, Shakespeare set an example which no later dramatist could emulate either in variety or subtlety. The problems which a writer faces in creating a historical world are particularly discernible in the work of Goethe, who made serious approaches to history at various intervals in his long career, yet never in his later work created as fully a historical world as he did in his play *Götz von Berlichingen*, written in his early twenties. *Götz* is the first great work of European literature consciously to attempt "a picture of an era," namely, the declining feudal world of sixteenth-century Germany, and as such it stands at the head of a tradition which includes not only those various pilgrimages (whether in the form of medievalism or Hellenism) to recapture a lost past, but also that central strain of nineteenth-century fiction which, in novelists from Balzac to Joyce, sought to picture a contemporary world in the most meticulous detail. Despite the fact that Goethe conceived *Götz* on what he took to be a Shakespearean (as against a neoclassical) model, the historical world of the play does not, as in Shakespeare, emerge out of a confrontation of disparate worlds; in fact, with its sprawling view of various segments of a changing world, it is singularly lacking in dramatic confrontations.

What makes Goethe's play historical in a profoundly new way is its concentration on the very process of change, its sense of time passing, of one set of human values gradually, though inevitably, giving way to another.[30] Goethe's greatness in this play — a kind of greatness he shares less with other dramatists than with such writers of epic as Homer and Tolstoy — lies in the sense of life with which he endowed the multitude of characters within his panorama, and, even more remarkably, in the love he was able to breathe into characters representing the most diverse points of view. In Goethe, as in

114

the great writers of epic, diverse worlds exist side by side rather than in dramatic confrontation with each other; although the subplot centered around those two characters out of romance, the siren Adelheid and the villain Weislingen, lacks that dramatic relevance to the main action which we expect in a Shakespearean double plot, it at least maintains a charming coexistence with the play's historical interests. If we experience any complexity of attitude toward the action, it does not, as in Shakespeare, come from our recognition of the ambiguities inherent in all political situations, but in our regret at the passing of a noble old order together with a grudging acceptance of the inevitability of change. "The times of deceit are coming," the dying Götz announces in his final speech; "the unworthy will rule with cunning and the worthy will fall into their nets."[31] As with the Highlands heroes of Walter Scott (who, as I mentioned earlier, translated *Götz* in his youth),[32] the high-minded, if also outmoded, values of a lost past are meant to serve as a means of moral reawakening for the present; insofar as the best of the past can be made to live in the present, historical continuity itself becomes a value.

In *Egmont*, with its lovingly depicted ordinary people, its ruthless foreign ruler (whom we see only through his regents and whose policies are incomprehensible to his victims), its hero striving to assert principles of freedom in a great moment of crisis, one expects a fully realized historical world in which the various dramatic conflicts might serve as a testing ground of values. Yet the testing never really takes place, for each segment of Goethe's world exists serenely independent of every other. Goethe has, in fact, chosen a hero who was legendary for his nonchalance in the face of unbending political repression; when Egmont finally faces the fact of his imminent execution, Goethe allows the play to resolve itself not within the confines of the historical world, but, as I indicated earlier in discussing the operatic quality of the ending, by invoking a "higher" level of reality with music, an allegorical vision, and a paean to the idea of freedom. The traditional freedoms which Egmont seeks to restore, like the heroic individualism of which Götz von Berlichingen is the last representative, leave the impression (despite the historical framework in which Goethe places them) of residing in an idyllic, timeless realm that somehow exists beyond history.

One could, in fact, adapt Erich Heller's catchy phrase about Goethe's "avoidance of tragedy"[33] (a characteristic, incidentally, which he shared with such major contemporaries as Rousseau and Wordsworth) and speak as well of a certain "avoidance of history," a tendency to skirt the complexities of the historical world in favor of some "higher" and less time-bound mode of thinking and feeling. When the well-meaning but ineffectual regent in *Egmont*, Margaret of Parma, states, "I know that politics can rarely maintain loyalty and faith, that it excludes openness, good-heartedness and flexibility from our hearts,"[34] she voices a disdain for the public world characteristic of Goethe's own approach to history. Goethe's tendency to retreat from history,

115

in fact that typical hankering after timelessness which stands behind all his work, seems particularly noteworthy when we realize that in his role as administrator for the duke of Weimar he doubtless surpassed all other great writers of history plays in practical experience in the inner workings of government. (Is it possible that the public world loses its fascination for those who have lived within it, or was the Duchy of Weimar too small and isolated a spot to kindle the historical imagination?)

Goethe's difficulties in coping in dramatic terms with the tensions of history are especially evident in a group of plays that attempt to deal, in one way or another, with the French Revolution. The first of these, *Der Gross-Cophta* (begun before the Revolution and finished in 1791) uses a celebrated scandal to analyze the corruptions within the ancien régime. As a Ben Jonson-like comedy about tricksters out-tricking each other, the play is wonderfully worked out, though Goethe's intended historical task was scarcely in tune with his comic purpose: since his comic structure demands an authority at the end who punishes the criminals and restores order, he comes up with the only plausible authorities he can invoke — the prince and police of the regime whose corruptions he was exposing! *Der Bürgergeneral* (*The Citizen-General* — 1793) uses the conventions of comedy to make fun of French notions of freedom, equality, and the like, yet it also displays the inappropriateness of these conventions to an imaginative understanding of political realities; when, at the end, the spokesman for revolutionary ideals is unmasked as an imposter, we recognize that the same mechanism which creates a comic resolution can also work to prevent any serious resolution of the political conflicts with which the play is concerned.

Die Aufgeregten (*The Enraged* — 1793), an uncompleted play which Goethe labeled a "political drama," makes an honest if not very convincing attempt to deal with class conflict; indeed, Goethe's inability to finish the play reflects his difficulty in finding an adequate dramatic and, for that matter, human resolution to the problems he chose to raise. As spokesman for the third estate Goethe presents the upright but comically boastful surgeon Breme, who, caught up in the revolutionary fever of the time, decides to lead a revolt in a small German state to settle what we are to see as traditional and genuine grievances. Throughout the play Goethe dreams of a reconciliation of classes which can take place without violence, and he manipulates his comic plot — which is to be resolved through the discovery of a document deliberately misplaced by an ill-motivated official — so that a social resolution will seem to follow naturally from a dramatic resolution. The narrow conception of social conflict characteristic of the play as a whole is exemplified by Goethe's own spokesman, the lovely aristocratic lady who has been influenced by the humanitarianism of the Enlightenment, but horrified by the violence she has witnessed in Paris, and who, though sympathetic to the people's grievances, believes that social problems could be solved on a

116

personal level if individuals would learn to behave sensibly and decently toward one another.[35] It is significant that among the scenes which Goethe did not write (but for which he left detailed summaries) are two which must have made him recognize the limitations of his social vision—the final reconciliation, in which the armed and angry rebels are calmed down through the showing of the old document, and an earlier scene (which a Genet or a Peter Weiss would have carried out with a self-conscious decadence impossible for Goethe) in which the whole cast gathers around a tea table to enact roles at a mock National Convention.[36]

The specificities of history which find their way—even without satisfactory resolution—into these three plays are notably missing in *Die natürliche Tochter* (*The Natural Daughter*—1799-1803), the last and also the most distinguished of the four dramas that reflect his preoccupation with the Revolution. In its refusal to name particular people, places, or events (except for the heroine, all the characters are known only by their class or occupational titles—king, secretary, preceptress, monk) it seeks an illusion of timelessness and placelessness with a rigor that the classicism of the preceding two centuries had never known. The fact that the play is based on an emigrée's memoir gives some indication of the peculiarly personal (and conservative) approach it takes to social change. The political world exists as a sinister force somewhere in the distance, while the fate of the heroine, Eugenie, whose life has been shattered by this force, exists not to be explored or understood but as something to elegize, though in noble and often quite moving verses.

There is one work, however, in which Goethe achieved an understanding of the Revolution not to be found in any of these plays. Significantly, it is not a drama at all, but a long pastoral poem, *Hermann und Dorothea* (1796-97), and it was precisely because he viewed the historical world through the timeless perspective of pastoral that he was able to evoke that world with a particularity and an intensity missing in the other works. (After *Götz*, which, after all, was written long before the Revolution, Goethe could deal adequately with history only in forms which did not demand a rendering of the public and all too often violent events which are the staple of historical drama.) As in the pastoral soliloquy of *Henry VI*, history and pastoral in *Hermann und Dorothea* assume a dialectical relationship to one another: Goethe's idyllic picture of life in a contemporary German small town achieves its intensity only through our awareness of the larger historical world—the world of the spreading French Revolution with its refugees encamped at the town's edge as a visible reminder of the breakdown of order—which is constantly threatening to intrude. By reminding us constantly of the revolutionary changes threatening his idyll, Goethe gives us an image of the small town—with its surrounding fields awaiting their rich harvest, its age-old domestic routine, its characters (like those of *Die natürliche Tochter*) known to us not by name but by their tradition-bound occupations, innkeeper, druggist, preacher — which comes to seem a kind of bastion against history, a goodly place which will pursue its timelessness despite the threat of a fast-moving, destructive new temporal order.

If Goethe was able in the 1790s to fashion an image of timelessness which was the more convincing for the threat it was able to withstand, at the end of his life, in the final act of *Faust, Part 2*, he chose to stress the precariousness of pastoral in the face of historical change. An aged couple, Philemon and Baucis, whom Goethe endowed with classical names to indicate their archetypal character and their distance from modern life, inhabit a quaint and archaic world characterized by such traditional pastoral virtues as rootedness, kindliness, independence, and resistance to change. The historical world intrudes when Faust determines to take over their land to pursue his "progressive" colonizing schemes. Faust's idealism about progress is put to a bitter test when, despite his admonitions to spare the old couple by relocating them, Mephistopheles, in the interest of efficiency, ruthlessly destroys them. In this confrontation between pastoral and historical worlds, Goethe was able to create a complex image which contains within itself such diverse perspectives as regret at the passing of a benign and seemingly timeless old order, a recognition that idealism in the modern world manifests itself in the form not of timelessness but belief in progress, and a sense of shock at the disruptions which progress inevitably entails. Although the symbolic terms in which this confrontation is presented are far removed from the historical particularities of *Götz* (or of Shakespeare's histories), in these scenes written in his eighties Goethe hints at a complexity of conception and an engagement with contemporary reality which most of his earlier approaches to history went to great pains to avoid.

THE PUBLIC AND THE PRIVATE

> What infinite heart's ease
> Must kings neglect that private men enjoy!
>> Henry V before Agincourt

> Vous êtes empereur, Seigneur, et vous pleurez!
>> Bérénice to Titus

> Denn die Weltgeschichte bewegt sich auf einem höheren Boden, als der ist, auf dem die Moralität ihre eigentliche Stätte hat, welche die Privatgesinnung, das Gewissen der Individuen, ihr eigentümlicher Wille und ihre Handlungsweise ist....
>> Hegel, Introduction to *Philosophy of History*

Like the mind-body problem in philosophy, or the heredity-environment argument in the social sciences, the conflict between public and private values

provides a continuing dialogue within many forms of literature, most conspicuously perhaps within historical drama. Just as the characteristic shapes of
conspiracy, tyrant, and martyr plays have determined the plotting of history
plays, the relation of public and private has provided a thematic framework
around which historical events could be organized. As an intellectual
construct, the relationship has tended to center around such problems as
accommodating one's personal inclinations to the demands of a public role
(*Richard II, Cinna, Prinz Friedrich von Homburg*), of satisfying one's private
conscience in spite of irreconcilable public demands (*Le Cid, Horace,
Polyeucte*), of determining what precisely are one's private and public rights
and obligations (*Coriolanus, Wallenstein, Dantons Tod, Galileo,* and, for
that matter, nearly all the great historical dramas). Indeed, the complexity of
attitude with which we are expected to respond to dramas centered in the
historical world is a complexity built into the very relationship (or, more
precisely, set of relationships) implied by public and private. If the conflict of
public and private seems in every way natural and appropriate to plays about
rulers and the problems of ruling, this is because any serious discussion of the
public realm plays upon that traditional distinction within political theory
between the "king's two bodies"—his "personal" or mortal body and his
eternal body which derives from his office. Out of this concept a dramatist
can readily exploit such themes as the respectability which office confers upon
a reprehensible human being, or the private pathos which accompanies a
ruler's loss of his office. Ernst Kantorowicz's use of *Richard II* to set up a
model at the start of his massive historical study of this concept testifies to the
ability of drama to clarify an issue with the intensity and concision which,
according to Aristotle and innumerable later commentators, make poetry
more philosophical than history.[37]

Like any convention, however, the relationship between public and private
can serve simply as an unthinking gesture, as in the many seventeenth-century
plays which pit love and honor automatically against one another, or it can
serve the interests of the most profound explorations of history, for instance in
Richard II's lament for the loss of his immortal body in his deposition scene
(IV.i), or in that monologue in *Cinna* (IV.ii) in which Augustus moves back
and forth debating the particular agonies that accompany both vengeance
and magnanimity. The vast majority of historical plays are weighted heavily
toward one or the other extreme within the public-private antithesis.
Ceremonial dramas by nature work to affirm public values; one could look at
the characteristic features of plays such as *Henry V* and *Numancia*—the
pageantry, the high rhetoric, the unleashing of hate against those who
threaten the national cause—as attempts to coax the members of the audience to suppress the individual will in favor of communal solidarity. But even
the most publicly centered plays retain a place for the private dimension,

though principally as something to be overcome, as when Henry V briefly laments the private sacrifice a king must make to fulfill his public role (IV.i.236-90) and then proceeds to fight the battle of Agincourt.

Except for ceremonial plays, most historical drama has opted to defend the private realm against the demands and threats of the public. To the extent that a writer seeks to exalt the heroism of his main character he is forced to set him in opposition to an outside world which resists or, in the end, acknowledges his supremacy. In such Renaissance advocates of the heroic as Marlowe and Chapman the public world has little substantiality of its own but exists largely to counterbalance the hero. *Tamburlaine* cultivates an extreme position which no later historical play has taken: the public world, what little we see of it, comes into being simply to be devoured by the hero, who, in effect, creates his own public reality as he goes about his conquests; history in *Tamburlaine* is neither narrated nor dramatized in the usual sense but becomes something improvised by the hero. But Marlowe, though he possessed an imagination for much else, had no real imagination for the public world. Even a deliberately "unheroic" play such as *Edward II* is notable for its conspicuous lack of a public context: Marlowe's impatience with the public realm is symbolized for us when, after Young Mortimer has announced, "The King of France sets foot in Normandy," Edward answers according to the dictates of a private whim, "A trifle! we'll expel him when we please" (unlike Tamburlaine, the passive Edward cannot put his whims into operation and absorb the public realm within himself).[38]

The public world which Chapman creates in his plays on recent French history exists primarily to demonstrate the difficulties of being heroic in a world which refuses to endure heroism. If heroes such as Bussy and Byron are unable, like Tamburlaine, to devour the public world, they can at least — with the help of stoic doctrine and some of the most splendid language in Renaissance drama — assert their independence from history. The separation of a Chapman hero from any significant social context is evident from the fact that Shelley chose these lines from *The Conspiracy and Tragedy of Byron* as the epigraph to his revolutionary and apocalyptic poem *The Revolt of Islam*:

> There is no danger to a man, that knows
> What life and death is: there's not any law
> Exceeds his knowledge; neither is it lawful
> That he should stoop to any other law.[39]

(Few if any such representative passages from Shakespeare's history plays would fit so romantic a context as Shelley's poem.)

Whenever a writer attempts to concentrate our sympathies on the fate of a hero (even if he carefully provides him with "flaws"), it becomes difficult to endow the surrounding historical context with sufficient life of its own for us to take it seriously except in its effect on the hero. Shakespeare's innovation in the treatment of the hero could be described as an attempt to balance the hero against his historical context, indeed to disperse our interests (and often our sympathies) so that we become unable to experience the hero or his context independently of one another. As David Riggs puts it in his study of *Henry VI*, "Shakespeare recognized that wherever the personal destiny of an heroic man might lie, he also could be understood, and desperately needed to be understood, as a more restrictively 'historical' phenomenon."[40] The "restrictive" role on which Shakespeare insists is evident in the fact that the reigning monarchs who give their names to the titles of his history plays of the 1590s are either subordinate figures within a larger action (Henry VI, King John, Henry IV) or figures for whom our sympathies are sharply qualified (Richard III, Richard II) by the context of the plays in which they appear (the exception is of course *Henry V*, whose ceremonial character allows both the king and the social context he represents to remain uncomplicatedly heroic).

Ever since the public realm became suspect during the Enlightenment, almost any historical character has been able to attract our fascination and sympathy through his defiance of, or victimization by, the historical forces surrounding him. One could speak of a characteristically modern genre called the "biographical" play, ranging from such relatively distinguished examples as *Egmont* and *Maria Stuart* to the middlebrow plays of recent decades on such historical culture heroes as Joan of Arc, Martin Luther, and Thomas More. The central direction of the play is the illumination and vindication of some famous historical personality. In such a play the public order in which the hero lives is doomed from the start; its triumphs, even if it asserts its power and sends the hero to his death, are Pyrrhic victories, for in the course of the play, as the audience comes to admire the hero's fortitude and spiritual power, it also comes to recognize the public realm as spiritually despicable or meaningless.[41] To the extent that the dramatist plays on some notion of historical progress or process, the audience can also gloat over its knowledge that the triumphant public power will soon (or at least eventually) disintegrate, like Ozymandias's kingdom, among the innumerable ruins of history.

The characteristic structure of a biographical play is that of a martyr play, from whose specifically Christian models it adopts the pattern of a dialectical relationship between an exemplary individual and a persecuting external world. But the Christian martyr does not, like many of his secularized successors, simply declare the primacy of private over public values; rather, his private spiritual values emerge as essentially public values, though of a "higher" kind than those of the pagan world. Whereas the Christian martyr play drives unrelentingly toward the demonstration of its hero's martyrdom, secular plays are often more concerned with portraying the hero's personality in the most vivid light than with depicting the coming (or avoidance) of his doom. Although Goethe certainly means for us to be moved by Egmont's martyr-death, fundamentally he seeks to arouse our fascination for his hero's personality, which he characterizes with the term "Dämonisch" (defined in a famous passage of his autobiography as the "tremendous energy" he observes in certain figures and the "unbelievable power they exercise over all creatures").[42] Once we recognize the "demonic" quality of Egmont, it becomes evident that every element in the play is designed to develop and sustain our interest in him; even the vivid crowd scenes and the discussions among the rulers — not to speak of the love scenes with the charming and swooning girl whom Goethe invented (without historical basis) to stand in awe of him — work less to create a political or social context than to define his "demonic" qualities.

The biographical emphasis of modern historical plays (whether or not they portray martyrs) is an extension of the psychological inquisitiveness which has accompanied the domination of private (as against public) experience within all forms of literature during the last two centuries. Goethe's investigation of the "demonic" is simply an early (and from a contemporary point of view a relatively crude) attempt to describe a psychological phenomenon. Among modern writers of historical plays, none is as thoroughgoingly psychological as Strindberg, each of whose plays is essentially a psychological biography of some great personage in Swedish (or world) history. Yet Strindberg's commitment to private experience also goes with a lack of interest in the public world. Indeed, Strindberg's dozen plays on Swedish rulers from the thirteenth through the eighteenth centuries are not, like Shakespeare's English histories, built on a larger controlling myth, but are essentially a series of significant psychological moments in history. Strindberg enjoyed great advantages such as no major nineteenth-century dramatist possessed — a colorful, long, and continuous national history and no Shakespeare, Calderón, Corneille, or Racine before him to stake out all existing claims on the language of drama; yet his obsession with private phenomena (his great strength in his naturalistic and expressionist plays) made him view history with an intensely private bias. When her chancellor, Oxenstjerna, calls Queen Christina an "artist" type who is not fit to govern, Strindberg is clearly not much concerned with the problems of governing yet very much concerned with the pathology of artist types.[43] The whole historical framework of *Charles XII* serves primarily to illuminate the neuroses of an unpleasant and broken man who unluckily (for future Swedish history) happens to be the king.

Just as a biographical emphasis can work to glorify a figure in our eyes, it can also — especially when a writer is prone to irony or psychological analysis — work to undo a hero's greatness for us. If I may play upon a term I used earlier, in the hands of a psychologizing writer history can very easily (though also quite intentionally) "de-magnify" a famous man. Note, for instance, the spectacle of a clever woman driving the newly victorious

Napoleon into a jealous frenzy in Shaw's *The Man of Destiny*. Hegel, who maintained a particularly lofty view of the great men who have helped the historical process along, solemnly warned against the psychologizing bent which stands behind Shaw's jeu d'esprit (and whose limitations Shaw himself advertised when he subtitled it "A Trifle"):

> What school master has not demonstrated that Alexander the Great and Julius Caesar were driven by such passions and were, consequently, immoral? From which it immediately follows that the school master is a finer man than they because he has no such passions, and proves it by the fact that he does not conquer Asia or vanquish Darius or Porus, but instead lives well and lets live. These psychologists are particularly prone to contemplating those peculiarities of great historical figures which belong to their role as private persons.[44]

Needless to say, a drama which aims primarily to uncover the private foibles (or, for that matter, the "endearing" qualities) of the great is scarcely capable of creating a historical world. This does not of course mean that a serious historical drama cannot also be thoroughly analytical of its heroes: in *Dantons Tod*, while unmasking Robespierre's moral pretensions and exposing the clichés of his language, Büchner is also able to treat the public realm (which he ultimately rejects) with a subtlety and seriousness one rarely finds in dramas of the last two centuries.

Among all the impediments that hinder or distort the portrayal of public realities, none has been so persistent as the prevalence of the "love interest" among dramatic conventions since the seventeenth century. In its most "private" form the love interest can reduce history simply to what Corneille, in a passage from which I quoted earlier, disparagingly calls "a simple love intrigue between kings...[who] run no risk either of their life or of their state." To Corneille, for whom the very idea of tragedy was dependent upon the more public (and catastrophic) aspects of history, the love interest must always remain subordinate: "The dignity of tragedy needs some great state interest, or some passion more noble and virile than love, such as ambition or vengeance, and which makes us fear greater misfortunes than the loss of a mistress. It is fit to mix love in it because it is always very attractive, and can serve as a basis to those interests and other passions of which I speak."[45] The love intrigue must not only remain subordinate, but it can also be integrated with historical matters ("peut servir de fondement à ces intérêts"). Corneille, in fact, took great pride in the integration he achieved between private and public in his tragedies. In his best plays the various love entanglements become a means for the serious exploration of those larger entanglements between private and public worlds in which the values attached to each world are challenged and questioned: one thinks, for instance, of Camille's moving outcry, in *Horace*, against the brutality inherent in the Roman virtue which sacrifices her fiancé (IV.iv); or one thinks of the succeeding scenes in which our initial sense of the situation is jolted, first, by her brother's murdering her in the name of this virtue and, second, by their father's eloquent speech which works to exonerate the son by redefining and reconciling the values that have collided in the course of the play.

Yet a successful integration of love with what Corneille calls the "intérêt d'État" has been rare in historical drama. Not only have many overtly historical plays — above all, historical operas, for which love provides the staple nourishment of arias and duets — been centered around "un simple intrigue d'amour entre des rois," but many plays with an otherwise weighty political content depend upon love intrigues to "lighten" the entertainment they have to offer. Love becomes a kind of dessert to counteract the effects of too heavy a historical meal. As Voltaire's Mohammed puts it after reporting his labors in politics and war-making,

> L'amour seul me console; il est ma récompense,
> L'objet de mes travaux, l'idole que j'encense;
> Le dieu de Mahomet; et cette passion
> Est égale aux fureurs de mon ambition.[46]

Yet by refusing to be integrated into the political action, love can also provide a serious perspective on this action. In *Wallenstein*, for instance, the love intrigue involving Max Piccolomini and Wallenstein's daughter Thekla (for which there was no precedent in Schiller's sources) serves as a model of possible simplicity within a complex and intriguing political world; it is essentially an idyll which, like Henry VI's fantasy about himself as a shepherd, provides a confrontation of pastoral and historical worlds. (If the Max-Thekla romance strikes us as the weakest element in *Wallenstein*, this is due not to Schiller's intentions but to his usual awkwardness in dealing with private passions.) The limitless conjugal devotion of Danton's and Camille's wives in *Dantons Tod* provides about the only "positive" note within an otherwise doomed world; similarly, the tenderness which Racine portrays between Britannicus and Junie is meant to seem like a slowly dimming light within the encroaching darkness of Nero's reign. But the complicated love intrigue in Schiller's *Don Carlos* (King Philip wants the princess Eboli, who wants Don Carlos, who, in turn, wants his stepmother, the queen) serves neither as a diversion from politics nor as a perspective upon it; rather, it is a result of Schiller's shifting his conception of the play, during his many years of work on it, from the relatively simple love-and-political conspiracy in his source (the Abbé de Saint-Réal's "exposure" of scandalous intrigues in the Spanish court) to the high-minded exposition of political idealism which was central to his final intention. The result is an unfortunate failure to integrate private and public in what might have otherwise become the great historical drama of the Enlightenment.

The difficulty of integrating private and public, even when both perspectives are present in a play, is especially obvious in those works which set antitheses such as love and honor baldly against one another. Violent oppositions, though they may make for a powerful and mercurial theatricality, rarely provide the best atmosphere for serious thought within an audience. Being greatly "moved" in the theater can sometimes (though not in the greatest plays) be at odds with the analytical faculty. The oppositions which Dryden manipulates with consummate theatricality in *All for Love* come to seem rather simplistic under close scrutiny. The private world, which we associate with love and Egypt, competes for dominance over Antony with the public world of honor, duty, and everything else that is Roman. In virtual morality-play fashion Ventidius plays Good Angel and Cleopatra Bad Angel as they work successively on a malleable Antony. With each act, in fact, the balance of private and public shifts with a teeter-totter effect from one side to the other: if in the first act Antony is won over by public virtue, love conquers in the second, while honor and duty take over again in the third; two shifts occur in the fourth act, while the play resolves itself in the fifth with the ultimate, though "tragic," triumph of love. Despite Dryden's attempt to maintain a neat antithesis between public and private, the play is not fundamentally concerned with the public world; indeed, when we note these lines from his preface, "for the crimes of love which they [Antony and Cleopatra] both committed were not occasioned by any necessity, or fatal ignorance, but were wholly voluntary; since our passions are, or ought to be, within our power,"[47] it is clear that *All for Love* is essentially a tragedy of the passions, that it is centered, moreover, in an ethical rather than a historical world. The public idea that stands behind the play is by and large an abstraction that is never embodied in concrete political actions: what we experience above all in the play is the private games which Cleopatra (and Octavia as well) play with Antony.

Like *All for Love* many plays since the Restoration which purport to deal with the conflict of public and private values have failed to project a powerful dramatic image of the public world. In Nicholas Rowe's *Jane Shore*, which on the surface reads much more like a Shakespearean history play than does *All for Love*, everything is so centered around a domestic revenge that the historical dimension, except on the most superficial level, is totally missing. Such nineteenth-century Shakespearean imitations as Tennyson's *Queen Mary* and *Becket*, though they are full of historical minutiae, are notably unable to project a vital public idea (those moments when they come to life at all are devoted to the voicing of personal sentiments). Readers of Hebbel's *Herodes und Mariamne* doubtless have a hard time making the connections

125

between the "private" battle of the sexes in which the play's public figures engage and the great Hegelian collision of historical epochs which this battle is supposed to represent. It could be argued, in fact, that Hebbel made the bridge from private to public more successfully in his study of "private" life, *Maria Magdalene* (about sexual and generational conflict in a lowly carpenter's family), than in his plays about the problems of great personages in distant times; for his bourgeois tragedy treats private matters as representative of what the nineteenth century could recognize as a public theme, namely, the tragic consequences of the imposition of an "older" morality in changing times. Once our conception of public matters comes to include the social problems that manifest themselves in everyday domestic life, the centers of high political power no longer have exclusive dominance over what we take to be the public world; moreover, when social changes from one generation to the next become central to our conception of history, we are much less likely to think that we are experiencing history in tales of distant ages than in plays — one thinks of Arthur Miller's or those of the English realists of the 1950s — which purport to tell us the changes we ourselves have been passing through.

Although *Maria Magdalene* is famous today largely because it anticipates the plays of Ibsen's realistic period, as a "bourgeois tragedy" it is actually a late example of a German form which, deriving from Lillo and Diderot, includes such distinguished examples as Lessing's *Emilia Galotti*, the early Schiller's *Kabale und Liebe*, and, to name a work which easily towers over its predecessors, Büchner's *Woyzeck*. In each of these works the private doings of ordinary citizens assume public significance through our consciousness that the oppression of a lower by a higher class — in *Woyzeck* the victims are not even bourgeois, but lower-class, characters, for whom the middle class assumes the oppressive role — is a more appropriately public matter than, say, the private woes of real-life kings; private and public become fused through the *representative* quality which a fiction about unknown and seemingly unimportant persons assumes for us. The first audiences of *A Doll's House*, to judge from the uproar that the play created, must have judged Nora Helmer's squabbles with her husband as matters of public import (as have more recent audiences who find the play relevant to the women's movement of the 1970s). The fusion of private and public in the great realistic dramas from Lessing to Ibsen and Chekhov is paralleled on a far grander scale by a similar fusion in the major novels of the last two centuries. If eighteenth-century novels claimed to be histories in order to establish their veracity in the eyes of readers, the genre as a whole can claim to be historical in the sense that novels have become a principal means of disseminating representative information about (as well as manipulating attitudes toward) the public world. Through those theories of fiction which view the novel as the characteristic expression of middle-class culture,[48] we have looked to the great representative scenes in novels — Clarissa Harlowe defiantly refusing to marry Mr. Solmes, Rastignac vowing to make war on Paris, Anna Karenina going to the opera in full knowledge that she will be snubbed, Thomas Sutpen building his manor house out of the Mississippi wilderness — to tell us about matters such as the class struggle and the repressive effect of manners, above all to remind us that our culture cannot be understood simply in political terms, but through those economic, social, and psychological phenomena which we are able to observe with a special precision within a fictive private world.[49]

Every age, of course, has made its own adjustments in defining the particular relationship between public and private. The violation of a peasant girl in Spanish Golden Age drama is of greater public (even religious) import than the loss of a royal mistress would be for Corneille, and although a non-Spanish audience (or even a twentieth-century Spaniard) might find it difficult to experience the public meanings of such an act, plays such as *Fuenteovejuna* and *El alcalde de Zalamea* can celebrate the fall of public officials who exercise their lasciviousness on lowly virgins. Antigone's conflict with Creon is not a simple battle between public and private values in the modern sense, but, to use one of Hegel's characteristic terms about his model tragedy, a "collision" between antithetical concepts of the public world (the special fascination which *Antigone* has had over the centuries doubtless has something to do with the possibilities it offers for reinterpreting the relationship of private and public). Among the many reasons one can cite for the loss of interest in *Venice Preserved*, after it had held the stage for a century as a major classic, are the changing conceptions of what constitutes private and public values; thus, when a late Victorian critic complained of the play that "the revenge of a merely private wrong upon a whole commonwealth is scarcely sane enough for the dignity of tragedy," he was in effect reminding us that the gentleman's code of honor shifted from the public to the private realm between the seventeenth and nineteenth centuries, that what we today view as strictly private matters may once have had considerable public import.[50] One of the central difficulties of modern Shakespeare interpretation lies in determining precisely where along the scale between private and public the ideal Elizabethan — who may never have existed — would have placed such actions as Hal's rejection of Falstaff and Hamlet's father's demand for vengeance.

To the extent that Western intellectuals have come to view the state as oppressive, modern dramatists have been forced to favor the private over the public — to the point, in fact, that it often becomes all too easy for us to predict how they will tip the balance; a Marxist writer such as Brecht (and even a Fabian such as Shaw) had the enviable advantage of being able to project the possibility of a future nonoppressive public order within plays that unambiguously depict the oppressiveness of a capitalist world. From the point of view of the poetic imagination, the English Renaissance offered a writer perhaps a better opportunity than any other age to explore public and private and to keep the two orders in an engrossingly uneasy balance at the same time. Not only was the public order an authority whose demand for allegiance one could take seriously (as one could not, say, in the Middle Ages or our own day), but the individual had a relatively large range of loyalties—God, king, family (which could include other feudal nobility to whom he was bound), lover, his own self-interest—whose varying combinations of conflicts could make for ideal theatrical exploitation. Given this range of socially acceptable loyalties (some, of course, more acceptable than others), a figure such as Richard III could hypocritically assert his loyalty to his God, to his royal brother and other members of his family, to the woman he professed to love— and all while working to wrest the crown in his own behalf. The implicit comparison we make among the three centers of force in Henry IV, Part 1— Hotspur, Prince Hal, Falstaff—is all the richer because each espouses a different range of loyalties. Much of our fascination with Shakespeare's histories as a whole, moreover, comes from the discrepancies we note within the plays between official Elizabethan doctrines on the relation of private ethics to public order and the ways we see characters translate these doctrines into action. The private-public conflict within medieval drama was limited largely to that between the individual will and divine authority, and with the coming of Puritanism the range of possible loyalties once again became circumscribed: in his study of the Puritan Revolution, Michael Walzer quotes an aphorism of 1654, "Public persons with private aims are monsters in church and state" as an early expression of what he calls "the modern notion that a public servant must divest himself of all private connections."[51] Whichever side within the conflict becomes suspect—whether the private will, as in Puritanism, or the public authority, as for most modern intellectuals—the imaginative freedom with which a writer can weigh seemingly opposed values against one another sharply diminishes.

No single work of literature manifests the imaginative freedom with which private and public are weighed against one another to the extent of Antony and Cleopatra. In the way that it is constantly forcing us to rethink our conceptions of private and public, the play is as mercurial as the personality of its heroine. The opening scene, in which two of Antony's soldiers comment disparagingly on the lovemaking they witness, is deceptive in the simplicity with which the two realms confront each other; if Shakespeare had proceeded according to the terms of this confrontation—with the public world represented by Roman duty and honor, the private world by the degradations and triumphs of Egyptian love—we should have a play something on the order of All for Love. But Shakespeare goes on to confound our expectations at every turn; in fact, the organization of the play—so different from that of the other tragedies—could be described in terms of the readjustments in perspective into which we are forced from one scene to the next. Long before the apotheosis of

love which Cleopatra talks herself (and us) into at the end of the play, we
have come to shift our evaluation of her world — which ranges symbolically
from the Nile's slime she occasionally invokes to those higher elements of air
and fire with which she finally identifies — several times in the course of the
play. By the same token, our evaluation of the public world shifts back and
forth from admiration for Antony's earlier heroism and for Caesar's gifts at
political accommodation (amply demonstrated within the dramatic action) to
an impatience with the oppressiveness and the imaginative limitations of these
Roman virtues.

But Shakespeare does more than simply manipulate our relative evaluations of the two worlds: fundamentally, he makes us question what appropriately belongs to the private and what to the public sphere. As Eugene M.
Waith writes, tracing the Herculean analogy which Shakespeare uses to
define Antony, "Antony's reassertion of his heroic self in the latter part of the
play is entirely personal. What he asserts is individual integrity, not the
integrity of a Roman general."[52] Yet if the Herculean analogy at the end
serves to assert the private self, it also represents a new conception of what is
private, for now the historical (Antony's actual deeds performed in a "real"
world) is transformed into the mythical: the earlier public image comes to
structure and imaginatively to color the individual and private image. Thus,
when the dying Antony tells Cleopatra to "please your thoughts / In feeding
them with those my former fortunes (IV.xv.52-53), he is setting up the
mechanism whereby he can be transformed from a defeated and demoralized
ex-hero into that mythical figure whose "legs bestrid the ocean" and whose
"rear'd arm / Crested the world" (V.ii.82-83).

And just as the heroic moves out of the public into a mythically magnified
private sphere, so the relation between the lovers shifts from what is simply
illicit sensuality to what, in the gorgeous imagery of Cleopatra's speeches
during the last two acts (though anticipated by the equally gorgeous imagery
of Enobarbus's famous description of her), comes to have distinctly imperial
attributes; the empire, in the course of the play, changes its locus from
Rome to Egypt, from what comes to seem merely an impermanent temporal
domain to the new and peculiarly spiritual place over which the dead,
imaginatively tranformed lovers preside at the end. Power is transferred from
something exercised by arms and crafty governing to a verbal force which
becomes all the more awesome for the transcendental significance it can
claim. Yet we remain aware of the illusory quality of this verbal force at the
same time that we acknowledge its power. As we listen, for instance, to those
splendid lines of Cleopatra's grand finale —

> Give me my robe, put on my crown, I have
> Immortal longings in me. Now no more
> The juice of Egypt's grape shall moist this lip. . . .

> Husband, I come:
> Now to that name, my courage prove my title!
> I am fire, and air; my other elements
> I give to baser life. . . .
>
> (V.ii.279-81, 286-89)

we recognize that foolishness and awe are fused for us in a single image which comes to seem sublime through our ability (like that of Cleopatra herself) to remain self-conscious about the play-acting in the very process of falling under its spell.

If the triumphant, though illusory, new world which *Antony and Cleopatra* celebrates makes the play a "transition" (as critics tend to treat it)[53] from the tragedies to the late romances, one should note that, quite in contrast to the romances, the historical world of this play is treated with the amplitude and understanding that one can find only in the histories of the 1590s and in the other Roman plays. Yet in this, one of the last, and certainly the most geographically all-encompassing, of his historical plays, the confrontation between history and romance does not work ultimately to establish the reality and worth of the historical world which Shakespeare has so meticulously created in the course of the drama; indeed, he uses the most considerable imaginative resources to demonstrate resoundingly that the historical world, however mighty in its pretensions and subtle in its workings, is a thoroughly unimaginative place.

FIVE

HISTORICAL DRAMA
AS HISTORICAL THOUGHT

DRAMA AND HISTORICAL PROCESS

In meiner Brust war meine Tat noch mein:
Einmal entlassen aus dem sichern Winkel
Des Herzens, ihrem mütterlichen Boden,
Hinausgegeben in des Lebens Fremde,
Gehört sie jenen tückschen Mächten an,
Die keines Menschen Kunst vertraulich macht.

> Wallenstein, in soliloquy after
> the arrest of his emissary

Let us think of drama as essentially a mode of thought that suggests the processes through which we can connect and make some ultimate sense out of the diverse persons and events we see represented on stage. Historical drama, insofar as it reflects upon and interprets past events, can be considered a branch of historical thought, though one which projects hypotheses and individual theories about history more than it does fully worked out philosophies. Serge Doubrovsky's statement about Corneille, "L'histoire cornélienne est une histoire de philosophe," and his insistence that Corneille does not simply "utilize" history but meditates upon it could be made of the other major dramatists who have created what I have called a historical world in their plays.[1] The distinction that Doubrovsky makes between events in themselves and those that have been subjected to reflection is similar to a dichotomy made by most modern commentators on the nature of historical writing. For instance, Morton White distinguishes between "chronicle," which he defines as essentially a "conjunction of statements," and "history," which he sees as "predominantly . . . integrated from a causal point of view."[2] White's dichotomy is similar to that of R. G. Collingwood, who contrasts Herodotus and Thucydides: the first of these he finds episodic in nature, while the latter is concerned with "the laws according to which [things] happen."[3] Robert A. Nisbet distinguishes between "history," which stresses events in their concreteness as discrete entities (and is thus closer to White's "chronicle" than to his "history"), and "change," which looks at events primarily to link them to other, earlier (or later) events.[4] However different the purposes and emphases of all these distinctions may be (Nisbet, for instance, attempts primarily to expose the metaphorical traps into which he sees the various analysts of "change" fall), each is intent on separating the notion of history as a series of relatively "raw," none too closely connected events from the notion of an intricate and intensely meditated concatenation of events. My concern here is not with the validity of these distinctions in the abstract, though I suspect that even the chronicler of "raw" events tends to color his narration with his particular notion of their ultimate "meaning." I am interested, rather, in the bearing of these distinctions on historical drama, which, needless to say, has traditionally gravitated toward the second and more "philosophical" side of the antithesis: Aristotle's statement that poetry is more philosophical than history is also a way of saying that philosophical history, whether in the form of drama or narrative prose, is more philosophical than chronical history.

By the same token, philosophical history is more "poetical" than chronicle history, if only in the sense that it sets up the kinds of problems which are, in the final analysis, unresolvable and which are meant to leave us with a sense of vastness and mystery. The great philosophers of history from Hegel to Toynbee, for all the rational explanations to which they subject the historical processes they describe, create an air of profundity and mystification through the high level of abstraction with which they treat the raw phenomena of history. (Hegel, one remembers, ended his philosophy of history with a statement that the historical process is ultimately in the hands of God.) The attitude toward history most favorable to the historical dramatist (whose first loyalty, after all, has traditionally been to poetry rather than to history) is one which leaves several explanations open at once. When a scholar prefacing an edition of Marlowe's *Edward II* writes, "For the Elizabethan the moving forces of history were three in number: Providence, Fortune ... and human character,"[5] his explanation is less interesting for what it tells us of Elizabethan doctrines about the ultimate causes of things than for the fact that the Elizabethans left three potentially conflicting possibilities open. The writer who opts too rigidly for a single explanation risks losing that sense of mystery which sustains our interest in the historical process. Standing at one rigid extreme is the Hardy of *The Dynasts,* whose Napoleon despairs of the efficacy of human agency:

> History makes use of me to weave her web
> To her long while aforetime-figured mesh
> And contemplated charactery: no more.[6]

The various choruses of Fates hovering in the air throughout *The Dynasts* — their utterances are by far the weakest aspect of Hardy's drama — never seem as mysterious as Hardy would like them to be, for we know full well from the start how surely they are in control of things. At the other unmysterious extreme one finds Marlowe's Tamburlaine, whose statement —

132

> I hold the Fates bound fast in iron chains,
> And with my hand turn Fortune's wheel about[7]

gains its fascination through its brash defiance of "standard" Elizabethan ideas about the various motive forces of history; as it turns out, of course, when Tamburlaine's mortality finally catches up with him at the end of the long play, Fortune is able once again to challenge the high claims of human character and, in effect, reassert the mysteries of historical process.

Most plays, of course, seek a middle ground between particular motive forces and, as a result, leave us with unanswered (and unanswerable) questions. In *Wallenstein,* for instance, to what extent is the protagonist's break with the Austrian emperor (out of which his tragedy necessarily follows) the result of fate (that is, the "accidental" arrest of his emissary to the Swedes or his misreading of the stars) or the result of his character (which, insofar as he was toying with the idea of a break, was implicated in a potential act against the imperial authority)? To what extent are the events of Shakespeare's English historical cycle a working out of providential design (by which the deposition of Richard II must result in the ultimate downfall of the successors of Henry IV until the restoration of order by the first Tudor king) or a result of the weaknesses in character of the various kings (or, for that matter, the stroke of Fortune which cut off Henry V in his prime)? All these questions must, of course, remain unanswered—or, at best, tentatively answered, with new answers following to modify or contradict earlier ones. One could speak of a kind of intellectual suspense about the ultimate causes of action: it is a suspense essentially different from the ordinary suspense of plot, though a drama's plot, through its particular juxtaposition of events, usually works to generate those larger questions which the play then refuses to answer. The particular "wisdom" of historical drama comes from the insight that the springs of human action are unfathomable, that there is no necessary correlation, for instance, between intention and event, between the ability of the human will to govern action and the power of actual circumstances.

Historical drama, like all drama, is "philosophical" in still another sense, namely, its ability to make connections between what might otherwise be a disparate series of events. Drama abhors contingency with something of the tenacity with which nature proverbially abhors a vacuum. Seemingly accidental happenings which may at first surprise us, by hindsight come to seem, if not precisely inevitable, at least a natural part of the chain of events we see enacted. Our consciousness is able to absorb the surprise we experience at the arrest of the emissary in *Wallenstein* through the connections we quickly make with what we know of Wallenstein's character and the role of the stars in the play. If Cleopatra suddenly and capriciously changes the course of history by fleeing in the middle of the battle of Actium, everything we have seen of her in the play serves to confirm the "naturalness" of the event, which, after all, is reported to us as a characteristically "feminine" act in which the

133

queen, "The breeze upon her, like a cow in June, / Hoists sails, and flies" (III.x.14–15). Few if any plays, for that matter, are as full of sudden and unexpected turns as *Antony and Cleopatra,* yet by means of our hindsight we manage to absorb them within a seemingly logical pattern which we create for ourselves in the course of the play. Our tendency to readjust our sense of reality in order to accommodate new and unexpected events is, I suspect, as operative in life as in art: consider, for example, how we have accommodated the American political assassinations of the 1960s within the conceptions we have created of recent history; the capriciousness of the various assassins becomes an expression of the anomie within modern American society, while our image of the famous victims — men who once seemed to be creating a future which would powerfully implicate us all — has readjusted itself so that their sudden and early deaths have become central to the image. (The subjects of the real-life Henry V doubtless projected a long life of continued heroic feats for him, but the Elizabethans witnessing his feats in the theater must have remembered all the while that he would be cut off in his prime.)

Drama, with its two-to-four-hour span, allows considerably less time than life for such readjustments, and writers have had to manipulate the facts of history to tighten the chain of events represented in the theater. Kenneth Burke, in a searching essay on *Coriolanus,* has described this tightening process while accounting for the difference in Plutarch's and Shakespeare's treatment of Valeria:

> The most notable thing about Valeria, from the standpoint of Shakespearean dramaturgy, is the fact that, though this friend of the family serves well for handling the relation between mother-in-law and daughter, she has a much less active role in the play than she does in Plutarch. For in Plutarch, *she* suggests that the women go to plead with Coriolanus and dissuade him from attacking Rome, whereas the full musculature of Shakespeare's play requires maximum stress upon his mother's role in this development.[8]

Burke's term "musculature" provides an apt image of the tight and intricate connections characteristic of many great plays. The tightness of these connections is perhaps most conspicuous within plays in the classical tradition, which, with its unities, its *liaison des scènes,* and its demand for probability, shapes the materials of history to create the illusion that events follow one another with the utmost logical rigor. Above all in Racine the linkages of events are so intense that history comes to seem an inescapable burden; the intensity comes not only from the tightly wrought structure of his plays but from the extreme rhetorical condensation of his language, as in Hippolyte's recital of his father's exploits in *Phèdre*:

> Quand tu me dépeignais ce héros intrépide
> Consolant les mortels de l'absence d'Alcide,

Les monstres étouffés et les brigands punis,
Procruste, Cercyon, et Scirron, et Sinnis,
Et les os dispersés du géant d'Epidaure,
Et la Crète fumant du sang du Minotaure.[9]

Through the syntactical parallels—"les monstres étouffés," "les brigands punis," "les os dispersés," and, with only a change from past to present participle, "la Crète fumant"—events which in other forms of narration might simply count as isolated episodes assume the most intimate connection with one another. Leo Spitzer has compared a similar passage in *Athalie* with the climactic lines of Yeats's "Leda and the Swan"—

A shudder in the loins engenders there
The broken wall, the burning roof and tower
And Agamemnon dead

to suggest "the correspondence ... of content and form offered by the construction of the participles ..., whose epigrammatic concentration reflects the inevitability of Fate."[10] Through the suggestive power of his language, together with the compression demanded by a short poem, Yeats was able, not only in "Leda and the Swan," but in lyrics such as "Two Songs from a Play" (on Christ's death as the end and beginning of a historical cycle), and "The Second Coming" (on the violent end of our current cycle) to render the drama inherent in historical crises with a concentrated force impossible within drama itself: without the distractions of characters and plot, Yeats's lyrics can give us the illusion that, for a brief moment at least, we are experiencing the essence of the historical process.

The single-minded forward movement of drama in the classical tradition, whether it seeks to express the race of events toward an inevitable doom, as in Racine, or to reenact the process whereby the individual will can master or transcend events, as in Corneille's major plays, is ideally suited to an image of history as a linear and fast moving process. Quite in contrast, a play such as *Henry IV* sacrifices the unbending swiftness of events in classical drama for an image of history in which events are embedded in a rich network of diverse contexts, as in the various concepts of time which exist side by side in the play—the slow-moving world of Falstaff, in which "hours [are] cups of sack, and minutes capons, and clocks the tongues of bawds" (Pt. 1.I.ii.7-8); the impetuous world of Hotspur ("he that kills me some six or seven dozen of Scots at a breakfast"—Pt. 1.II.iv.100-101); the king's world with its mysteries about the "hatch and brood of time" (Pt. 2.III.i.86); and the gradually shaping but ultimately triumphant world of Prince Hal, who in his first soliloquy speaks of "redeeming time when men think least I will" (Pt. 1.I.ii.212). The sense of fullness and diversity which derives from the interaction of the play's various worlds reminds us that the historical process can reveal itself in a spatial as well as a linear way, and that it does not, moreover, have to overwhelm us with its inexorability or the swiftness of its doom. In *Dantons Tod*, to cite one of the great works within the Shakespearean tradition, Büchner pursues a method even less linear than that of any Shakespeare play to create a sense of doom which is distributed spatially among the diverse places within which the play moves—the streets of Paris with their bourgeois promenaders and angry crowds, the brothels, the places of high power, the prisons packed with men awaiting the guillotine; the chief agony of the play's main characters becomes the slowness of the process which will bring about what they know to be their doom.

Whether in the racing time-processes of the classical tradition or in Shakespearean slow time, history can be said to manifest itself in the very form of a play. A relatively "episodic" play such as *Edward II*—not to speak of many other early Elizabethan chronicle plays—suggests little about the processes of history. Rather, we concentrate primarily on the personal conflicts within the individual episode, which in Marlowe's play could be said to repeat itself with variations—Edward attempts to exert his will, only to find it thwarted in one way or another by those around him—throughout the course of the play. With this episodic focus the play does nothing to make us look before or after—or at those other, parallel worlds, as in Shakespeare's greatest histories, to which the individual episode implicitly refers. The greatness of *Edward II* lies not in its historical vision but in the way it renders the pathos of personal relationships. It does not seem accidental, moreover, that the young Brecht was attracted by the episodic nature of Marlowe's play (not to speak of the earlier writer's interest in passive heroes with homosexual inclinations) in his attempt to find an alternative to the classical structure dominant within German drama. In his rewriting of Marlowe's play Brecht goes Marlowe one better in every respect: the king becomes even more passive than in the original (Brecht had him played by an actress in the first production), Gaveston is reduced to the vulgar son of a butcher, and each episode cultivates anticlimax to give maximum emphasis to the discontinuity—and meaninglessness—of history.[11] The historical, or rather antihistorical, statements of Brecht's play achieve much of their impact through the audience's consciousness that the historical dramas it was accustomed to—tightly integrated and driving unrelentingly to their grand climaxes—could all too automatically utilize the tricks of plot to conjure up profound-sounding visions of history. It is as though drama had to go back to its pre-Shakespearean beginnings after more than three centuries during which the intimate connection of dramatic form and historical process could be taken for granted.

Brecht's *Leben Eduards des Zweiten von England* was of course written before his conversion to Marxism; yet his pursuit of episodic modes of organization was no less zealous after he had committed himself to the most influential of modern doctrines about the historical process. Although in his early Marxist years he created such rigidly ordered fables as *Die Massnahme*

(*The Measures Taken*) and *Die Ausnahme und die Regel* (*The Exception and the Rule*) to articulate the principles, as well as the dilemmas, within Marxist-Leninist doctrine, the great historical plays of his years in exile, *Mutter Courage* and *Galileo,* are notable for their refusal to force dramatic structure to enact historical process. For one thing, Brecht associated classical dramatic structure with a conception of man which viewed human nature as everywhere the same; the history enacted in the classical plays of Goethe and Schiller, which Brecht sought to parody at various times during his career, was meant to be universal in its applications. Brecht, on the other hand, was intent on stressing historical particularities. As he wrote in praising a Piscator version of *An American Tragedy,* "The idea of man as one of the variables of the environment, the environment as one of the variables of man—which means the dissolution of the environment into relationships between men— corresponds to a new way of thinking, the historical way.... The histori- cizing theater ... concentrates entirely on whatever in this everyday event is peculiar, particular, and demanding inquiry."[12] The "historical way" which Brecht is advocating stresses the role of particular persons in particular historical situations: the greed of Mother Courage becomes a "variable" of her role in an exploitative economic situation, and Galileo's great capitu- lation to the forces of reaction becomes a "variable" of his particular weakness (a gluttony for food and knowledge) which is unable to withstand the pressures of a particular and powerful ruling class.

Yet within the individual episodes of his plays these particularities work in a peculiarly exemplary fashion: although the play in its total structure does not, like many earlier plays, attempt to enact the historical process, each episode provides an exemplary situation (for instance, Mother Courage unwittingly sacrifices one of her children while her greed distracts her; or the bell tolls to announce Galileo's recantation while his idealizing followers stand surprised and disillusioned) which is meant to lead us toward Brecht's particular view of the process. And if the play as a whole is deliberately broken up through its episodic organization and the various "alienation" techniques, each of the major episodes stands as a finely (one might almost say "classically") wrought drama exemplifying and enacting a moment within the historical process. One scarcely needs to add that everything about a Brecht play—not only the exemplary situations that make up the individual episodes, but the interspersed songs, the messages in the filmed projections, the appendices for the reader, as well as the knowledge of audiences East and West that the public figure Bertolt Brecht was a Marxist who fully intended to make claims on them—is designed to actively propagate a particular view of history.

The medieval audiences witnessing the Corpus Christi cycles did not need to have the dramatic structure of the individual episode imitate any larger historical process, for they were well aware, from the start, of the universal

Christian historical pattern within which each episode was simply a type prefiguring the whole. If throughout this section I have stressed the ways in which plays create a sense of historical process in their very form, this is not to deny the power of those larger historical patterns whose presence we recognize *outside* the framework of a play. Indeed, every historical drama in one way or another calls upon our knowledge of some particular historical pattern against which the action can be read—though this pattern need not be the "central" meaning which the play seeks to articulate. Shakespeare's English histories, especially the second tetralogy, tell us considerably more about history and politics than the notions embedded in the Tudor myth about England's fall from grace at the time of Richard II and its happy restoration under Henry Tudor. It is as though the human mind needs a larger framework within which it can assimilate the progress of events it sees enacted. Beyond their obvious ceremonial functions, the various curses and prophecies that run through Shakespeare's histories act as signals to show us where, precisely, an event fits into the framework, and, perhaps even more important, to remind us in what direction the play is going. (In something of the same way, the particular ideological framework—whether conservative, middle-of-the-road, radical, or whatever—which we adopt in the "real" world provides us with the signals we need to make sense out of the chaos of political events that we observe, or participate in, from day to day.)

The various historical frameworks which plays invoke to assimilate and make sense out of events tend to be built out of a sharp antithesis between "good" and "bad" times. Collingwood's definition of Christian apocalyptic history as "a history . . . divided into two periods, a period of darkness and a period of light,"[13] could well be applied to the governing framework of most historical dramas. Whether or not in specifically Christian guise, apocalyptic contrasts of good and evil, darkness and light, destruction and renewal are the stuff that history plays are characteristically made of. What I earlier pointed out as an obvious and natural attribute of ceremonial drama such as the medieval cycles and patriotic plays can be said as well of most plays which are in no way ceremonial. Indeed, some of the world's subtlest dramas cling to the crudest of historical frameworks. Modern attempts to stress the Christian meanings of Shakespeare's histories reveal a failure to distinguish the unmistakably Christian larger framework from the moment-to-moment historical thinking which gives the plays their particular distinction but which is not always in tune with the abstractions that govern the framework. The need for crude structures has insured the survival of apocalyptic imagery even when the Christian belief which was once essential to it is missing. In a note on *Emperor and Galilean* the nonbelieving Ibsen unashamedly inserts a Christian image within his Hegelian framework: "When the world spirit no longer finds souls to tempt and lead astray . . . then the Last Day has come."[14] Although Büchner was an atheist writing about atheist revolutionaries, the coming

doom which so dominates *Dantons Tod* expresses itself in insistently apocalyptic terms, as in that beautiful image (just before the guillotining of the
Dantonists) which, despite the classical allusion, reminds us of those symbolic
signs in the sky within the Book of Revelation: "The clouds are hanging in the
quiet evening sky like a dying Olympus with fading, sinking, godlike forms."[15]
(We need no longer be reminded, as in Carl Becker's day, that post-Christian
philosophies of history are suffused with apocalyptic imagery; indeed, to
move to a not so philosophical level, witness the apocalyptic imagery of
destruction and renewal to which the American public is subjected at every
presidential election.)

The power of the antitheses between darkness and light is so fundamental a
part of the historical imagination that every play could be said to move in one
or the other of these directions. The light at the end of Shakespeare's cycle
does not prevent many individual moments of darkness, especially in the
backward-and-forward movement of the *Henry VI* plays. A ceremonial play
such as Grillparzer's *König Ottokar* moves unabashedly toward the light as
Rudolf of Hapsburg celebrates the institution of the new dynasty with
apocalyptic images of youth and renewal:

> Der Jugendtraum der Erde ist geträumt . . .
> Und nach dem Zeichen sollt es fast mich dünken
> Wir stehn am Eingang einer neuen Zeit.[16]

In *Götz von Berlichingen*, not to speak of *Dantons Tod*, we are always aware
of the darkness which characterizes the coming new age. In *Dantons Tod*, the
darkness manifests itself not only in the end of revolutionary hope and the
unnatural deaths of the central characters but in the recognition of the
impossibility, even uselessness, of love, of human communication, and of all
hope, whether in life or in death. A "tragically" directed play can, of course,
remind us of the light that will dawn far in the future through the sacrifices of
those who embody an idea whose time has not yet come. "Das Jahrhundert /
Ist meinem Ideal nicht reif,"[17] Schiller's Marquis Posa, that Enlightenment
liberal in King Philip's court, tells his eighteenth-century audience, which
happily can compliment itself on the progressive ideas it is practicing when it
criticizes absolute monarchy.

Frank Kermode, in one of the most subtle explorations of the relation of
literary fictions to historical thinking, has called attention to Wallace
Stevens's adage "The imagination is always at the end of an era."[18] To the
extent that drama by its very nature thrives on crisis, the end of a historical
era provides the ideal temporal location in which to situate a play. Although
such longer cycles as Shakespeare's histories and the Corpus Christi plays start
out well before the end (at Genesis, in fact, in the medieval cycles), we receive
reminders throughout the plays of the providential end toward which
everything is pointing. Yeats's historical lyrics, by contrast, are able to

he long preparations for the end and concentrate instead on the
a of rapist swans and slouching beasts that accompany the end
Yeats, as for any apocalyptic thinker, also means the beginning of
. Although the apocalyptic antitheses have maintained their hold
on the modern historical imagination, the historicist doctrines which developed in the late eighteenth century have distinctly colored the images with
which writers perceive and define particular eras. Thus, every era has become
a cultural entity in its own right, with its own configuration of values,
customs, and social relationships. And since every era was distinct from those
preceding and following it, writers could search avidly throughout world
history for the crises which accompany each moment of transition: Hebbel
could exploit the shift from Hebraism to Christianity (*Herodes und
Mariamne*); Ibsen, from the new pagan age which Julian the Apostate
unsuccessfully sought to institute to the return of Christianity; Shaw, from a
benighted medieval order to "the Reformation, which Joan had unconsciously
anticipated," as he tells us in the preface to *Saint Joan*.[19]

Although the cultural relativism implicit in historicism would seem to be at
odds with the moral coloring of apocalyptic thinking, historical dramas
usually manage to have it both ways. Thus, in *Götz* the benign outgoing order
is associated with medieval individualism and Rousseauistic simplicity, while
the dark times about to come are to be dreaded because they bring in the
highly organized, unheroic forms of modern society. Needless to say, *Götz* was
immensely influential on that aspect of romanticism which rejected the
present in favor of an idealized medievalism. Insofar as dramatists have
sought allegiance to various theories of human progress, most "world-historical" plays, as I indicated in the first chapter, have placed the darkness in the
past and lauded those ages which lead up to the more enlightened present.
"There is a new spirit rising in men," the Archbishop, with admirable
historical foresight, says early in *Saint Joan*; "we are at the dawning of a wider
epoch."[20] Although the dark side of the Apocalypse may be in the past, the
coming of a new age still has its apocalyptic terrors, as we see in the execution
of Joan and all the other martyrs whom the partisans of progress have
celebrated as harbingers of "wider epochs." Brecht, calling upon all the
sophisticated historical machinery of Marxism, was able in *Galileo* not only to
dramatize the transition from an aristocratic (and narrow) Renaissance world
to the "wider" world of bourgeois individualism but by implication to suggest
the end of the latter world through the dropping of the first atomic bomb
(which, by further implication, would be followed by the still wider world
which Marxist doctrine could institute).

If men are "products" or "variables" of the age in which they live, as
historicist doctrines have insisted, the dramatist obviously faces a problem in
placing moral evaluations on them. It is hard to condemn a king's or a
husband's tyrannical acts if we are constantly reminded that these acts were

standard behavior at a more barbarous time than ours. Yeats was able to avoid the problem, for there was little room for exploration of character in the miniature historical dramas he created in his lyrics; indeed, we are doubtless meant to feel a certain shock at the moral indifference which the poet, like his character Zeus, shows to the world-historical collisions which he depicts with such zest. But modern dramatists have generally not hesitated to engage our moral sympathies with certain characters—or to excite our condemnation of others. We award our moral prizes to those heroes who, in the best apocalyptic way, represent the epochs of light, whether these are located in a lost past, as in *Götz,* or in a progressively more enlightened future; the morally distinguished characters are those, like Götz, willing to resist the encroaching darkness or those, like Shaw's Joan, who sacrifice themselves for the enlightened notions whose time is still to come. The moral coloring which historicist-minded authors attach to their characters is especially evident in Brecht's attitude to Galileo: in a note entitled "Praise or Condemnation of Galileo?" Brecht resorts to theological terminology in describing Galileo's recantation as "the 'original sin' of modern science" and refers to the atom bomb "both as a technical and social phenomenon as the classical end product of [Galileo's] scientific achievement and his failure in relation to society."[21] Although we can rightly accuse the great modern dramatists of lacking historical "objectivity," we must also remember (as they themselves luckily did) that drama has never thrived well on moral neutrality.

HISTORY AND HIERARCHY

Drama as growth

For God doth know, so shall the world perceive,
That I have turn'd away my former self.
Henry V rejecting Falstaff

Je suis maître de moi comme de l'univers;
Je le suis; je veux l'être.
Augustus at the end of Corneille's *Cinna*

Throughout most of the history of drama one discerns a tendency to draw the consciousness of the audience from "lower" to "higher" things, to trick it out of the ties it feels with the "meaner" aspects of existence (whether in the form of sensuality, egotism, or small-mindedness) and raise it to such "lofty" stances as love of God, devotion to the state, and the overcoming of pride. In its most obvious form, this movement manifests itself in martyr plays, which, as I have described in an earlier chapter, are distinguished by readily discernible "stages" of development as the martyr-figure moves upward from

141

relatively secular to more spiritual concerns. In a larger sense one could speak of an upward movement that governs the structure of most of those works we dignify these days with the term "landmarks of Western literature" — in Aeneas's "growth" from his dalliance with Dido to his acceptance of his public mission, in Faust's "ascent" from the "little world" of Gretchen to the "big world" of high political power, and, to cite the perfect model of ascent, in Dante's journey through what is made to seem every possible stage from the lowest depths to his confrontation with God. One could speak of a similar movement governing many of the major philosophical systems from Plato to Hegel. Projecting hierarchies, and establishing models for ascending them, has been a characteristic and constant habit within our cultural tradition. My concern here is not with the larger aspects of this theme — one can imagine a treatise on hierarchy and upward movement as metaphors in Western philosophy[22] — but with the way that this mode of thought has given shape to many historical dramas. I am thinking particularly of those dramas concerned with the growth of an individual — what the Germans, with their penchant for endowing all manner of subgenres with names, call *Entwicklungsdramen*. Take, for instance, the growth enacted within Kleist's Prince Friedrich, whom we first see dreaming of glory in war within a moonlit garden, but who, in the course of the play, moves through a quick succession of stages — a rash heroic action which violates battle orders, an execution sentence for disobedience, an open show of fear in which he pleads for his life, and a final pardon after he has demonstrated an inward acceptance of the justness of the punishment he was about to receive. Or take the growth of the Emperor Augustus in Corneille's *Cinna* — from uncertainty about his will to maintain the responsibilities of power, to a desire for vengeance against the members of a conspiracy threatening him, to thoughts of suicide, and to a final act of magnanimity against the conspirators which is at the same time an acceptance of the responsibilities of his imperial role. Or take the best-known instance of growth in drama, that of Shakespeare's Prince Hal, whose father, even before the prince's first appearance, compares him unfavorably to Hotspur (I.i.77–89), yet who, by the end of Part 1, has emerged as an exemplar of valor in battle, with the heroic Hotspur himself as his victim.

The growth we see enacted in these plays is perhaps best described as dialectical in nature. If by dialectical (to cite the *O.E.D.*'s definition of Hegel's method) we mean "the process of thought by which contradictions seem to merge themselves in a higher truth which comprehends them," these plays are dialectical by virtue of the sharp and sudden turns that occur as one stage in a character's development (for instance, the self-contained egotism of Prince Friedrich at the start of Kleist's play) is replaced by a later, seemingly contradictory, stage (the prince's acceptance of his guilt and his subordination of self to the state), while the contradictions are resolved for us at the end with a sudden and final logical stroke (in *Prinz Friedrich* through the act of pardon which, as we quickly recognize, is a just, though unexpected, reward for the growth which the prince has achieved).[23] Although the stages of growth in Kleist's play, as in Corneille's and Shakespeare's, are doubtless more complex than I have indicated (above all, in the subtle ways with which each author prepares the next stage while focusing on an earlier one), these plays are also notable for the clarity with which each stage is distinguishable from the last and the sharpness of the turns as the play moves from one stage to the next. (If there is more clarity and sharpness in Corneille and Kleist than in Shakespeare, this is a consequence of the sharply focused "classical" dramatic structure used by the two later writers.)

Whatever theories of human growth we may adhere to, growth in drama is by necessity a swift-moving process, for we must experience a person's coming to maturity in the course of a single evening in the theater. The dialectical contradictions that jolt us along the way can, in fact, be viewed as a means of speeding up a process which, in other forms of literature or in "life itself," may proceed in a far more gradual and continuous way. In the many *Bildungsromane* from Goethe's *Wilhelm Meister* to our own day, we are meant to perceive growth as a slow and gradually unfolding process defined by means of a vast number of incidents which the protagonist of each novel experiences: the frequent lack of clarity we note when we try to distinguish the stages in a hero's growth is, in fact, a way of simulating its gradualness and creating the illusion of slow evolution from a lower to a higher stage of existence. Between *Stephen Hero* and *A Portrait of the Artist as a Young Man* Joyce shifts from a traditionally novelistic, slowly evolving conception of growth to one which is essentially dramatic and dialectical. In *The Prelude,* which Wordsworth conceived as an epic-like poem on the growth of his own mind, the growth process is rendered for us through the accumulation of what Wordsworth calls "spots of time" (short and precise descriptions of significant moments of illumination) as well as through long, distinctly undramatic discursive passages which chart the intricate and often mysterious movements of a gradually developing consciousness; yet in its larger framework *The Prelude,* like such shorter poems as "Tintern Abbey" and the Immortality Ode, also charts a typically dramatic, dialectical pattern of growth — what M. H. Abrams, in his exhaustive study of the characteristic structure of romantic poems and philosophical treatises, calls the "circuitous journey" from primal unity through division and ultimately toward a "higher" synthesis.[24]

In their attempts to create a swiftly moving series of stages, dramatists have set up closely organized structures to draw the audience into the processes they are portraying. A verbally oriented critic would describe these processes by pointing out words that generate new meanings at different points along the hierarchy: in *Henry IV,* for instance, the word "honor," which has distinctly separate meanings for Falstaff, Hotspur, and Prince Hal; in *Prinz Friedrich von Homburg,* the word "gleichviel" ("It's all the same") which, as the protagonist uses it during the earlier stages of his growth process, gives us signals about his attempts to suppress the inward crisis he is undergoing; in *Cinna,* the word "empire," which moves from its very personal use by the vengeful Emilie in the opening lines ("Vous [les desirs d'une illustre vengeance] prenez sur mon âme un trop puissant empire")[25] to its constantly more public meaning as Augustus grows into his imperial role.

The psychological or existential critic would speak of shifting images of the self: in *Henry IV,* the way in which the self is defined through the various father-son conflicts; in *Prinz Friedrich,* the way the protagonist's sense of self moves from total obliviousness to the outside world in the opening scene to total subordination at the end; in *Cinna,* the way that the statements of self-assertion shift from the unchangeableness of Emilie ("Je suis ce que j'étais")[26] to the painfully achieved and all-encompassing selfhood of Augustus in the celebrated lines quoted at the head of this section —

> Je suis maître de moi comme de l'univers;
> Je le suis; je veux l'être.[27]

The same critic might point out the centrality of what could be called "testing" scenes, in which the main issues of the play are tested on a fictive level before they are made to count as "reality" — in *Henry IV,* for instance, the play-acting scene in which Falstaff plays first the king and then Prince Hal (Pt. 1.II.iv.371–475), or that later scene in Part 2 in which Hal tries on the crown while his father is asleep (IV.v.20–224); in *Cinna,* the scene in which Augustus calls the conspirators (their role still unknown to him) before him for advice as to whether he should abdicate or not (II.i); or the scene at the end in which Emilie and Cinna, expecting death at his hands, are treated to his generosity (V.ii); in *Prinz Friedrich,* the whole dénouement, in which the protagonist is given the final say on his own death sentence, passes the test by assenting to the sentence, and then, while standing blindfolded awaiting his execution, is awarded his life in return for his show of maturity.

Those critics who stress the way an audience or reader perceives a text would remind us that the growth process does not take place so much within the characters of the play as in our own consciousness. In *Cinna,* for instance, Augustus, whose growth is the thematic center of the play, does not even appear until the second act. But if the notion of growth is transferred from character to audience, the process starts at the opening of the play as Emilie attempts to "trick" us into assenting to the vengeance she desires against Augustus for her father's death during the recent civil wars; the progress of the play then becomes a movement from sympathy with the victim of a private wrong toward a recognition that the wrong can be righted only by threatening the stability of the public order, and finally (by one of those dialectical resolutions typical of plays about growth) toward our admiration for Augustus's statesmanship, which succeeds in converting the conspirators to his conception of order. In *Henry IV,* similarly, we are tricked into Falstaff's and Hotspur's worlds only to find ourselves increasingly aware of their limitations. In *Prinz Friedrich* we give our sympathy wholeheartedly to the protagonist within each stage through which he passes: we are charmed by his self-absorption in the garden, for instance; we admire his heroism in battle, and we share his fear of death and his resentment toward a repressive higher authority — after all of which he convinces us that we have misplaced our sympathies for a faulty set of values!

Indeed, the process that we (by analogy to the protagonists) are meant to undergo demands a continuing reassessment of values throughout the course of each play. If we feel we are tricked along the way, this is because we must first be attracted to the "lower" values before we are ready to accept the "higher" ones toward which we are being led. By the time we reach the end of *Cinna,* for instance, we note something a bit bogus about those once-persuasive early speeches in which Emilie sought to make us share her sense of being wronged. If historical drama is a mode of historical thought, it is thought in the most active sense of the word — a growth in consciousness where values are constantly put to the test and where the frameworks within which we are first taught to think are replaced by other frameworks that are better able than the earlier ones to accommodate the diversity of problems raised by the play. Yet despite the surprises to which we are subjected as we reassess the changing frameworks within the play, the direction of growth within historical drama is fairly predictable, for we are made to grow from an adherence to essentially private values toward an acceptance of public ones. The private realm comes to be associated with the disorder which, as we come to see, results from the desire of an individual (however attractive he may be) to exert his will at all costs.

The plays about growth which I have used as examples are all, in one way or another, concerned not simply with growth and order as general principles but with the stability of particular political orders: *Henry IV* (whatever we may say about its "ambivalence") and *Cinna* with newly consolidated national states for which civil disorders were a recent and frightening memory, *Prinz Friedrich* with a Prussia which, during the French occupation, was beginning to experience the force of a new national idea (an idea, incidentally, whose most thoughtful exponent happened to be an associate of Kleist's, the political theorist Adam Müller). Moreover, each writer maintained the sort of connections with his government which would be rare for any major contemporary writer in the West: Elizabethan acting companies were patronized by the monarch, Corneille was one of the group known as *Les cinq auteurs* under Richelieu's employ, Kleist received a small pension from the Prussian queen. We know enough about Kleist's private life (as we do not about Shakespeare's or Corneille's) to infer that Prince Friedrich's growth from self-absorption to subservience to an external and public idea is related to Kleist's own search for stability. (That he committed suicide soon after finishing the play tells us simply that the stability he was reaching for was not long-lasting — or perhaps was beyond his grasp!)

Within dramas centered in the historical world the education or redirection of the audience's consciousness is often overtly part of the play's intent. The didacticism of Caesar's speeches in *Caesar and Cleopatra* is directed not only at Cleopatra (who in the course of the play grows from a giggly girl to what Caesar hopes may be a wise ruler) but also at the audience on whom Shaw is trying out his ideas about government. However much they may entertain us, Brecht's later plays are designed to give us what he conceived to be a Marxist education. Plays that propagate an idea or mood of disillusionment derive much of their deflating force from the implicit comparisons we make between them and earlier plays which had succeeded in inducing a sense of growth and expansiveness within an audience. The horror we are meant to feel as we witness Nero's growth into a total tyrant in *Britannicus* (Racine's reference to him as "un monstre naissant" suggests the actively developing aspect of his role)[28] gains in intensity through out sense that his "growth" is a negative version of that of Augustus and other upward-moving Corneillian heroes; Agrippine's phrase, "l'avenir détruisant le passé,"[29] which voices her fears that her son Nero will undo Augustus's historical achievements, is emblematic of the negative direction which his growth into power will take in the course of the play. The static quality that characterizes the plot of *Dantons Tod,* a play in which we recognize from the start that no growth (whether on a political, personal, or metaphysical level) is possible, gains something of its disillusioning force through the deliberate absence of that spiritual uplift which Goethe and Schiller so assiduously built into their plays. (Brecht's continued parodying of the various techniques of uplift within German classical drama was a necessary preparation for, and a complement to, the Marxist edification his own plays were attempting.) The idea of uplifting an audience is, for that matter, built into most theories which attempt to describe and justify the effects which art exerts upon those who experience it: witness, for instance, Aristotle's theory of catharsis or Horace's notion of instruction going on in the very process of delighting, or, to cite one of the most influential modern examples, the elaborate and very abstract argument of Schiller's *Ueber die ästhetische Erziehung des Menschen* (*On the Aesthetic Education of Man*), which sanctifies art as an instrument of ethical growth. If art can be justified only through its ability to move us upward through some hierarchical structure or other, it is no wonder that individual works cultivate structures that can help set the upward process in motion.

History from below

What is the city but the people?
The tribune Sicinius in *Coriolanus*

146

The upward bias which has traditionally characterized hierarchical thinking has been sharply questioned as a result of the various democratic movements of the last two centuries. During this time our conception of what appropriately belongs to the domain of history has widened from a narrow focus on those who wield political power to include not only the social and economic factors which determine their actions but also, in more recent years, the role of the powerless within the life of a culture. Among Western intellectuals hostility toward the public realm and even toward the very idea of order has often been so pronounced that the only ways of confronting history were to view it with the biases of the private world or from the point of view of those who have been oppressed by order. Our sentiments, in contrast to those of the Elizabethans, are all with the lower links of the great chain of being. This tendency of ours to look at history "from below" is evident, for instance, in the difficulties we often experience with the great plays about growth which I discussed in the preceding section. Thus, Maurice Morgann's celebrated defense of Falstaff, published in 1777, can be linked with those various attempts, during the succeeding half century, to defend the Satan of *Paradise Lost* against the oppression from above to which Milton had subjected him. If Morgann at least sought to raise Falstaff's status in our eyes by calling him a man of courage, a modern writer such as Brecht could discard courage as a virtue altogether — indeed, much of his writing demonstrates the sheer ridiculousness of being brave. Heroes who become spokesmen for public order (even if we are made to experience their painful growth into this role) are always likely to arouse our suspicions; thus we are likely to dismiss Prince Hal as a prig, Augustus as a canny political manipulator (a view held by Napoleon, who knew a thing or two about such matters),[30] Prince Friedrich as a conformist who was far more appealing at an earlier, less mature stage. I myself can testify to the strange effect of teaching *Prinz Friedrich von Homburg* in the volatile political atmosphere common to American campuses at the end of the 1960s. The students simply dismissed the play as absurd, while they were able to respond enthusiastically to that grim parody of a play on growth, *Britannicus,* which, with its atmosphere of political terror and its exploration of the relationship of power and sexuality, corresponded precisely with, indeed gave a shape to, what was most pressing on their minds. A modern commentator has argued that Kleist intended his play as a direct answer to *Egmont,*[31] whose hostility toward the public realm I cited earlier as a characteristic modern attitude; indeed, *Prinz Friedrich* must be accepted as thoroughly counterrevolutionary in spirit, for it questions the Enlightenment critique of political tyranny, discredits our faith in the reliability of the individual will, and propounds a doctrine of subservience to established authority (it is no wonder we are forced to translate it from political into existential terms to experience its greatness).

Our modern bias in favor of the lower members of the social scale manifests itself especially in our attitude to the anonymous crowds which appear in many historical dramas. Brecht happily assented to his friend Walter Benjamin's remark that the hero of *Galileo* is not the title figure but the people ("Das Volk"),[32] yet the uninformed reader or viewer would be hard pressed to assent so quickly unless his view of history allows the masses a decisive role even when they are not very visible. Max Reinhardt's productions of *Dantons Tod* early in this century were notable for the powerful stage effects he achieved with the restless crowds on the streets—to the point, in fact, that the play's political and philosophical discussions were relegated to a strictly subordinate role.[33] The contemporary audience watching angry and surging crowds feels that it is getting "close" to history in something of the way a sixteenth- or seventeenth-century audience must have felt when a royal figure appeared on stage in all his regalia. (Peter Weiss in *Marat/Sade* took advantage of the magical effect we feel in crowds by creating a play-within-a-play in which the revolutionary crowd is played by madmen; if *this* is what history is all about, we are meant to tell ourselves, then the historical process is simply another manifestation of the irrational.)

Despite our special fascination with the various anonymous forces in history, a glance through the history of drama reveals that the crowd has rarely been treated with sympathy and that its dramatic role, moreover, has been very limited. An analyst of dramatic structure might note that in plays such as *Julius Caesar, Coriolanus, Götz von Berlichingen, Egmont,* and *Murder in the Cathedral* crowds have been used at the outset to provide "exposition"—in much the same way that the gossiping servants do at the beginning of Ibsen's realistic plays. Goethe himself admitted that the Brussels populace, who occupy the stage for about a quarter of *Egmont,* do not play a significant role in the action.[34] As I indicated earlier, its chief function is to help build up the hero in our eyes—and, incidentally, to convince us that ordinary citizens are not by nature disorderly; indeed, as spokesmen for their author, who possessed an uncommon disdain for violence, they can in no way satisfy a modern audience's desire to experience a surging revolutionary force.

The undeniable unpleasantness of the crowd in *Coriolanus* (whether an expression of Shakespeare's ideology or simply a dramatic expedient to provide a foil for the protagonist) has posed a special challenge for those who cannot abide a Shakespeare totally out of tune with twentieth-century realities. Brecht, as I indicated earlier, solved the problem in his adaptation by tipping the play's balance against the patricians in favor of the crowd—with the risk, as it turned out, of the intrusion of those "real" working-class Berliners whom Günter Grass, in his play about Brecht rehearsing *Coriolanus* during the 1953 riots, introduces to put the master's compassion for working people to a test. In a discussion of the play's first scene appended to his adaptation Brecht goes to great lengths to point out evidences of Shakespeare's sympathy for the poor.[35] The question has obviously been a touchy one for Marxist critics. At its crudest extreme one finds the wishful interpreting of an early Soviet Shakespeare specialist, A. A. Smirnov, who quotes out of context from the citizens' grievances in *Coriolanus* and quickly concludes that "Shakespeare's sympathies are all on their side."[36] The eminent East German scholar Robert Weimann, who in his massive and impressive historical study *Shakespeare und die Tradition des Volkstheaters* portrays Shakespeare as the heir to the medieval and early Renaissance popular theater, carefully avoids extended commentary on those plays which portray the populace, except to argue briefly that Shakespeare's conception of "plebeian immaturity and fickleness is something more than *destructive* criticism, for it can also be seen as a contribution to the *overcoming* of this immaturity and ignorance" (italics Weimann's).[37] Weimann's honesty about Shakespeare's attitude, combined though it is with a Marxist faith that this attitude can help prepare the way for a more effective role of the crowd at a later stage in the historical process, at least admits the truth of what even the most untutored reader or audience perceives.

But the question of whether Shakespeare cared much for the common people is a trivial one, if only because it applies a central modern prejudice to an alien historical situation.[38] An issue of far greater import and interest is the way that Shakespeare utilized what Weimann called the crowd's "immaturity" and "fickleness" to provide insights into the nature of politics. In all three plays in which the crowd plays a major role — *Henry VI, Part 2, Julius Caesar,* and *Coriolanus* — the crowd is worked upon with the most elaborate rhetorical tools to achieve crucial shifts of allegiance. The shift of allegiance in the scenes depicting the Jack Cade rebellion in *Henry VI* is so swift, in fact, that the crowd emerges as ridiculous — or, to use the apt analogy from painting which A. P. Rossiter applied to these scenes, as Bosch-like grotesques.[39] The crowd scenes in the two Roman plays, however, are among Shakespeare's most complex explorations of politics. In Mark Antony's great oration in *Julius Caesar,* during which the crowd sways from whole-hearted support of Brutus to an acceptance of Caesar as martyr, we become aware that the dramatic shift of political allegiance we witness is not simply a comment on the fickle nature of the crowd but on the volatility and instability inherent in the political realm as a whole. Indeed, Antony's rhetoric is directed at two crowds at once — the populace on the stage and the audience only a short distance beyond.[40] Through its powerful effect on us we come to understand its ability to manipulate the populace so resoundingly; in fact, the effects we see in the crowd on stage become an exaggerated version, almost a parody, of the manipulation to which we allow ourselves to be subjected simultaneously.

The political process that Shakespeare portrays in *Julius Caesar* is relatively simple compared to that in *Coriolanus,* in which the crowd scenes not only extend over a considerably greater part of the play but in which a larger and more varied combination of forces contends for the crowd's favor: thus, the crowd serves as an unstable political arbiter in the rhetorical war between Menenius and the two tribunes, while the situation becomes further complicated by the willful political (not to speak of verbal) ineptness of Coriolanus and the powerful Oedipal tug to which Volumnia subjects the action from behind the scenes (one might add that Shakespeare quite clearly acknowledges that the crowd, unpleasant and foul-smelling though it may be, has some genuine economic grievances). A "sympathetic," "wise," or "stable" crowd in these plays would provide a very different sort of insight into politics (a look at the history of crowds — and their leaders — in our own century might yield insights unpleasantly close to Shakespeare's).

Almost everything one can say of the crowd in these two plays — its instability, its proneness to manipulation, even its relationships with the political leaders and the audience — can be said of the crowd in *Dantons Tod*. However much Büchner may have learned about French crowds from the chronicles of the Revolution he consulted, or about the Hessian peasants who failed to support the rebellion he sought to organize during the month before he wrote the play, he must have recognized that Shakespeare provided an image of political action persuasive enough to undo whatever influence might come from his own radical ideas or his observations on the difference between the Elizabethan and the nineteenth-century populace. The changeable nature of crowds occasionally plays a role even in French neoclassical plays, whose conventions rigorously exclude the crowd's presence on stage: in the closing scenes of Corneille's *Nicomède,* for instance, we are constantly aware that the offstage crowd, whose favor is desperately coveted by the various characters of high station we see, can influence the course of the play's action as surely as though it were surging before the spectators' eyes.

Though a long-standing goal of liberal and radical writers, the portrayal of a "positive" crowd, like that of a "positive" hero, runs into all the difficulties writers have always had in persuading the reader or audience to lend (and sustain) its sympathy to the characters they have created. In a ceremonial drama such as *Numancia,* the audience is prepared to give its sympathy wholeheartedly to its starving compatriots even before it enters the theater; when an anonymous mother comes on stage with a dying child in her arms the audience responds as automatically as a participant in communion. Our attitude is quite different, however, in a play which makes no ceremonial claims on us, for we go to the theater expecting our sympathies (and hostilities) gradually to be coaxed out of us. If an anonymous mother with a dying child enters in a nonceremonial play, we ask ourselves if the writer is not perhaps toying with our capacity for sentimentality. And if the writer proceeds to develop the mother as a central character, he may succeed in making a "believable" and even moving heroine out of her, but he has also sacrificed the anonymity which gives her membership in the crowd. Moreover, anonymous persons do not easily arouse an audience's sympathy or interest. One problem is the difficulty of finding an authentic language which they can speak. What we take to be authenticity of language comes more readily out of the nastier and more strident members of a crowd (if only because dialect has been traditionally associated with comic types) than out of those who might arouse our compassion. To the extent that it does not depend on verbal communication, film offers perhaps the best means of eliciting sympathy and concern for the anonymous populace: witness the powerful effect that Eisenstein achieved both in the close-ups of faces and panoramic views of the crowd in the Odessa steps episode of *Potemkin;* the repeated shots of the baby carriage rolling down what seems an unbearable and interminable number of steps make an immediate claim on our emotions similar to the symbolic scenes of horror in a ceremonial drama such as *Numancia.*

The greatest modern example of history seen from the viewpoint of the masses is doubtless *Mutter Courage,* in which the Thirty Years' War is chronicled without the appearance of a single public personage; it is as though the crowds and the representative common folk who people *Wallensteins Lager,* the short first play of Schiller's trilogy, were to displace the great figures around whom the final two plays are centered. Brecht's heroine is neither anonymous (though she has no historical basis) nor "positive"; indeed, as a mother who allows herself to sacrifice her children for her own survival, she is the total antithesis of the symbolic suffering mother who elicits our sympathy so automatically in *Numancia.* But for Brecht she emerges as a great representative figure of the populace under a repressive economic system: if we are horrified by her mean-spirited and callous behavior, then we should blame the system which shaped her and which sustains her throughout the play—and which the author consequently advises us to overthrow.

Among modern plays that seek to portray a "positive" view of the common people, none is so persuasive or moving as Gerhart Hauptmann's *Die Weber* (*The Weavers*), which chronicles episodes from an unsuccessful revolt of Silesian weavers against their capitalist masters in 1844. Hauptmann had advantages which few dramatists have possessed for the task: a native tie to the people and place of the drama (his grandfather had even been a weaver); a naturalistic method which encouraged him to portray the milieu in a direct and concrete way without idealizing it; a compassion (without condescension) for the poor which he refused to make fit the needs of any single ideology; and, at least as important as these other advantages, a crude enough sense of theater so that he was not inhibited from seeking out powerful effects—for instance the violent ending in which a naive old religious man too much removed from the world to approve of the revolt is the first to be gunned down by the troops who come in to suppress it. The play avoids most of the pitfalls of a socially conscious drama: the capitalist figure Dreissiger is never reduced to caricature; the violence committed by the rebels is not glossed over; the

151

common people are not treated as an abstraction, and a goodly number are characterized to the point that we can remember particular individuals. Above all, Hauptmann was able to give them authenticity of language without making them ridiculous; one suspects, in fact, that the sufferings of a person speaking a local dialect are less likely to ring sentimental than those of someone who speaks as we do (the Silesian dialect of the original version was so authentic that Hauptmann had to exchange it for a dialect-colored High German in order to communicate with a non-Silesian audience). Through Hauptmann's refusal to create a single rebel leader and through his repetition, at crucial moments, of the revolutionary hymn (itself an authentic relic of the weavers' revolt), we retain an image of the weavers as a powerful but doomed collective force who not only function as the play's "hero"—in the sense both of protagonist and bearer of heroic qualities—but whose political actions seem to follow naturally and inevitably out of the material conditions we are shown without the need of revolutionary rhetoric from "above."

There is one other drama in Western literature, Lope's *Fuenteovejuna,* in which the common people emerge as a collectivity to perform the heroic (again in both senses of the term) actions of the play. The drama, based on an incident from late fifteenth-century Spanish history, depicts the assassination, by the villagers of Fuenteovejuna, of the local feudal chieftain who had abducted one of their girls from her wedding festivities. The whole focus of the drama is, to use Leo Spitzer's words, on "the solidarity of the village in its own group spirit as it grew before us during the play."[41] Like *Die Weber, Fuenteovejuna* is thus a play about growth—not the growth of a single hero preparing for the responsibilities of governing but rather that of a collective force at the lowest level of society. Yet the resemblance between the plays ends here, for *Fuenteovejuna* is in no sense revolutionary in sentiment or intention. As I indicated in the first chapter while discussing the difficulty of assigning modern political meanings to older works, the play is the product of a unique historical situation in which the Spanish monarchy allied itself with the peasantry in opposition to the remaining vestiges of feudal power. Lope goes to great lengths to justify the rebellion from the point of view of the monarchy, which is represented conspicuously through the appearance of Ferdinand and Isabella in the play; thus the feudal chieftain is shown from the start as disloyal to the interests of the newly unified Spanish state, and his sexual crime has the overtones of a sacrilegious act which threatens the established order (politics, sex, and religion are inextricably tied together in Spanish drama of the Golden Age). But Lope's care in fixing the limits of rebellion in no way detracts from his great success in creating a group of common people, who, even in our own very different historical situation, can excite interest and sympathy in a most powerful way. Though the individuals are scarcely characterized (except for the rape victim, Laurencia, who emerges as a veritable Amazon after the crime), they achieve a collective impressiveness—in the earthiness, for instance, with which they discuss their daily domestic routine, in the honor and dignity which motivates their actions, in the ballad-like tone (the historical incident in which they took part was the subject of popular ballads before Lope wrote his play) which often characterizes their talk. Spitzer specifically ties Lope's treatment of the populace to the pastoral tradition[42]—yet the very mention of pastoral can serve to remind us of the gap that separates Lope's attitude from our own conceptions of common people. Traditional pastoral, after all, asserts an image of unchangeableness and stability; if it is able to endow the lowest orders of society with dignity, virtue, and charm, it does so on the premise that they emphatically know their place within the hierarchy of things. Indeed, the rebellion staged by the villagers of Fuenteovejuna is in no sense of the word a revolution but a restoration of what they see as their traditional rights—an interpretation to which the king (though he admonishes them for the seriousness of their offense) gives his blessing at the end of the play. The social order which we see through their eyes is unchanging and ultimately benefi- cent; and, unlike the order which constrains the social forces whose rights modern writers attempt to defend, its stability is predicated on the notion that these charming and honorable peasants will make no claims to any higher niche within the hierarchy.[43]

Drama and Power

> Cet empire absolu sur la terre et sur l'onde,
> Ce pouvoir souverain que j'ai sur tout le monde,
> Cette grandeur sans borne et cet illustre rang,
> Qui m'a jadis coûté tant de peine et de sang,
> Enfin tout ce qu'adore en ma haute fortune
> D'un courtisan flatteur la présence importune,
> N'est que de ces beautés dont l'éclat éblouit,
> Et qu'on cesse d'aimer sitôt qu'on en jouit.
>
> Augustus contemplating the
> possibility of abdication in *Cinna*

> Then am I king'd again, and by and by
> Think that I am unking'd by Bolingbroke,
> And straight am nothing.
>
> Richard II after his deposition

You see, when one wields power, and when one has it for a long time, one ends up thinking one has a right to it. I'm sure that when I leave this job I shall feel the lack of power. However, power as an instrument in its own right has no fascination for

me.... What interests me is what one can achieve with power.
Splendid things, believe me....

Henry Kissinger in an interview of November 4, 1972

If one can judge from the success with which historical plays, both old and new, have flourished in recent centuries, power exerts its fascination even on those who profess to despise it and identify with the powerless. The thinking and writing we do about history are in one sense a contemplation of the magic which we feel inheres in persons who hold power and the situations in which they wield it. Drama can contemplate this magic directly through the portrayal of royal figures on stage with all the visual symbols — crown, costly robes, throne, scepter — which we traditionally associate with them. "The sovereign represents [repräsentiert] history," wrote Walter Benjamin; "he holds the course of history in his hand like a scepter."[44] Benjamin's remark, though especially relevant to those symbol-laden German baroque tragedies of which he wrote so brilliantly, is applicable to all historical drama, if only because power can be depicted more readily at its source than in its more distant manifestations. Observing power at its royal source means in a sense to participate in it: we become privy to secrets that would otherwise be withheld from us; we share vicariously in the triumphs a monarch enjoys when he victimizes others to maintain or increase his power; and we share as well the terrors he experiences when his power is threatened and removed. (If the French Revolution deprived *Dantons Tod* of the colorful royal symbols which traditionally marked the seat of power, the play's six prison scenes and its scenes in the courtroom and at the guillotine provide an ample visual show of power within a totalitarian regime.)

Shakespeare's Richard III is palatable as a character only because his author has established a special relationship between him and us: thus, by taking us into his confidence, Richard allows us to view the play's actions from his own perverted point of view and, in effect, to share in the fears and thrills (though emphatically not the responsibilities) which power entails. The ambivalent attitudes into which we are forced as we experience this play (we enjoy something of the protagonist's power at the same time that we are horrified by his use of it) are an exaggerated version of the ambivalence that marks all our encounters with power in drama. The vicarious triumphs we feel may be tempered by our qualms about the amorality (or immorality, however we may choose to put it) of what we are approving; our fascination for power may be qualified by the guilt we feel for taking it as seriously as we do; and our compassion for the victims of power may be colored by our recognition that it derives from a fellow-feeling of powerlessness. Through our confrontation of power in drama (a confrontation we can experience in the "real" world only if we ourselves hold power), we are able to perceive a reality that exists separate from our accustomed moral categories; yet in the very act of perception these moral categories intrude to complicate our attitude and, at certain moments, may even jar us into a new understanding both of the nature of power and of the moral categories we take for granted (as well as remind us, incidentally, that we do not go the the theater simply to confirm the principles we already hold).

To portray power in drama a writer cannot simply place a ruler on stage and let him wave his scepter back and forth. Power, after all, can manifest itself only in the relationships between those exercising it and those upon whom it is exercised. Yet no drama can portray the total network of relationships within which power — whether in autocratic ancient Persia or democratic contemporary America — exists in particular historical situations (though a panoramic drama such as *Die letzten Tage der Menschheit,* with its 220 scenes ranging across what seems the whole of Viennese society during World War I, gives every impression of exposing such a network). Thus, historical drama has traditionally turned to the complicated power relationships within ruling families to create paradigms of the ways that power is exercised within society as a whole. A recent study of Shakespeare's history plays has suggested a relationship between family and state applicable to history plays of all times: "In a kind of drama shaped by Tudor political ideas, Shakespeare makes the family a microcosm of the state and an echo of its values. Marriage and the relationship of father and son, brother and brother, the noble and his house — these are the stuff of a personal drama. He relies on them to give immediacy to his panoramic views of the rise and fall of kings and kingdoms." [45]

The analogy between family relationships and those that define society as a whole is by no means limited to drama or even to literature (the great nineteenth-century social novels can, for instance, be seen as attempts to define a larger social network through the networks existing within individual families) but is something natural to "common-sense" thinking, as when a citizen demands that the government clamp down on dissident youth just as a parent would (or should) punish his disobedient child. Freud's theory of the Oedipal family network (in its very name, of course, a literary analogy for what Freud had earlier discovered in his clinical experience) is the model for the theory of society which he later worked out in *Totem and Taboo* and *Civilization and Its Discontents.* And the limitations of Freud's social vision, built as it is on the premise of "the similarity between the process of civilization and the libidinal development of the individual," [46] are akin to the limitations of the social vision we find in drama. We do not go to Freud or the great dramatists to learn how the mode of production helps determine social relationships; if they have anything to tell us about the economic or technological aspects of society, they will tell it in terms of personal idiosyncrasies and conflicts — the anal behavior of Molière's Harpagon, the Oedipal problems of Coriolanus and Racine's Nero, the gluttony of Brecht's

Galileo (whose author, despite his allegiance to Marx, was not entirely able to escape the tendency of drama to read social phenomena in terms of private conduct). And if historical drama puts a special stress on power relationships —more so, for instance, than some historians would do—this is because the family model on which it depends is itself fraught with power conflicts.

Power relationships are at their most blatant in tyrant plays such as *Richard III* and *Britannicus,* in which outrageous violations of family bonds become the norm: thus, the tyrant can murder close relatives (including innocent children), seduce the wife (or, as in *Britannicus,* attempt to seduce the lover) of someone he has murdered (or will murder), betray those who helped make possible the act of power he exercised scarcely a moment before. Yet one of the central insights we gain from such plays is that even the most ruthless wielders of power are forced to adopt ruses, make alliances (temporary though these may be), and engage in all manner of manipulation to achieve and exercise power. Indeed, compared to the elaborate preparations we witness, the actual murders and moments of betrayal take up very little of the dramatic action of these plays. The famous scene in which Nero plays voyeur at the interview of the lovers Britannicus and Junie [47] can be taken as an emblem both of the elaborateness of a tyrant's devices and of the perversity which accompanies his exercise of power. It would be easy to dismiss Racine as a dramatist who, in contrast to Corneille, is concerned primarily with court intrigues and private relationships: indeed, his own statement in the preface to *Britannicus,* "Néron est ici dans son particulier et dans sa famille,"[48] would seem to support such a view. But Racine concentrates on intense family relationships precisely because they provide the ideal model for the brutal, though overtly civilized, power relationships which are at the center of his historical vision; among the great dramatists before Büchner, Racine is unique for the sense of claustrophobia, the constraints on action, and the utter hopelessness that characterize the historical world he has created.

Hegel's reference to the prevalence of fraternal enmity (usually culminating in murder) among the major themes of world literature[49] is a reminder of the special meaning we seek in extreme instances: murdering one's brother is a more potent act than murdering one's friend, while the latter act, in turn, carries more meaning for us than the murder of a stranger. However much our notions of kinship have changed since the Greeks, Aristotle's discussion of the power that emanates from crimes committed within a family is applicable to all drama since his time: "When the painful deed is done in the context of close family relationships, for example when a brother kills or intends to kill a brother, or a son a father, or a mother a son, or a son a mother, or does something else of that kind—those are the acts one should look for."[50] The closer the relationship between murderer and victim, the greater the outrage we feel, while, by a strange sort of paradox, the more outrage we express, the more emphatically we recognize the murderer's power.

156

Drama, moreover, has a way of "compressing" relationships in order to simulate the tightest possible bond between potential antagonists. Although Britannicus is technically Nero's half brother, Nero's murder of him has the force of a thoroughgoing fratricide. In Kleist's *Prinz Friedrich,* though the Elector who trains the prince into subservience to the organic state is actually his uncle, the relationship emerges psychologically as that of father and son. Falstaff would have no place in *Henry IV* if he were not a rival vying with the king for fathership over Prince Hal; indeed, the most obvious of the many themes holding the diverse "worlds" of the play together is the various father-son relationships within each world. Richard II not only stresses his cousinhood to Bolingbroke (which the latter, eager to keep his usurpation on a nonfamilial basis, tries to underplay) but at one point (III.iii.204-6) even invokes a father-son analogy to compress the relationship. Historical plays whose political settings preclude the use of ruling families often define friendship in terms of familial bonds. Caesar's dying cry "Et tu, Brute" impresses on us the idea that we have just witnessed a violation akin to patricide. Büchner echoes these famous words in *Dantons Tod* with Robespierre's "Also auch du Camille," spoken when Robespierre hears that Camille Desmoulins has attacked him in his journal; and Camille later stresses the fraternal relationship by reminding us that he had formerly shared the same bench with Robespierre in school.[51]

The power relationships with which drama is concerned are in no sense static; indeed, as an art enacting events passing through time, drama can focus above all on the shifting nature of these relationships. The famous horse-and-rider statues of Donatello and Verrocchio can freeze an image of heroic power to retain an illusion of its permanence — a permanence all the more convincing because the energy and movement we perceive in the poses tell us that the power can forever renew itself. But drama is incapable of such illusions of permanence. In an earlier context I spoke of the difficulty of "sustaining the heroic" in a play, by which I referred to the problem every dramatist meets in finding a language and a plot structure which can retain the illusion that his characters and their actions are greater than the life we ordinarily know. A central means of giving an individual a heroic dimension is to place him in a position of publicly acknowledged power. Even at his most maudlin moments, Richard II retains a trace of the heroic bearings which we naturally associate with royal office — until, of course, he hands the crown to Bolingbroke, after which the new king achieves a nobility in our eyes which we had denied him all the time he was pursuing the crown. (Even in our democratic culture, with its absence of royal symbols to adorn and elevate an otherwise commonplace person, we come to see dignity, if not precisely heroism, in those holding high office whom we formerly treated with contempt or disgust.)

The medieval notion of the king's two bodies, in separating the impermanence of a ruler as a person from the permanence of his office, provides a superb metaphor for drama, which can exploit the idea that the coexistence of person and office is never permanent, indeed that it is among the more unstable relationships within the social order. If power inheres in the office and not the person, a character in drama is able to radiate the magic of power only when he has secure control of the office. The plots of most history plays could be retold in terms of the transfer of power which occurs as one character seeks to displace another from office, or of a character's efforts to tighten the security with which he controls his office. The suspense in history plays often consists of a certain nervousness (experienced both by characters and audience) as to whether a particular character can wrest a prized office or whether another character can maintain an office already in his possession. For example, Henry IV's line, "Uneasy lies the head that wears a crown" (Pt. 2.III.i.31), though we recognize it as a commonplace when we hear it, conveys something of the nervousness we seek to experience in history plays.

When viewed as battles for offices, history plays assume the aspect of games (though unlike sports events, games in which we hope to recognize that the issues at stake, and their outcome, have somehow affected our lives). The game analogy has recently been used to describe the struggle for power not in those secular dramas which we ordinarily classify as historical, but in the medieval Corpus Christi cycles: "[Their] great subject was a struggle for power played out as game but in fact deadly serious—a battle between God and Satan for man's soul, in which the outcome is never in doubt, but where the price of victory is a terrible one."[52] In historical drama we reserve a special fascination for those players of the game who are at the brink of achieving power or who are about to lose it. Drama, moreover, cultivates crises in which a particular office—whether through the ambitions of someone without power or the weakness of the holder of power—has become vulnerable to change. A character incapable of managing power is of little interest unless, like Richard II, he already has the crown and we witness the agony of his losing it; by the same token, a dictator whose regime is totally secure is unable to generate enough struggle to keep a drama going (a modern dramatist might, of course, subject his regime to satire to demonstrate that mediocrity lies at the heart of power).

No play visualizes the shifts in the game so forcefully or movingly as *Richard II,* whose prevailing images of "up" and "down"—tersely described by the twin buckets (IV.i.184-89), one of which must move to the bottom of the well as the other mounts—are a constant reminder of the precariousness, as well as enchantment, which belongs to the power of high office. The visual force is evident, for instance, in Shakespeare's use of upper and lower stages in the scene at Flint Castle, in which Richard, anticipating the fall from power that takes most of the play to complete, enacts this fall symbolically through his descent from the high walls to the low courtyard in which he sees the man who will soon depose him waiting. As in innumerable other passages which play upon the opposition of height and depth, the characteristic movements of the drama are condensed in these few lines which Richard speaks just before he comes down from the upper stage:

> Down, down I come, like glist'ring Phaeton,
> Wanting the manage of unruly jades.
> In the base court? Base court, where kings grow base,
> To come at traitors' calls, and do them grace!
> In the base court? Come down? Down, court! down, king!
> For night-owls shriek where mounting larks should sing.
>
> (III.iii.178-83)

With the calculation characteristic of a figure contemplating possible martyr-dom, Richard sees to it that the words "base" and "down" retain their physical and moral meanings at once.

The up-and-down movement is evident, as well, in the visual symbols of the deposition scene, in which Richard holds onto the crown for what every audience must experience as an unbearably long time while he voices all the hierarchical inplications of his act — after which he calls for a mirror, which he dashes to the ground to demonstrate the "brittleness" of his glory and the loss of identity which automatically follows loss of office. Shakespeare also makes a visual point through the painful symmetry of the opening and closing scenes: in the first scene Richard, as impersonal as his office, sits adjudicating on his throne with Bolingbroke before him as a supplicant for justice, while at the end Bolingbroke, ennobled by his new office (though tinged with the guilt which, in the final lines, he hopes to expiate through his "voyage to the Holy Land") sits on the throne with Richard's coffin directly before him. In this play, moreover, as well as in *Henry VI* and *Richard III*, the long prison scene serves as a necessary antithesis to the scenes at court: it is as though the seat of power achieves its allure only through a visual reminder of the abjectness with which those who have lost their offices can fall.

The transfer of power which we witness in drama is determined not simply by a blind struggle between the various rivals for office but, at least in those dramas which are set where hereditary rule prevails, by the principle of succession. If the determination of which heir is to succeed a ruler (and at what point in time he may succeed!) were a purely mechanical and uncontroversial exercise, we should have few historical dramas except for such modern plays as *Mutter Courage* and *Galileo,* which focus on the power of economic and social forces rather than on the power of office. (Even many of the great martyr plays, to the extent that they record a shift of allegiance from a secular to a spiritual power, are modeled on the idea of succession.) But in drama, at least as much as in life, determining succession is a process which is anything but mechanical: it is in fact fraught with all the difficulties that make possible those examinations of human motivation, patterns of action, depravity, and the like on which literature has traditionally thrived. Sigurd Burckhardt has shrewdly described the disorder that stands behind the apparent order in the idea of succession in Shakespeare's English histories:

> At first glance it seems obvious that Shakespeare's histories recognize only one mode of succession as truly legitimate: primo-geniture. Other modes—particularly succession by combat, as described in Frazer's *Golden Bough*—seem clearly illegitimate; indeed they are not alternate modes so much as lapses into chaos. (Succession by popular election can readily be interpreted as a variant of succession by combat.) All the same it would be very easy for an anthropological critic to read the history plays as recording a series of successions by combat, in which kings who are lacking in potency are supplanted (and usually killed) by others who prove their right to the title by their ability to seize it. Indeed, if this critic were rigorously descriptive and inferred the law of succession in the histories strictly from the actual events, he could not possibly arrive at the law of primogeniture.[53]

If what Burckhardt describes as succession by combat is the actual mode of succession even in plays which pretend to follow as mechanical a rule as primogeniture, the "lapses into chaos" to which he refers are really the norm in all plays dealing with the transfer of power. To put it another way, the actions of most historical dramas can be described as attempts to provide semblances of order which can disguise (and also legitimize) the chaos and barbarism which characterize the various struggles for power. To the extent that the legal right which a person holds to an office is always somewhat in doubt (at least in drama, if not necessarily in life), power is never fully secure. The power of the Lancastrians, even when it is as vigorously defended as it is in *Henry IV* and *Henry V,* is always compromised by the very real doubts surrounding their legitimacy. The action of historical drama is more precisely a struggle for legitimacy than a struggle for power as such. Dramas that depict a hereditary throne generally present sharply divergent readings of genealogies to justify the rights of various contenders for the throne. Before Henry V has the archbishop of Canterbury serve up the genealogy he has ordered to legitimize his right to France, he warns him not to "fashion, wrest, or bow [his] reading" (I.ii.14) with misinterpretation, yet long before we have heard the whole of the archbishop's lengthy speech we recognize the extreme casuistry out of which it is built.

The semblances of order which are set up in historical contexts without primogeniture allow far more elaborate (and often farfetched) rational-izations by which a ruler or pretender may legitimize himself. Racine took brilliant advantage of the uncertainties regarding succession in imperial Rome to dramatize the break between an "ungrateful" Nero and the power-craving and possessive mother who has gone to the most ruthless lengths to secure the throne for him; many of the richest passages in the play, in fact, come from the self-justifications, the search for earlier imperial precedents, the reproaches, the intricate manipulations, and the efforts to secure new alliances that accompany the break. In lines such as these, as Nero is about to accuse his mother of trying to displace him with her other son—

> Je me souviens toujours que je vous dois l'Empire;
> Et sans vous fatiguer du soin de le redire,
> Votre bonté, Madame, avec tranquillité
> Pouvait se reposer sur ma fidélité.
> Aussi bien ces soupçons, ces plaintes assidues
> Ont fait croire à tous ceux qui les ont entendues
> Que jadis (j'ose ici vous le dire entre nous)
> Vous n'aviez, sous mon nom, travaillé que pour vous [54]

we are aware, first of all, of the extraordinary civility with which personal relationships are conducted: note, for instance, the formal terms of address, the initial expression of gratitude, the innumerable qualifications before Nero comes home for the kill ("Vous n'aviez, sous mon nom, travaillé que pour vous"). Much of the impact which Racine, in fact, achieves comes from the great gap we feel between these expressions of outward civility and the barbarity of the actual struggle for power which is taking place. By means of this gap Racine is able to convey a maximum shock effect with minimal physical means; indeed, the "actual" violence (all of it, of course, offstage) within the time-span of the play is limited to one abduction (Junie), one premeditated murder (Britannicus), and one killing by a mob (Narcisse).

The potential ferocity of struggles for power is at its most open (though not necessarily most honest) in actions demanding that the voice of the people be consulted for legitimacy to be conferred upon a prospective ruler. *Dantons Tod,* for instance, portrays a world in which, since the commencement of the Republic, the traditional rules of succession have been replaced by a mode dependent on a repeated show of popular support. The dramatic function of Robespierre's long speeches—on the streets, at the Jacobin Club, in the National Convention[55]—is to ratify his power anew from moment to moment. Danton's eloquence before the Revolutionary Tribunal, though it fails to prevent his execution, earns him at least temporary popular support, which he loses soon after through a speech by one of Robespierre's adherents. [56] In plays such as *Dantons Tod, Julius Caesar,* and *Coriolanus,* political power can be earned through the power of rhetoric, but its staying power is as limited as the ability of words to maintain their persuasiveness. The snarling line of the tribune Sicinius in *Coriolanus,* "What is the city but the people?" (III.i.198 — a statement which, incidentally, could be uttered by most any contemporary radical, or even liberal), indicates what we cynically recognize to be the ultimate source of sovereignty in these plays. With his notorious oratorical incompetence, Coriolanus is the perfect tragic hero for a play in which deeds, no matter how heroically performed, must invariably be supplemented by words as a prerequisite to attaining power. As a verbal art, drama is ideally suited to staging a show of verbal eloquence (or awkwardness) as a means of determining the transfer of power. One suspects that verbal power cannot lead to political power in the "real" world as readily as it can in the fictive world of plays. The whole question of whether Shakespeare and Büchner were "unsympathetic" to the crowds they depicted states the problem too exclusively from the point of view of the "real" world: from a "fictive" point of view a malleable crowd upon whom words could work their magic with maximum effectiveness was the theatrically most suitable instrument for the transfer of power.

As a verbal art, drama also has a penchant for finding words to express the agonies experienced by those who have lost their power. The eloquence that comes so much more easily to writers than to most public figures can, when put in the mouths of the latter, come to seem virtually a substitute for the real power which they have left behind. The dread curses which the aged Queen Margaret levels at the usurping Gloucester in *Richard III* (I.iii.111-303), or Agrippine at Nero in *Britannicus,*[57] are expressions of the only power that remains to those who have been rendered impotent (and since the dire predictions they make are to come true, the power they exercise in these curses is real and not simply verbal). Agrippine's role in the play consists both of an attempt to hold on to her power (which she has maintained through intrigue and through her Oedipal hold on her son) and to make words simulate the power which we see gradually waning in the course of the play. The eloquent line she speaks early in the play to Nero's confidant, "Moi, fille, femme, soeur, et mère de vos maîtres,"[58] is a desperate, though quite useless, assertion of power by virtue of her blood ties; and in the beautiful Racinian paradox within her line, "Je vois mes honneurs croître, et tomber mon crédit,"[59] she expresses her realization that the ceremonial attributes that are heaped upon her are, like the words she utters, superficially attractive substitutes for the power she so longs for.

Since Nero emerges as the absolute center of power in the play, every character becomes a study of some variety of impotence. Thus, when Britannicus defies Nero in his major confrontation with him,[60] we recognize what might be called the "idealist's" power — a purely moral and verbal form of power used to counter the thrusts of those who hold the real power (as might be expected, Nero can end the scene by having his opponent arrested). From the point of view of the person holding real power, an idealist's power is nothing more than a luxury in which the idealist indulges to make himself feel better and perhaps flatter the audience for its good taste in identifying with him (his opponent, moreover, can remain impervious to his insults in full knowledge that they are simply expressions of his impotence).

162

Every martyr play depends upon the eloquence of the idealist to pit his special and unworldly power (often quite insolently) against that of the secular authority, and to the extent that we are receptive to the martyr's religious or moral claims, we come to recognize the validity of a spiritual power which transcends the usual secular forms. The spiritual power which martyrs invoke to counter the secular power that sends them to their death is analogous perhaps to the mental power which that would-be martyr, Richard II, finds is all he has left when, in his prison soliloquy, he decides to people his own world out of his thoughts:

> I have been studying how I may compare
> This prison where I live unto the world;
> And, for because the world is populous
> And here is not a creature but myself,
> I cannot do it. Yet I'll hammer it out.
> My brain I'll prove the female to my soul,
> My soul the father, and these two beget
> A generation of still-breeding thoughts,
> And these same thoughts people this little world,
> In humours like the people of this world;
> For no thought is contented. . . .
>
> (V.v.1-11)

Though we can sometimes share a martyr's belief in his own spiritual power, we quickly become aware of the ridiculousness of Richard's creation, which is notable for the poverty of the materials over which he asserts his power; indeed, in the course of the speech, Richard himself moves to a realization that his thoughts have no function except to idle away a life made useless by its total powerlessness.

One could, in fact, look at his speeches throughout the play as a long, slow elegy on his loss of power (the fact that he still possessed real power at the start of his elegiac progress tells us simply that the drive to powerlessness was more central to his nature than the temptations of power). The extraordinary sympathy which we feel toward Richard (tempered, of course, by our insight into what we would today call his self-destructiveness) has, I suspect, much to do with the immense verbal skill with which his verbally illustrious creator invested him. The power which Richard, in his final soliloquy, commands to people a world out of his thoughts is strictly an artist's power, though one which, in retrospect, we recognize that we have seen at work in his speeches throughout the play. In the very process of voicing his obsession with power (or, more precisely, with powerlessness, and in particular his own powerlessness) he becomes an exemplar of what De Quincey, in defending the greatest literature for the energies it succeeded in unleashing, called the "literature of power."[61]

Since the romantics we have, in fact, become accustomed to invoking (and experiencing) the power of art as a substitute for, or even "higher" form of the political power which we, like Richard II, despair of achieving. Shakespeare and his contemporaries at least possessed an imagination for political power, which they were able to embody in the lives and struggles of great men and the manifestations of which, short-lived and tragic though they may be, could strike us with an awe which we assume to be commensurate with their manifestations in reality. Although we can still imaginatively experience the agonies of the power struggles in the great historical dramas of the sixteenth and seventeenth centuries, the conception of power which emerges in that diverse body of literature which we call "modern" (and whose exemplifications we locate in works since the mid-eighteenth century) is quite foreign to what we find in Shakespeare and Racine. For we no longer see power as a property (if ever so temporary) of great individuals, but as a generally diffused force which, whether we translate it into social or economic (or even psychological) terms, is notable above all for its oppressiveness.[62] Brecht, in a note appended to *Arturo Ui,* the play in which he parodies *Richard III* as a means of defining Hitler's rise to power, expresses the modern inability to conceive of powerful individuals on a serious level: "The great political criminals must be given up completely, and primarily to ridicule. For they are above all not great political criminals, but the perpetrators of great political crimes, which is something quite different."[63] Brecht puts the stress on *acts* of power rather than on their *agents,* and in his "imitations" of earlier plays such as *Richard III* and *Coriolanus* he makes his point by systematically robbing his heroes of what awe they possessed and reducing them to common criminals.

Our difficulty in conceiving that a man can achieve the autonomy which power confers (and that he can do so nobly!) is of course a part of our skepticism toward the possibility of heroic action and our general suspicion of the public realm. If we assume that modern drama "begins" with the writing of *Dantons Tod,* we can isolate the peculiarly modern quality that distinguishes the play from earlier historical dramas in Büchner's refusal to locate power within an individual and his determination to diffuse it throughout the fearfully oppressive atmosphere which he establishes throughout the play. Büchner even gives Robespierre a touch of that ridiculousness which Brecht was to exploit much more fully as he reduced his heroes and villains to size. The source of power does not lie in any office, but rather in what Büchner, in the letter I quoted earlier, called "the frightful fatalism of history" which he experienced, "as though utterly crushed," while reading about the French Revolution and in which, as he discovered, the individual was "a mere froth on the wave, greatness a mere chance, the dominance of genius a puppet's game."[64] The inertia which Danton manifests so consistently and wittily from the start of the play follows naturally from this recognition that power was both useless to attain and too oppressive to bear.

The oppressiveness which we attribute to the forces which shape our lives helps us in a sense to cope with the feeling that we live in a world too complex for us to hope to participate in significantly. Büchner's "frightful fatalism of history" could thus be seen as a typical modern myth which we invoke to explain or justify our helplessness or inertia; or we can twist the myth around and look at history as a force which, by virtue of some change in consciousness or economic arrangements, can be rechanneled and, as a happy future result, ultimately lose its oppressiveness. Either way, whether we consider ourselves oppressed or prospectively content, we adjust our sights to remaining powerless and small, indeed mere instruments of some larger force, beneficent or malign though it may be. Dramas about power, we must remember, are written from a very limited point of view, that of authors who have themselves never tasted significant political power. Their envy, fear, and awe at the spectacle of power, whether the power of great individuals or impersonal forces, are expressions of powerless men writing for audiences as powerless as themselves and finding their ideas about power transmitted to posterity by equally powerless critics. Yet one could argue that the powerless are privileged with a special insight into that which is different from them; such, at least, was the notion voiced by Machiavelli when, in dedicating *The Prince* to the grandson of Lorenzo the Magnificent, he sought to excuse his presumptuousness in writing about (indeed, also *for*) rulers:

> Nor will it, I trust, be deemed presumptuous on the part of a man of humble and obscure condition to attempt to discuss and direct the government of princes; for in the same way that landscape painters station themselves in the valleys in order to draw mountains or high ground, or ascend an eminence, in order to get a good view of the plains, so it is necessary to be a prince to know thoroughly the nature of the people, and one of the populace to know the nature of princes.[65]

In claiming his special insight into the great, Machiavelli fully recognized that the tables could be turned, that men of power could portray the rest of us in ways we could never ourselves conceive. Rulers have, in fact, occasionally distinguished themselves as writers — Lorenzo the Magnificent was himself a fine poet — but I know of none who have written dramas about ordinary life comparable to the dramas which ordinary men write about the great. If any were to take up the challenge implicit in Machiavelli's dedication, they might, like many of our own recent authors, simply tell us how banal we all are.

NOTES

CHAPTER ONE

1. "De Arte Poetica," in *Satires, Epistles and Ars Poetica*, ed. H. R. Fairclough, Loeb Classical Library (London: William Heinemann, 1926), p. 460 (l. 131).

2. Corneille recognized the difference in attitude between antiquity and his own time in the following lines from his "Discours de la tragédie": "la fable et l'histoire de l'antiquité sont si mêlées ensemble, que pour n'être pas en péril d'en faire un faux discernement, nous leur donnons une égale autorité sur nos théâtres" (in Corneille, p. 101). What matters to a modern audience (whether in the seventeenth or the twentieth century) is not the historical accuracy of the fable, but the fact that, whether historical or mythical, the material is "publicly known."

3.   scriptor honoratum si forte reponis Achillem,
           impiger, iracundus, inexorabilis, acer,
           iura neget sibi nata, nihil non arroget armis.
           sit Medea ferox invictaque . . . (ll. 120-23).

4. "Kein Dichter hat je die historischen Charactere gekannt, die er darstellte, hätte er sie aber gekannt, so hätte er sie schwerlich so gebrauchen können" (in J. P. Eckermann, *Gespräche mit Goethe,* ed. H.H. Houben [Leipzig: Brockhaus, 1916], p. 182 [Jan. 31, 1827]).

5. *Four Tragedies*, ed. L. A. Beaurline and Fredson T. Bowers (Chicago: University of Chicago Press, 1967), p. 287.

6. "Dating" a change of sensibility is one of the more exhilarating, yet also riskier, activities of the historical imagination. Although we conventionally pick the seventeenth century as the time when people "began" to feel self-conscious about separating truth from fiction, the distinction goes back in varying ways to ancient literary theory. See Herschel Baker's discussion of the distinction during the Renaissance (as well as in antiquity) in *The Race of Time: Three Lectures on Renaissance Historiography* (Toronto: University of Toronto Press, 1967), esp. pp. 79-89; for a discussion of the origins of the distinction in antiquity, see Wesley Trimpi, *The Ancient Hypothesis of Fiction: An Essay on the Origins of Literary Theory*, vol. 27 in the monograph series *Traditio* (New York: Fordham University Press, 1971).

7. ". . . je fais entrer Junie dans les Vestales, où, selon Aulu-Gelle, on ne recevait personne au-dessous de six ans, ni au-dessus de dix. Mais le peuple prend ici Junie sous sa protection, et j'ai cru qu'en considération de sa naissance, de sa vertu et de son malheur, il pouvait la dispenser de l'âge prescrit par les lois, comme il a dispensé de l'âge pour le consulat tant de grands hommes qui avaient mérité ce privilège" (Racine, p. 406).

8. For an edition of *Dantons Tod* which provides easy reference to the relevant passages which Büchner took over, see *La Mort de Danton*, ed. Richard Thieberger (Paris: Presses Universitaires de France, 1953).

9. Racine, p. 483. Modern scholarship, as one might expect, has come up with additional source material; for summaries of source studies of *Bérénice* and *Cinna*, see Henry Carrington Lancaster, *A History of French Dramatic Literature in the Seventeenth Century*, pt. 4, vol. 1 (Baltimore: Johns Hopkins Press, 1940): 71, and pt. 2, vol. 1 (1932): 314, respectively.

10. See *Richard the Third* (London: Allen and Unwin, 1955) and also the same author's *Richard III: The Great Debate* (London: Folio Society, 1965), esp. pp. 5-20 of the Introduction.

11. Note, for instance, the comparisons of text and sources in *Sejanus,* ed. Jonas Barish (New Haven: Yale University Press, 1965), pp. 181-203. The classical sources which Jonson himself listed in the margins of the *Sejanus* quarto provide a display of learning that would have done honor to any humanist scholar.

12. For discussions of Jonson's attitude to the relation of poetry and history, see the articles by J.T. Bryant, Jr., "The Significance of Ben Jonson's First Requirement for Tragedy: 'Truth of Argument'," *SP* 49 (1952): 195-213, and *"Catiline* and the Nature of Jonson's Tragic Fable," *PMLA* 69 (1954): 265-77.

13. *From "Mankind" to Marlowe* (Cambridge: Harvard University Press, 1962), pp. 234-44.

14. One is especially aware of the differences in those instances when Elizabethan and Spanish plays have been "rewritten" in neoclassical terms: comparing Guillén de Castro's *Las mocedades del Cid* with Corneille's play, or *Antony and Cleopatra* with *All for Love,* makes for an ideal school exercise.

15. " . . . we may take notice that where the poet ought to have preserved the character as it was delivered to us by antiquity, when he should have given us the picture of a rough young man of the Amazonian strain, a jolly huntsman, and both by his profession and his early rising a mortal enemy to love, he has chosen to give him the turn of gallantry, sent him to travel from Athens to Paris, taught him to make love, and transformed the Hippolytus of Euripides into Monsieur Hippolyte" (*All for Love,* ed. David M. Vieth [Lincoln: University of Nebraska Press, 1972], pp. 16-17 [Preface]). Needless to say, Dryden himself had few compunctions about modernizing older texts for his own imitations. Racine's audiences, incidentally, might well have viewed his characters as existing in a timeless world, at least if one can judge from the costumes, which, as John C. Lapp explains, "artfully combined the Roman costume . . . with the dress of the time" (*Aspects of Racinian Tragedy* [Toronto: University of Toronto Press, 1955], p. 191).

16. See Racine, p. 549 and pp. 1139-40, and Lancaster, *History of French Dramatic Literature,* pt. 4, vol. 1: 82.

17. See Barbara N. De Luna, *Jonson's Romish Plot: A Study of 'Catiline' and Its Historical Context* (Oxford: Clarendon Press, 1967).

18. The contemporary Elizabethan political meanings of the history plays are central to books such as Campbell's *Shakespeare's "Histories": Mirrors of Elizabethan Policy* (San Marino: Huntington Library, 1947); E. M. W. Tillyard's *Shakespeare's History Plays* (1944; reprint ed., New York: Collier Books, 1962); Irving Ribner's *The English History Play in the Age of Shakespeare* (Princeton: Princeton University Press, 1957); and M.M. Reese's *The Cease of Majesty* (New York: St. Martin's Press, 1961). Whereas Campbell stresses the impact on the plays of specific political events during Elizabeth's reign, the others stress the influence of political thought and of ideologically colored earlier literature.

19. *Die Hermannsschlacht* is exhortative by its very nature, but *Prinz Friedrich,* a much "cooler" play, demands political action largely by implication (though its final line, "In Staub mit allen Feinden Brandenburgs!" is as exhortative as any line in the history of drama).

20. Corneille, p. 869 (III.v).

21. Racine, p. 468 (V.vi).

22. Büchner, 1: 70 (IV.v).

23. *Coleridge's Shakespearean Criticism,* ed. T. M. Raysor (Cambridge: Harvard University Press, 1930), 1: 138.

24. For an extended commentary on the ways that audiences experience their national past, see the section entitled "History as Ceremony" in Chapter 3.

25. Within the neoclassical system, the depiction of a recent historical event could be taken as a violation of the decorum proper to tragedy. Racine, in his preface to *Bajazet,* a play based on a quite recent incident in Turkish history, sought to excuse himself by asserting that distance in place could substitute for distance in time and then cited *The Persians* as precedent for a play on recent history set in a distant place (Racine, pp. 548-49).

26. *An Apology for Actors,* cited from the photo-facsimile of Richard H. Perkinson (New York: Scholars' Facsimiles and Reprints, 1941), sig. F3ᵛ.

27. "Gegen das Stück lässt sich anführen . . . Dass es fremd und ausländisch ist" (Schiller, 11: 179).

28. "Man sieht aber, was die englische Geschichte ist, und was, es sagen will, wenn einem tüchtigen Poeten eine solche Erbschaft zu Theil wird. Unsere deutsche Geschichte in fünf

Bänden ist dagegen eine wahre Armuth, so dass man auch, nach dem *Götz von Berlichingen,* sogleich ins Privatleben ging, und eine *Agnes Bernauerin* und einen *Otto von Wittelsbach* schrieb, womit freylich nicht viel gethan war" (in Eckermann, pp. 376-77 [March 9, 1831]).

29. "Ich studirte die Geschichte der Revolution. Ich fühlte mich wie zernichtet unter dem grässlichen Fatalismus der Geschichte. . . . Der Einzelne nur Schaum auf der Welle, die Grösse ein blosser Zufall, die Herrschaft des Genies ein Puppenspiel, ein lächerliches Ringen gegen ein ehernes Gesetz, es zu erkennen das Höchste, es zu beherrschen unmöglich" (Büchner, 2: 425-26).

30. *The Oxford Ibsen,* 4 (1963), ed. and trans. James Walter McFarlane and Graham Orton (London: Oxford University Press): 603. Although Ibsen drew from late Roman history for this play, his use of Rome is distinctly different from that in, say, *Julius Caesar* or *Britannicus,* for the conflict of Julian's paganism with Christianity is seen as a dialectical development in which one form of order confronts another and then leads to a still newer form — which is only to say that Hegel (as well as those eighteenth-century thinkers who had laid the groundwork for "universal" history) had helped create a new conception of the role of Rome in world history. Ibsen, incidentally, subtitled the play "A World-Historic Drama."

31. The role of the interpreter's historical situation in his apprehension of a work of the past is of course a central issue in contemporary literary theory, notably in the writings of Hans-Georg Gadamer and E. D. Hirsch, Jr. My present concern is less with the theoretical aspects of this thorny question than with its practical implications, above all the ways that readers, audiences, stage directors, and dramatists have habitually (and often gleefully) read the present into earlier historical works.

32. For a discussion of recent attempts to find additional political effects the play may have had between the time of its composition and the Essex Rebellion, see the introduction to the New Arden edition, pp. lvii-lxii.

33. The Goethe and Coleridge interpretations can be found, among many other places, in the *Hamlet* variorum, ed. H. H. Furness (1877; reprint ed., New York: Dover, 1963), 2: 272-75, and 152-55, respectively. Kott's essay, entitled *"King Lear* or *Endgame,"* is in his *Shakespeare: Our Contemporary,* trans. B. Taborski (New York: Doubleday, 1966), pp. 127-68; for Kott's description of Brook's production ("It sufficed to discover Beckett in Shakespeare" — p. 365), see pp. 363-66.

34. "Ich bin fleissig, mein 'Egmont' rückt sehr vor. Sonderbar ist's, dass sie eben jetzt in Brüssel die Szene spielen, wie ich sie vor zwölf Jahren aufschrieb, man wird vieles jetzt für Pasquill halten" (Goethe, 12: 367 [*Italienische Reise,* July 9, 1787]).

35. Quoted in *Ben Jonson,* ed. C. H. Herford and Percy Simpson, 5 (Oxford: Clarendon Press, 1937): 415. One cannot predict what plays may generate new meanings any more than one can predict what political events will take place at any given time. While I was at work on this book, I learned about the uproar in Warsaw created by a new production in 1968 of *Forefathers Eve,* a play which, among its various apocalyptic concerns, contains a bitter and brilliant denunciation of the Russian repressions that took place in Poland well over a century before, at the time Mickiewicz was writing the play. Similarly, Musset's *Lorenzaccio,* a play written during the post Napoleonic period about the repressive effect of Medici absolutism, generated distinctly contemporary meanings when performed in Prague a year after the suppression of the liberalized Czech regime of 1968.

36. See John Loftis, *The Politics of Drama in Augustan England* (Oxford: Clarendon Press, 1963), pp. 57-60.

37. *Estudios sobre el teatro español* (Madrid: Gredos, 1962), pp. 9-44.

38. For an exhaustive study of the social, economic and political background of these plays, see Noël Salomon, *Recherches sur le thème paysan dans la "comedia" au temps de Lope de Vega* (Bordeaux: Institut d'Etudes ibériques et ibéro-américaines de l'Université de Bordeaux, 1965), especially pt. 4, pp. 741-911. The fact that this learned study was written by an avowedly Marxist scholar should remind us that the historicist bias central to Marxism can help motivate, as it does here, a thoroughly researched investigation of what must seem a strange historical situation to the modern mind.

39. "Der faschistisch verfälschte und der wirkliche Georg Büchner," in *Deutsche Realisten des 19. Jahrhunderts* (Bern: Francke, 1951). pp. 66-88.

40. See Beard, *An Economic Interpretation of the Constitution of the United States* (New York: Macmillan, 1913), with its Populist-inspired image of urban mercantile interests opposed to agrarian ones; Boorstin, *The Genius of American Politics* (Chicago: University of Chicago

Press, 1953), especially the chapter entitled "The American Revolution: Revolution without Dogma," pp. 66-98, with its post-World War II image of compromise and accommodation as the guiding spirit of the nation's early years — an image, incidentally, shared by a multitude of specialized research studies produced at the time, for instance Robert E. Brown, *Middle-Class Democracy and the Revolution in Massachusetts, 1691-1780* (Ithaca: Cornell University Press, 1955), which emphasizes the "conservatism" and "continuity" of the Revolution; and Lynd, *Class Conflict, Slavery, and the American Constitution* (Indianapolis: Bobbs-Merrill, 1967), with its New Left image clearly expressed in its very title. For a recent, more academically "respectable" study that stresses the radical nature of the Revolution, see Bernard Bailyn, *The Ideological Origins of the American Revolution* (Cambridge: Harvard University Press, 1967); unlike Lynd, who presents an image of economic and social conflict sharply opposed to the optimistic image of the consensus historians, Bailyn is concerned with the Revolution's political ideology, which he sees as stressing disruption rather than continuity.

41. *Shakspere: His Mind and Art* (1872; reprint ed., New York: Capricorn, 1962), p. 283.

42. *Shakespeare's History Plays*, p. 330.

43. *Angel with Horns*, ed. Graham Storey (New York: Theatre Arts Books, 1961), p. 59.

44. See Ornstein, *A Kingdom for a Stage: The Achievement of Shakespeare's History Plays* (Cambridge: Harvard University Press, 1972), pp. 1-32, and Lever, *The Tragedy of State* (London: Methuen, 1971), p. 5. Lever's study is not, properly speaking, about Shakespeare's histories, but about the Jacobean historical tragedies of the succeeding decade; yet the context surrounding the remark I quote indicates that he is referring to the period of Shakespeare's histories as well. In a study which appeared after my own had been completed, Moody E. Prior locates the ideological background of Shakespeare's histories in "practical-minded" historians such as Machiavelli and Guicciardini rather than in the providential historians whom Tillyard stressed (see *The Drama of Power: Studies in Shakespeare's History Plays* [Evanston: Northwestern University Press, 1973]).

45. "Preface to Shakespeare," in *Johnson on Shakespeare*, ed. Arthur Sherbo (New Haven: Yale University Press, 1968), 1: 77. The novelty of Johnson's argument lies, of course, in its liberal approach to the unities. Sir Philip Sidney, who did not share Johnson's view on the unities, would at least have agreed with his "common-sense" attitude toward theatrical illusion: note, for instance, the remark "What child is there, that, coming to a play, and seeing *Thebes* written in great letters upon an old door, doth believe that it is Thebes?" (*A Defense of Poetry*, ed. J. A. Van Dorsten [London: Oxford University Press, 1966], p. 53).

46. "The poet is now setting you in the midst of that war. Sixteen years of devastation, of plundering, of misery have fled away, the world is still fermenting in dark masses, and no hope of peace radiates from afar. The Empire is an arena of arms, the cities are deserted, Magdeburg is rubble" (Schiller, 8: 5 [Prologue, 79-86]).

47. "It is not *he* who will appear on this stage today. But among the bold forces which his command powerfully directs, which his spirit inspires, you will encounter his phantom, until such time that the shy muse will dare to bring him before you in living form" (p. 6, ll. 111-16).

48. "Therefore forgive the poet, if he does not draw you with a quick step to the action's goal *at once*" (ll. 119-21).

49. Goethe himself applied Schiller's distinction to *Wallenstein* while describing the function of *Wallensteins Lager* within the trilogy: "Wenn die alten Dichter ganz bekannte Mythen, und noch dazu theilweise, in ihren Dramen, vortrugen, so hat ein neuer Dichter, wie die Sachen stehen, immer den Nachtheil dass er erst die Exposition, die doch eigentlich nicht allein auf's Factum, sondern auf die ganze Breite der Existenz, und auf Stimmung geht, mit vortragen muss. Schiller hat deswegen einen sehr guten Gedanken gehabt dass er ein kleines Stück, die *Wallensteiner* [*Wallensteins Lager* — Goethe was writing before Schiller had completed the manuscript], als Prolog vorausschickt . . . (*Briefe*, Weimar ed., 12 [1893]: 142-43). Note Goethe's contrast of the "naive" writers ("die alten Dichter") and the modern "sentimental" one ("ein neurer Dichter"); his contrast, moreover, is based on the contention that the earlier writers could count on audiences who knew the stories ("bekannte Mythen") in advance, while the modern writer must lay his own groundwork for his fable.

50. I have used Savonarola as a hypothetical example because, despite the fact that he has often enough been treated dramatically, I know of no major plays centered around his role in Florentine history. At least two major writers have tried their hand (though none too successfully) at the material — George Eliot in her novel *Romola* (1863) and Thomas Mann in his only drama,

Fiorenza (1905). Mann's play, notably lacking in dramatic action, is formally perhaps closer to the manner of a Castiglione dialogue than to any standard theatrical convention. Mann translates Florentine history into cultural and psychological terms borrowed above all from Nietzsche. Thus, the Medicis, together with their court intellectuals, emerge as representatives of a splendid but decadent culture awaiting its apocalyptic doom at the hands of Savonarola; the latter, whose detailed characterization Mann was able to avoid by not introducing him until the final scene, becomes plausible to Mann's audience through the resemblances he bears to the ascetic type of priest figure for whom Nietzsche, in *Zur Genealogie der Moral,* had provided the classical analysis.

51. For a study of the relationship of Grass's play to Brecht's adaptation, and of the relationship of both to Shakespeare's play, see Andrzej Wirth, "Günter Grass and the Dilemma of Documentary Drama," *Dimension* (special issue, 1970) 22-35; for Grass's use of allusion and his play's relationship to the tradition of the so-called "rehearsal play," see Lore Metzger, "Günter Grass's Rehearsal Play," *Contemporary Literature* 14 (1973): 197-212.

52. For an interesting attempt to place German documentary dramas within the context of pop art and the "anti-aesthetic" movement of the 1960s, see Jost Hermand, "Wirklichkeit als Kunst: Pop, Dokumentation und Reportage," *Basis* 2 (1971): 33-52.

53. *The Village Voice* (New York), April 2, 1970, p. 11. I have found no evidence that these plans for a Chicago Eight play were ever implemented, though I know of at least two professional productions which utilized material from the trial transcripts.

54. *Pamoja Venceremos* (East Palo Alto, Calif.), August 12-25, 1971.

55. If I stress our tendency in recent years to define our actions as role-playing, I might add that we are also coming to interpret figures of the distant past in similar terms. Witness, for instance, an engaging recent book which views role-playing and theatricality as the key to an understanding of Sir Walter Ralegh (and also, by implication, of such other Renaissance figures as Sir Thomas More and Sir Philip Sidney): see Stephen J. Greenblatt, *Sir Walter Ralegh: The Renaissance Man and His Roles* (New Haven: Yale University Press, 1973), especially pp. ix-xii and 1-56. Could it be that life-as-theater is all-pervasive in human history or that we have simply learned to read the past through the framework of newly formulated insights?

56. *The Theatre of Commitment* (New York: Atheneum, 1967), p. 207.

57. Heywood, sig. B4^r.

58. *Goethe und seine Zeit* (Bern: Francke, 1947), pp. 157-58, 163, 175-76.

59. *"Ulysses,* Order and Myth," *The Dial* 75 (1923): 483

60. "A Note on 'The Tower'," in Hofmannsthal, *Selected Plays and Libretti,* ed. Michael Hamburger (New York: Pantheon, 1963), p. lxxiv.

61. "Mir ist ein historischer Augenblick, dass sie meiner Tochter übers Aug geschlagen haben" (Brecht, 7: 157 [sc. 6]).

62. "Spiel und Wirklichkeit in einigen Revolutionsdramen," *Basis* 1 (1970): 83.

63. Racine, p 538.

64. Schiller, 20: 432, 439, 471. Note the following statement: "Wir haben auch in neuern ja sogar in neuesten Zeiten naive Dichtugen in allen Klassen wenn gleich nicht mehr ganz reiner Art, und unter den alten lateinischen ja selbst griechischen Dichtern fehlt es nicht an sentimentalischen" (438n). Schiller unashamedly uses his distinction between naive and sentimental both as a description of the course of history and as a typological system.

65. *Must We Mean What We Say?* (New York: Scribner's, 1969), p. 337.

66. *European Literature and the Latin Middle Ages,* tr. W.R. Trask (New York: Pantheon, 1953), pp. 138-44. For a wide-ranging study of the implications of this figure for Italian, English, and Spanish drama during the Renaissance, see Jackson I. Cope, *The Theater and the Dream: From Metaphor to Form in Renaissance Drama* (Baltimore: Johns Hopkins Press, 1973).

67. "Der Geist ist aber auf dem Theater, auf dem wir ihn betrachten, in der Weltgeschichte, in seiner konkretesten Wirklichkeit" (*Werke* [Frankfurt: Suhrkamp, 1970], 12: 29).

68. Compare, for instance, the use of the word in these awesome lines from his philosophy of history, "Hier ist es gerade, wo die grossen Kollisionen zwischen den bestehenden, anerkannten Pflichten, Gesetzen und Rechten und den Möglichkeiten entstehen, welche diesem System entgegengesetzt sind, es verletzen, ja seine Grundlage und Wirklichkeit zerstören..." (*Werke,* 12: 44-45), and its use in these lines from his aesthetics about "collisions" in art, "Die Kollision hat ... ihren Grund in einer *Verletzung,* welche nicht als Verletzung bleiben kann, sondern aufgehoben werden muss" (*Werke,* 13: 267). The progress within history and within an

individual work of art is marked not only by a collision of discernible forces, but by a certain violence accompanying the whole process (note the word "verletzen" in each passage).

69. Hegel's descriptions of the spectacle of world history stress verbs of seeing, above all "sehen," "betrachten," and "erblicken," all of which occur in the following clauses within a single long sentence: "Wenn wir dieses Schauspiel der Leidenschaften *betrachten* und die Folgen ihrer Gewalttätigkeit, des Unverstandes *erblicken* . . ., wenn wir daraus das Uebel, das Böse, den Untergang der blühendsten Reiche, die der Menschengeist hervorgebracht hat, *sehen* . . ." (italics mine) (*Werke*, 12: 34). Note also the idea of seeing embedded in the very word for drama, "Schauspiel."

CHAPTER TWO

1. "I cannot easily excuse the printing of a play at so unseasonable a time, when the great plot of the nation, like one of Pharaoh's lean kine, has devoured its younger brethren of the stage" (*Works*, ed. Walter Scott and George Saintsbury [Edinburgh: William Paterson, 1883], 6: 5 [Dedication to *Limberham*]).

2. *Sejanus*, ed. Barish, p. 123 (IV. 140).

3. Byron, *Poetical Works* (1904; reprint ed., New York: Oxford University Press, 1946), p. 418 (II.i. 108-10).

4. Corneille, p. 909 (I.iii).

5. Otway, *Venice Preserved*, ed. Malcolm Kelsall (Lincoln: University of Nebraska Press, 1969), pp. 29-30 (II.iii. 51-57).

6. For an extended commentary on the tendency of history plays to seek out a middle ground — whether political, ethical, rhetorical or whatever — see the section "History as Middle Ground" in Chapter 4.

7. Among his notes toward *Demetrius* Schiller included two parallel columns entitled "Gegen Warbek" and "Für Warbek," in which he weighed the advantages and disadvantages of the Warbeck theme against one another (and by implication against the Demetrius theme) (Schiller, 11: 179).

8. One does not have to use Pirandello to read this problem into Renaissance plays, for, as Jackson I. Cope has shown in his discussion of Ford's Warbeck play, the problem belongs to the epistemological framework of Renaissance Platonism (see *The Theater and the Dream*, pp. 122-33).

9. Elida M. Szarota, *Künstler, Grübler und Rebellen: Studien zum europäischen Märtyrerdrama des 17. Jahrhunderts* (Bern: Francke, 1967), p. 257.

10. *Civilization and Its Discontents*, trans. James Strachey (New York: Norton, 1962), p. 61.

11. *Schriften*, ed. T.W. and G. Adorno (Frankfurt: Suhrkamp, 1955) 1: 234.

12. "Mais je ne puis pas te haïr puisque je ne te crois pas heureux" (in *Théâtre, Récits, Nouvelles*, ed. Roger Quilliot [Paris: Pléiade, 1962], p. 77 [III.vi]).

13. *Complete Plays with Prefaces* (New York: Dodd, Mead, 1962), 2: 312.

14. Racine, p. 959 (V.vi).

15. Quoted by Georges Mongrédien in "*Athalie de Racine* (Paris: Sfelt, 1946), p. 131. Voltaire's changing and quite ambiguous opinions of the play are recorded on pp. 127-39.

16. Racine, p. 892.

17. "Et l'Ecriture dit expressément que Dieu n'extermina pas toute la famille de Joram, voulant conserver à David la lampe qu'il lui avait promise. Or cette lampe, qu'était-ce autre chose que la lumière qui devait être un jour révélée aux nations?" (p. 892).

18. P. 909 (II.iii).

19. P. 926 (III.iii).

20. P. 961 (V.viii).

21. For a powerful argument that *Polyeucte* should be viewed primarily as a political rather than as a Christian drama, see Serge Doubrovsky, *Corneille et la dialectique du héros* (Paris: Gallimard, 1963), pp. 222-61. Martin Turnell gets around the conflict by avoiding the usual answers about what properly belongs to the political and to the religious realm: "Some critics have denied that [Corneille] is properly speaking a religious poet at all, while others have described *Polyeucte*, which is certainly his greatest play, as a masterpiece of religious poetry. . . . In spite of its subject it is neither more nor less religious than any of Corneille's other works. What is religious in all Corneille's best work is not the subject or the setting, but his sense of

society as an ordered whole and of man as a member of this hierarchy" (in *The Classical Moment* [1947; reprint ed., London: Hamish Hamilton, 1964], p. 39).

22. For a discussion of growth in plays which do not treat martyrdom, see the section "Drama as Growth" in Chapter 5.

23. Frank J. Warnke, *Versions of Baroque: European Literature in the Seventeenth Century* (New Haven: Yale University Press, 1972), p. 199.

24. For an extended discussion of ceremonial drama, see the section "History as Ceremony" in Chapter 3.

25. For a lucid explanation of what precisely separates the modern mind from Christian martyr stories in the *contemptus mundi* tradition, see Morton Bloomfield, "The Man of Law's Tale: A Tragedy of Victimization and a Christian Comedy," *PMLA* 87 (1972): 384-90. Bloomfield's term "tragedy of victimization," though he applies it specifically to a narrative poem, would be useful in discussing many martyr plays. One might also cite Robert B. Heilman's apt term "innocence neurosis" to describe the characters of martyr plays: "In defeat," Heilman writes, "the innocence neurosis makes one always a victim who does not deserve his fate, and who finds it irrational and untimely; in victory it makes one guiltless; and in all the actions of life . . . it makes one the voice of justice and honor" (in *Tragedy and Melodrama: Versions of Experience* [Seattle: University of Washington Press, 1968], p. 114).

26. *Complete Poems and Plays* (New York: Harcourt, Brace, 1952), p. 192.

27. A martyrdom that would have looked admirable in the hero of a seventeenth-century play might not necessarily have been so for a medieval figure. As Donald R. Howard reminds me, the Middle Ages could have interpreted Eliot's fourth temptation as leading to the sin of pride or vainglory.

28. Egmont's full line at the end is "Und euer Liebstes zu erretten, fallt freudig, wie ich euch ein Beispiel gebe" (in Goethe, 4: 454). Schiller's comment on the whole of Egmont's long final speech reads as follows, "Kurz, mitten aus der wahrsten und rührrensten Situation werden wir durch einen Salto mortale in eine Opernwelt versetzt, um einen Traum—zu *sehen*" (in Schiller, 22: 208).

29. "Mein Namen [ist bald] im Pantheon der Geschichte" (in Büchner, 1: 52 [III.iv]). "Wir wollen uns beieinandersetzen und schreien . . . Griechen und Götter schrieen, Römer und Stoiker machten die heroische Fratze." . . . "Die Einen waren so gut Epicuräer wie die Andern. Sie machten sich ein ganz behagliches Selbstgefühl zurecht. Es ist nicht so übel seine Toga zu drapieren und sich umzusehen ob man einen langen Schatten wirft" (p. 71 [IV.v]).

30. As Norman Rabkin reminds me, the modern skepticism toward martyrdom that we see in *Dantons Tod* and in many plays of our own century can also be seen in Shakespeare's treatment of the title character of *Richard II*. We do not have to view Shakespeare as a characteristic modern sensibility to account for this, but simply to note that an absolute attitude toward martyrdom would be thoroughly incompatible with the extraordinary complexity of attitude that Shakespeare takes to the political problem around which the play is centered.

31. Grotowski, *Towards a Poor Theatre* (New York: Simon and Schuster, 1968), pp. 98-99.

32. I can discuss Grotowski's production only by way of the theories expressed in his book, *Towards a Poor Theatre*, as well as the accounts of friends who have seen his productions. (I had hoped to attend a performance, in fact had even obtained a ticket for one he was to give nearby, but the famous director cancelled his whole engagement after learning that the theater management had sold more tickets than it had been instructed to: for Grotowski, a severely limited audience is necessary to insure the appropriate communal experience in his essentially ritual form of drama.) Those who have seen his performances tell me that verbal interchanges play a greater role than Grotowski's theories imply. Moreover, his version of *El príncipe constante* is not, properly speaking, based on Calderón's play, but on the adaptation of the play by the Polish Romantic poet Julius Slowacki. A German translation of Grotowski's original scenario, which later underwent considerable improvisation in performance and which was itself an extreme condensation of the Calderón-Slowacki play, has been published in *Theater Heute* 12 (August, 1971): 33-51.

33. Grotowski, *Towards A Poor Theatre*, p. 97.

34. *New Yorker*, October 25, 1969, p. 139.

35. Grotowski, p. 98.

36. The document is reprinted in Büchner, 1: 487-549.

37. See Murray's celebrated "Excursus on the Ritual Forms Preserved in Greek Tragedy" in Jane Harrison, *Themis,* 2d ed. (1927; reprint ed., Cleveland: World Publishing Co., 1962), pp. 341-63, and Frye, *Anatomy of Criticism* (Princeton: Princeton University Press, 1957), pp. 206-23.

CHAPTER THREE

1. *A Defense of Poetry,* ed. Van Dorsten, pp. 37-38.

2. The traditional comparison of history and poetry associates the former with the prosaic world of particularities, the latter with what Baxter Hathaway, in his study of Renaissance criticism, calls the "grandeur of generality" (see *The Age of Criticism: The Late Renaissance in Italy* [Ithaca: Cornell University Press, 1962], 189-202). In this chapter I argue that the very introduction of a historical perspective within drama helps create that sense of "grandeur" which poetry strives for.

3. From Robert Bolt's preface, printed with the play in *The New Theatre of Europe,* ed. Robert W. Corrigan (New York: Dell, 1962), p. 42.

4. "Die Geschichte ist nicht der Boden für das Glück. ... Die weltgeschichtlichen Individuen ... haben wohl sich befriedigt, aber sie haben nicht glücklich sein wollen" (in *Sämtliche Werke,* ed. Georg Lasson [Leipzig: Felix Meiner, 1920], vol. 8, pt. 2, p. 71).

5. *Essays of John Dryden,* ed. W. P. Ker (1900; reprint ed., Oxford: Clarendon Press, 1926), 1: 100-101.

6. *Four Tragedies,* p. 135 (II. 386).

7. I have used Dryden as an extreme instance of heroic assertion within drama, but I am also aware of recent attempts to show that Dryden intended the heroic element in his plays to be taken with a measure of irony. Thus, D. W. Jefferson, in an essay of 1940, claimed "that Dryden deliberately used heroic melodrama as a playground for his powers of wit and rhetoric" (in "The Significance of Dryden's Heroic Plays," in *Restoration Drama,* ed. John Loftis [New York: Oxford University Press, 1966], pp. 176-77). Jefferson's student Bruce King has pursued the argument considerably further — to the point where he views the heroic plays as essentially satires on heroic ideals (see *Dryden's Major Plays* [Edinburgh: Oliver and Boyd, 1966]). It is of course difficult to "restore" the consciousness of an audience as far removed from us in time as is that of the Restoration; indeed, we all too easily read aspects of our own consciousness into the earlier one. When King, in his conclusion, writes, "As our century progresses, our problems have come more and more to resemble Dryden's" (p. 204), it is clear to me that the prejudices of our own antiheroic age have been attributed to Dryden's time.

8. For a study of how powerfully the reference to an earlier mythic hero can shape an audience's responses to a dramatic character, see Eugene M. Waith, *The Herculean Hero in Marlowe, Chapman, Shakespeare and Dryden* (New York: Columbia University Press, 1962). As Waith observes, "The poet who associates his hero with Hercules or Achilles shows him, momentarily at least, in a pre-existing heroic form, as if already part of a great tradition. At the same time, the poet puts an important part of his meaning in code. It will only be understood by a reader familiar with mythology and with the further truths which it conceals" (pp. 49-50). Audiences during the Renaissance and seventeenth century could be expected to show a familiarity with this code in a way that those of our own time do not.

9. *Four Tragedies,* p. 141 (III. 85-86). For a subtle argument about how we are meant to take the heroic absoluteness of Marlowe's hero, see Thomas R. Edwards, *Imagination and Power: A Study of Poetry on Public Themes* (New York: Oxford University Press, 1971), pp. 16-24.

10. *Essays,* ed. Ker, 1: 155

11. *Four Tragedies,* p. 107.

12. Dryden defended his use of fighting on stage as a means of "raising the imagination of the audience, and to persuade them, for the time, that what they behold on the theatre is really performed" (in *Essays,* 1: 154-55). Violence thus becomes a means of establishing verisimilitude.

13. *Essays,* 1: 155. The ease with which Dryden can refer to heroes from epic and romance in the same breath is attributable to the fact that chivalric ideals were essential to the conception of heroism which prevailed in the seventeenth century. See Eugene M. Waith's chapter entitled "The Ideals of Chivalry" in *Ideas of Greatness: Heroic Drama in England* (New York: Barnes and Noble, 1971), pp. 1-34. I was unable to consult Waith's book, which traces the idea of

heroism in English drama from the Renaissance through the early eighteenth century, until I had completed this chapter; Waith's historical approach to the idea confirms much that I, with my more theoretical approach, was attempting to say.

14. "Die Malerei kann in ihren koexistierenden Kompositionen nur einen einzigen Augenblick der Handlung nutzen und muss daher den prägnantesten wählen, aus welchem das Vorhergehende und Folgende am begreiflichsten wird" (in Lessing, *Werke*, ed. Georg Witkowski [Leipzig: Bibliographisches Institut, n.d.], 4: 119 [*Laokoon*, sec. 16]).

15. *The Tatler and the Guardian* (Edinburgh: William P. Nimmo, 1880), p. 18 (April 26, 1709).

16. "Thomas Couture and the Theatricalization of Action in 19th Century French Painting," *Art Forum* 8 (June, 1970): 41.

17. The only oath in Livy's story of the Horatii is taken not by the brothers but by a priest and a spokesman for a delegation; the ceremony demands not the heroic pose depicted by David but the striking of a pig with a flint ("porcum saxo silice percussit" — in Livy, ed. B. O. Foster, Loeb Library [London: Heinemann, 1919], 1: 84 [bk. 1, chap. 24]) — scarcely an appropriate gesture for a solemn historical painting.

18. Fried, p. 46.

19. *L'Oeil vivant* (Paris: Gallimard, 1962), pp. 60-61.

20. Corneille, p. 866 (III.iv), p. 867 (III.iv), and p. 852 (II.iii).

21. P. 879 (IV.iv).

22. See *Corneille et la dialectique du héros*, pp. 87-261. The development which Doubrovsky traces in Corneille is indicated by his chapter titles: "Le Cid ou la conquête d'autrui," "Horace ou la conquête de soi," "Cinna ou la conquête du pouvoir," and "Polyeucte ou la conquête de Dieu."

23. Commenting on this passage of my manuscript, Charles R. Lyons writes of the Corneillian hero's "strong need to act in order that the action may be put into some rhetorical form: the particular quality desired only has life as it is being discussed, as it is being verbalized. Consequently, the characters are under awesome pressure to feed their dialogue with its basis, namely heroic action; but the action is not as important as the form it is given within the speech. The value achieved in the verbalization disappears immediately. The value is short-lived because it lives only in the saying." Through the skepticism toward both heroic action and heroic language implicit in this commentary, it is evident that the unself-conscious relation of words and actions which Corneille's audience could probably take for granted cannot be recaptured by a reader or audience today.

24. "Die Freiheit in himmlischem Gewande, von einer Klarheit umflossen, ruht auf einer Wolke" (in Goethe, 4: 453). For Schiller's comment on the "Opernwelt" which he found supplanting the more purely verbal drama of the rest of the play, see the section "Tyrant and Martyr Plays" in Chapter 2 (note 28).

25. I refer, of course, not to the "major" Mozart operas (which belong to distinctly nonheroic genres such as comedy and *Zauberspiel*), but to his two neglected masterpieces, *Idomeneo* and *La Clemenza di Tito*, the last great representatives of the genre of *opera seria*.

26. This statement does not apply, as David G. Halliburton reminds me, to the "heroic" symphonies of the later Prokofiev and Shostakovich. The burden of composing within a Stalinist cultural context, together with the nationalist reawakening which World War II called forth in Soviet artists, obviously sufficed to undo the powerfully ironic self-consciousness of the early, emigré Prokofiev and of the Shostakovich who aroused Stalin's disapproval during the 1930s.

27. See Igor Stravinsky and Robert Craft, *Conversations with Stravinsky* (New York: Doubleday, 1959), pp. 145-46; *Themes and Episodes* (New York: Knopf, 1966), p. 279; and *Dialogues and a Diary* (London: Faber, 1968), pp. 112-13. In his antiheroic enthusiasm Stravinsky continually lauded the Eighth (and sometimes the Second and Fourth as well), disparaged the Fifth for its "false ending" and totally dismissed the Ninth.

28. "Es sind nun die grossen welthistorischen Individuen, die solches höhere Allgemeine ergreifen und zu ihrem Zwecke machen, die den Zweck verwirklichen, der dem höhern Begriffe des Geistes gemäss ist" (in the Lasson edition, p. 75).

29. *Théâtre complet*, ed. J.-J. Thierry and Josette Mélèze (Paris: Pléiade, 1963), 1: 1227 (III.iv). Note the mysteriousness of the processes with which the hero, who describes himself as an "agent aveugle et sourd," identifies:

Je suis une force qui va!
Agent aveugle et sourd de mystères funèbres!
Une âme de malheur faite avec des ténèbres!
Où vais-je? je ne sais.

30. Racine, p. 489 (I.iii of *Bérénice*) and p. 777 (I.iii of *Phèdre*).

31. *Anatomy of Criticism*, pp. 33-34.

32. P. 35.

33. *Hero and Saint: Shakespeare and the Graeco-Roman Heroic Tradition* (New York: Oxford University Press, 1971), pp. 354-81.

34. *Lives of the English Poets*, ed. G. B. Hill (Oxford: Clarendon Press, 1905), 1: 360.

35. *Four Tragedies*, p. 285

36. See *The Perfect Wagnerite: A Commentary on the Niblung's Ring* (1898; reprint ed., New York: Dodd, Mead and Co., 1934), pp. 61-64, 81-99.

37. Buckingham actually began his parody some years before Dryden's play, which, as it turned out, supplied the appropriate concrete example he was obviously waiting for. The impulse to parody, one suspects, exists independently of its object.

38. For a fine discussion of how Shaw was able both to utilize and parody the conventions of nineteenth-century historical drama, see Martin Meisel, *Shaw and the Nineteenth-Century Theater* (Princeton: Princeton University Press, 1963), pp. 349-79.

39. See Harry Levin's classic explication of the Player's speech in *The Question of Hamlet* (1959; reprint ed., New York: Viking, 1961), pp. 138-64.

40. As editors like to remind us, the language which Falstaff is parodying is considerably closer to Kyd and Greene than it is to Preston, the author of *Cambises*. A writer feels a greater need to parody his immediate predecessors than those more distant in time.

41. Büchner, 1: 12-16 (I.ii).

42. "Ich habe auf dem Marsfelde dem Königthume den Krieg erklärt, ich habe es am 10. August geschlagen, ich habe es am 21. Januar getödtet und den Königen einen Königskopf als Fehdehandschuh hingeworfen" (Büchner, 1: 53 [III.iv]).

43. "Es kommen die Zeiten des Betrugs" (Goethe, 4: 175 [V.xiv]).

44. For a discussion of the problems which poets have encountered during recent centuries in the writing of long poems, see my chapter "The Possibility of a Long Poem" in *On Wordsworth's 'Prelude'* (Princeton: Princeton University Press, 1963), pp. 99-129.

45. The nature of Cervantes's achievement in respect to the old "conflict" between poetry and history is aptly described by E. C. Riley in his important study *Cervantes' Theory of the Novel:* "There is in the *Quixote* a practical solution to the problem which taxed the wits of Italian theorists of the Counter-Reformation: how to bring the universal and the particular into harmony. Here, for the first time, the novel triumphantly shows its range. It is not history and not poetry: its centre is somewhere in between and it includes both of them" (Oxford: Clarendon Press, 1962, pp. 177-78).

46. Leo Braudy, *Narrative Form in History and Fiction* (Princeton: Princeton University Press, 1970), p. 93.

47. "Alle erzählende Formen machen das Gegenwärtige zum Vergangenen; alle *dramatische* machen das Vergangene gegenwärtig" (from "Ueber die tragische Kunst," in Schiller, 20: 165).

48. *Der historische Roman* (Berlin: Aufbau-Verlag, 1955), pp. 129-32.

49. *Tom Jones*, ed. William Ernest Henley (London: Heinemann, 1903), 1: 143 (bk. 4, chap. 1).

50. For a study of "the psychological basis of the theory for historical realism in tragedy" during the Renaissance, see G. Giovannini, "Historical Realism and the Tragic Emotions in Renaissance Criticism," *PQ* 32 (1953): 304-20.

51. For some useful admonitions about the dangers of using drama to understand "the life of the times," see John Loftis, "The Limits of Historical Veracity in Neoclassical Drama," *England in the Restoration and Early Eighteenth Century*, ed. H. T. Swedenberg, Jr., (Berkeley: University of California Press, 1972), pp. 27-50.

52. "Sa dignité demande quelque grand intérêt d'Etat, ou quelque passion plus noble et plus mâle que l'amour ... et veut donner à craindre des malheurs plus grands que la perte d'une maîtresse" (Corneille, p. 67).

53. In his later justifications of his "licenses" Corneille, of course, cites literary and critical tradition — unpunished murders such as Orestes in the case of *Horace,* and a series of critics from Minturno to Grotius in the case of *Polyeucte.* (Corneille, p. 833 and p. 967 respectively.).

54. *Schriften,* 1: 180.

55. *Shakespearean and Other Studies,* ed. Helen Gardner (Oxford: Clarendon Press, 1969), pp. 1-2.

56. *Coleridge's Shakespearean Criticism,* ed. Raysor, 1: 143.

57. *The Early Shakespeare* (San Marino: Huntington Library, 1967), p. 87.

58. For an attempt to work in an opposite direction — that is to *separate* history from tragedy and other literary modes — see the sections "History as Middle Ground" and "Boundaries of the Historical World" of Chapter 4.

59. "O you who, in the sorrow-laden world, entwined with woe and ah and meager skeletons, seek me, where everything crumbles and falls . . ." (*Werke,* ed. Hermann Palm [1882; reprint ed., Hildesheim: Georg Olms, 1961] 2: 149.)

60. "Die Welt ist das Chaos. Das Nichts ist der zu gebärende Weltgott" (Büchner, 1: 72 [IV.v]).

61. See H. D. F. Kitto, *Greek Tragedy* (London: Methuen, 1939), p. 213, as well as the chapter on *The Suppliant Women* which he entitles "Lyrical Tragedy" (pp. 1-31).

62. For Goethe's comments on the problems Schiller encountered with a theme unfamiliar to audiences of the 1790s, see the section "Apprehending Reality" of Chapter 1 (note 49). In the same letter, however, Goethe cites a contemporary analogy, namely, "die Geschichte von Dumouriez," the French revolutionary general who defected to the Austrians in 1793. Whether or not Schiller's early audiences and readers would actually have had Dumouriez in mind, in a fundamental sense *Wallenstein* reflects the instabilities that marked power relationships throughout Europe during the decade in which it was written. For a discussion of *Wallenstein* by a distinguished modern historian, see Gordon A. Craig, "Friedrich Schiller and the Problems of Power," in *The Responsibility of Power: Historical Essays in Honor of Hajo Holborn,* ed. Leonard Krieger and Fritz Stern (New York: Doubleday, 1967), pp. 125-44.

63. ". . . manches will sich gar nicht in die engen Grenzen einer Tragödien-Oekonomie herein begeben," and "Das Ganze ist poetisch organisiert, und ich darf wohl sagen, der Stoff ist in eine rein tragische Fabel verwandelt" (in Schiller, 8: 400 and 402 respectively).

64. "Freylich hat das letzte Stück den grossen Vorzug dass alles aufhört politisch zu seyn und blos menschlich wird, ja das historische selbst ist nur ein leichter Schleyer wodurch das reinmenschliche durchblickt" (in *Briefe,* Weimar ed., 14: 46). Goethe's compliment, with its obvious preference for the universally "human" ("das reinmenschliche") over the historical ("das historische"), reflects the extreme classicism which marked his thinking during the 1790s.

65. The following evaluation of *Wallenstein* (in *Table Talk,* February 16, 1833), both in relation to works by other writers and to Schiller's own development, stands up very well today: "After this [Schiller's early period] he outgrew the composition of such plays as the Robbers, and at once took his true and only rightful stand in the grand historical drama — the Wallenstein; — not the intense drama of passion, — he was not master of that — but the diffused drama of history, in which alone he had ample scope for his varied powers. The Wallenstein is the greatest of his works: it is not unlike Shakspeare's historical plays — a species by itself. You may take up any scene, and it will please you by itself; just as you may in Don Quixote, which you read *through* once or twice only, but which you read *in* repeatedly. After this point it was, that Goethe and other writers injured by their theories the steadiness and originality of Schiller's mind; and in every one of his works after the Wallenstein you may perceive the fluctuations of his taste and principles of composition" (*Coleridge's Miscellaneous Criticism,* ed. T. M. Raysor [London: Constable, 1936], pp. 414-15).

66. Schiller, 8: 209 (*Wallensteins Tod,* II.ii. 835-43) and 188 (*Wallensteins Tod,* I.v. 285-87).

67. "Don't murder sacred sleep" (in Schiller, 8: 345 [*Wallensteins Tod,* V.vi. 3709]).

68. "This house of splendor and magnificence is now laid waste" (in Schiller, 8: 352 [*Wallensteins Tod,* V.xii. 3821-22]).

69. ". . . elevated through his ambition, destroyed by his ambition, still great and admirable despite all his flaws, unsurpassable if he had only observed some moderation" (in *Werke,* ed. Arthur Kutscher [Berlin: Deutsches Verlagshaus Bong, n.d.], 10: 303).

70. *Johnson on Shakespeare,* 2: 565; Hazlitt, *Complete Works,* ed. P. P. Howe, 4 (London: Dent, 1930): 289; Tillyard, *Shakespeare's History Plays,* p. 347; Van Doren, *Shakespeare* (1939; reprint ed., New York: Doubleday, 1954), pp. 143-52; Traversi, *Shakespeare from Richard II to Henry V* (Stanford: Stanford University Press, 1957), p. 196; Rossiter, *Angel with Horns,* p. 57.

71. *Shakespearean Meanings* (Princeton: Princeton University Press, 1968), p. 193.

72. *The Cease of Majesty,* p. 319.

73. See the section entitled "Specific Forms of Drama" in *Anatomy of Criticism* (pp. 282-93), in which Frye sets up a distinction between "mimetic" (more or less realistic) and "spectacular" forms. What I call "ceremonial" in this section belongs distinctly to Frye's concept of the spectacular.

74. *Sämtliche Werke,* ed. August Sauer and Reinhold Backmann (Vienna: Anton Schroll), pt. 1, vol. 3 (1931), p. 117 (III, after line 1960).

75. ". . . sale España, coronada con unas torres, y trae un castillo en la mano, que significa España" (Act I). "Sale el río Duero con otros tres ríos, que serán tres muchachos" (Act I). "Sale el cuerpo amortajado . . . y va saliendo poco a poco, y, en saliendo, déjase caer en el tablado" (Act II). ". . . sale una Mujer armada con una lanza en la mano y un escudo, que significa la Guerra, y trae consigo la Enfermedad y la Hambre" (Act IV) (in *Obras completas,* ed. A. Valbuena Prat [Madrid: Aguilar, 1960], pp. 151, 152, 159, and 170 respectively).

76. *Obras completas,* pp. 152-53 (end of Act I).

77. "Look round about, wherever your glance turns, [the river landscape] laughs as the bride facing the bridegroom! With bright lawn-green and grain-gold, embroidered yellow and blue with flax and saffron, sweetly scented with flowers and noble herbs, it roams onward in wide-stretching valleys" (in *Sämtliche Werke,* pt. 1, vol. 3, p. 103 [Act III, ll. 1674-79]).

78. "Er spricht das Folgende mit dem Ton eines Sehers—seine Rede steigt bis zur Begeisterung" (in *Werke,* ed. Kutscher, 6: 89 [IV.ii, after line 2437]).

79. For a fine analysis of the special relationship which existed between medieval drama and its audience, see V. A. Kolve's chapter entitled "The Drama as Play and Game" in *The Play Called Corpus Christi* (Stanford: Stanford University Press, 1966), pp. 8-32.

80. The advantages of producing a play in the place where its actions were once enacted are stressed in a recent handbook designed to encourage and instruct potential writers and producers of communal dramas. See George McCalmon and Christian Moe, *Creating Historical Drama: A Guide for the Community and the Interested Individual* (Carbondale: Southern Illinois University Press, 1965), p. 113. This whole huge book could in fact be looked upon as a colorful and also quite unsophisticated illustration of the central points I make in this section.

81. See the description in O. B. Hardison, Jr., *Christian Rite and Christian Drama in the Middle Ages* (Baltimore: Johns Hopkins Press, 1965), p. 112. Unlike Hardison, whose superb book is devoted to religious drama, I am concerned in this chapter with a particular kind of communal theatrical experience which is not necessarily religious in nature. Since this experience takes place both in secular and religious contexts, I have preferred to speak of ceremony rather than ritual to describe it.

82. See Kolve, pp. 33-56.

83. Racine, p. 911 (II.v).

84. *Poems of Shelley,* ed. Thomas Hutchinson (1905; reprint ed., London: Oxford University Press, 1960), p. 477 (ll. 1060-61).

85. For a description of Strindberg's plans for a cycle and the historical notions that stand behind these plans, see Walter Johnson, *Strindberg and the Historical Drama* (Seattle: University of Washington Press, 1963), pp. 3-17; for a description of O'Neill's projected cycle, which was to be entitled "A Tale of Possessors, Self-Dispossessed," see Travis Bogard, *Contour in Time: The Plays of Eugene O'Neill* (New York: Oxford University Press, 1972), pp. 368-407.

86. For a discussion of the apocalyptic tendencies that mark historical plays in general, see the section "Drama and Historical Process" in Chapter 5

87. *The Dynasts: An Epic-Drama of the War with Napoleon* (1904-8; reprint ed., London: Macmillan, 1965), p. xxv.

88. "Die Aufführung des Dramas, dessen Umfang nach irdischem Zeitmass etwa zehn Abende umfassen würde, ist einem Marstheater zugedacht" (1926; reprint ed., Munich: Kösel, 1957), p. 9.

89. Hardy, p. xxvi. It is indicative of the generic "uncertainty" of many panoramic dramas that they can be discussed profitably within histories of a number of genres, above all the long poem, drama, and the novel; Avrom Fleishman, for instance, finds an appropriate context for *The Dynasts* in his book *The English Historical Novel* (Baltimore: Johns Hopkins Press, 1971), pp. 197-207.

90. "Wenn wir nun einen Blick auf die Weltgeschichte überhaupt werfen, so sehen wir ein ungeheures Gemälde von Veränderungen und Taten, von unendlich mannigfaltigen Gestaltungen von Völkern, Staaten, Individuen, in rastloser Aufeinanderfolge. Alles, was in das Gemüt des Menschen eintreten und ihn interessieren kann, alle Empfindung des Guten, Schönen, Grossen wird in Anspruch genommen..." (*Werke,* Suhrkamp ed., 12: 97).

91. *The Oxford Ibsen,* 4: 563.

92. P. 608.

93. Johnson, *Strindberg and the Historical Drama,* pp. 15-17.

94. The comment was reported by that industrious intermediary between English and German literature, Henry Crabb Robinson. See *Henry Crabb Robinson on Books and Their Writers,* ed. Edith J. Morley (London: Dent, 1938), 1: 371.

95. "We'll see the small, then the large world" (in Goethe, 3: 66 [l. 2052]).

96. Hardy, p. 149 (pt. 2.I.ii)

97. "Everything transient is but a simile" (in Goethe, 3: 364 [ll.12104-5]).

98. "Ich bewahre Dokumente für eine Zeit, die sie nicht mehr fassen wird oder so weit vom Heute lebt, dass sie sagen wird, ich sei ein Fälscher gewesen. Doch nein, die Zeit wird nicht kommen, das zu sagen. Denn sie wird nicht sein" (Kraus, p. 671 [V.liv]).

99. "Dieses Drama war vor den welthistorischen Ereignissen des Juli vorigen Jahres vollendet. Seitdem ist manches eingetroffen, was in ihm vorausgesagt ist, — ebensoviel aber auch nicht. Man halte also den Verfasser an keiner Stelle für einen Propheten ex post" (*Werke und Briefe,* ed. Alfred Bergmann, 2 [Emsdetten: Lechte, 1963]: 317).

100. Ibsen, p. 608.

101. George Sand, "Essai sur le drame fantastique: Goethe, Byron, Mickiewicz," *La Revue des Deux Mondes* 20 (1839): 593-645.

102. "Ganz gemäss dem satanischen Verhängnis, das uns von den kleinen Tatsachen zu den grossen Erscheinungen der realen Tragödie geführt hat" (Kraus, p. 504 [IV.xxix]).

103. "*Saint Antoine* ne m'a pas demandé le quart de la tension d'esprit que la *Bovary* me cause" (in a letter to Louise Colet in *Correspondance,* augmented edition [Paris: Conard, 1927], 3: 156).

104. Ibsen declared *Emperor and Galilean* his masterpiece in a conversation reported by his masseur; he qualified his statement, however, by citing as the basis of his choice the fact that this play "is incontrovertibly the one that cost me the most work" (Ibsen, p. 609). If Flaubert had judged his own work by the same criteria as Ibsen, he would have had to prefer *Madame Bovary* to the *Tentation.*

105. Ibsen, pp. 336-37 (pt. 2.I).

106. *The Oxford Ibsen,* 7 (1966), trans. Jens Arup and J.W. McFarlane, pp. 231, 233, and 250.

107. Hardy, pp. xi-xii.

108. *Film Form,* ed. and trans. Jay Leyda (1949; reprint ed., Meridian, 1957), p. 62.

109. *The Film Sense,* ed. and trans. Jay Leyda (1942; reprint ed., Meridian, 1957), pp. 173-216.

110. For a shot-by-shot description, see David Mayer, *Sergei M. Eisenstein's Potemkin* (New York: Grossman, 1972).

Chapter Four

1. Quoted in the New Arden edition, p. 155.

2. "Falstaff, the Prince, and the History Play," *Shakespeare Quarterly* 16 (Winter 1965): 69.

3. See the documentation in the notes to the New Arden edition, p. 136.

4. *Some Shakespearean Themes* (1960; reprint ed., with *An Approach to 'Hamlet',* Stanford: Stanford University Press, 1966), p. 30.

5. The characteristic attitude toward the play during the last generation is evident from some of the section titles within the discussion of *Henry IV, Part I* in Cleanth Brooks's and Robert B. Heilman's influential school-text *Understanding Drama* (New York: Henry Holt, 1945), pp. 376-88: "The System of Contrasts in the Play," "The 'Immaturity' of Falstaff and Hotspur," "The Parallelism of Falstaff and Hotspur," *"Henry IV* as Mature Comedy," "Shakespeare's Balance," "Shakespeare's Irony." Although the New Critical model out of which their discussion is built has often been questioned in recent years, the central perspective through which we view this play has not changed substantially. It is the perspective which guides the analyses of L.C. Knights from which I quoted above, of A.P. Rossiter (especially the chapter "Ambivalence: The Dialectic of the Histories," *Angel with Horns,* pp. 40-64), C. L. Barber (in *Shakespeare's Festive Comedy* [1959; reprint ed., Cleveland: Meridian, 1967], pp. 192-221), and Norman Rabkin (in *Shakespeare and the Common Understanding* [New York: Free Press, 1967], pp. 80-101 — note, for instance, Rabkin's statement "There is only one constant in Shakespeare's political plays: the view of politics as problematic" [p. 81]). It is significant, I believe, that the East German scholar Robert Weimann, himself the author of a Marxist critique of the New Criticism, approvingly quotes Rossiter's statement about "two-eyedness" and "the constant doubleness of the Shakespearian vision" in his attempt to locate the origin of this doubleness in folk traditions (in *Shakespeare und die Tradition des Volkstheaters* [Berlin: Henschel, 1967], pp. 310-11). C. L. Barber, incidentally, has partially questioned his own earlier emphasis on the balances Shakespeare created in the play (in an informal talk at the Western Shakespeare Conference, Berkeley, California, February 1971). Needless to say, my guiding perspective throughout the present chapter derives from my reading of *Henry IV* — a reading that has been strongly influenced by the critics mentioned above (including Weimann).

6. Note Brooks's and Heilman's discussion of honor as a central theme in the play (p. 378) and note as well the questions they set up for student papers (for example, "Does [the structure] suggest that the meaning of Falstaff is narrow and easily definable, or rich and elusive?" — p. 387).

7. If I take something of a normative view throughout this chapter (saying, in effect, that I have a special preference for plays which create what I define as a "historical world"), this does not prevent my also responding to plays such as *Henry V* and others which I discussed in the preceding chapter. Indeed I have deliberately separated my discussion of plays which stress the "magnifying" possibilities of history from those rooted in the "historical world," for the context which I attempt to create in each chapter implies its own system of values and points of emphasis; these values and emphases will, I think, seem "inconsistent" with one another only if one removes them from the contexts within which they are articulated.

8. For a study of *Antony and Cleopatra* as a critique — and extension — of the public realm of the earlier histories (as well as of the major tragedies), see Julian Markels, *The Pillar of the World: 'Antony and Cleopatra' in Shakespeare's Development* (Columbus: Ohio State University Press, 1968).

9. The sympathy we feel for these characters — indeed, our whole attempt to find "holes" in Brecht's Marxist armor — may simply be a consequence of the bourgeois biases through which we view his work. Brecht could have countered that the ironic qualifications are central to his radical intent, to what Fredric Jameson, in his recent study of Marxist criticism, calls "the anti-idealistic thrust of Marxism (*Marxism and Form* [Princeton: Princeton University Press, 1971], p. 372). One could argue that Brecht was deliberately setting up figures whom we would feel tempted to see as martyrs (Mother Courage as a victim of larger forces she could not control, Galileo as a victim of papal and aristocratic repression) only to make us question the idealism which we all too automatically apply to situations in which we see a figure wronged. Brecht's Marxism is thus a critical tool which he employs to correct the idealizing tendencies of his bourgeois audiences. From a liberal bourgeois point of view (which is doubtless what a Marxist would see as the bias of the present study) the middle ground within which we locate Brecht's plays is a result of his ability to break down our idealistic absolutes as well as of our own ability to ignore the radical absolutes toward which the lessons of the plays are meant to point.

10. Needless to say, Büchner did not have access to that modern view of Robespierre which would see him as a skillful and pragmatic politician trying to cope from day to day with new and often unresolvable problems. (See, for instance, R. R. Palmer, *Twelve Who Ruled: The Year of*

the Terror in the French Revolution [Princeton: Princeton University Press, 1941].) Moreover, the histories of the Revolution which supplied him with most of the material for the play—those of François-Auguste Mignet and Adolphe Thiers—were notable for their anti-Robespierrist bias and their disdain for the mob.

11. For examples of such readings, see the section "Tyrant and Martyr Plays" of Chapter 2 (note 21).

12. The Shakespearean work which provides the best introduction on how to read many of the great Spanish plays is an "unpleasant" comedy such as *Measure for Measure,* whose political interest remains narrowly focused on the public consequences of private willfulness. Spanish dramas, though normally based on historical materials, tend to focus on what a northern European would view as the private rather than the public realm; even a political play such as Lope's *Fuenteovejuna* locates the source of the public disorders it depicts in the lustfulness and arrogance of the local ruler. Yet from the point of view established within the dramas themselves, private experience is fraught with public significance. The personal honor which Calderón's heroes defend with such intransigence cannot be separated from its larger political meanings. The hero of Lope's love tragedy *El cabellero de Olmedo,* a play which treats private matters similar to those of *Romeo and Juliet,* achieves public significance through his prowess in the bull ring and the recognition which the king accords him. Spanish drama creates its own, quite unique historical world; if I were to use it to view European drama as I use my Shakespearean model, the resulting image would be vastly different from the one that emerges within this chapter.

13. *Some Versions of Pastoral* (1935; reprint ed., Norfolk: New Directions, 1960), pp. 26, 41-44, 102-5.

14. Dryden, *Works,* Scott-Saintsbury edition, 4: 44 (*Conquest of Granada,* pt. 1.1.i).

15. I am aware of Anne T. Barbeau's recent reading of the heroic plays as "plays of ideas" (in *The Intellectual Design of John Dryden's Plays* [New Haven: Yale University Press, 1970]). Although she provides ample demonstration of her thesis that "the political ideas expounded in Dryden's heroic drama are not merely plaster decoration but an integral part of the design" (p. 6), the other aspects of Dryden's design—his attempt to evoke admiration for heroic endeavor and his use of epic to create a model for dramatic action—are antithetical to the type of political analysis characteristic of plays within what I call the historical world.

16. *Works,* 9, ed. John Loftis (Berkeley: University of California Press, 1966): 27.

17. *Dramatic Works* (London: Routledge, 1876), 1: 152.

18. *Comédies et Proverbes,* ed. Edmond Biré and Maurice Allem (Paris: Garnier, n.d.), 1: 67 (I.v).

19. "On allait à Montolivet tous les vendredis de certains mois; c'était à Florence ce que Longchamp était autrefois à Paris. Les marchands y trouvaient l'occasion d'une foire et y transportaient leurs boutiques" (p. 66n).

20. See Shaw's "defense" of his procedure in the notes entitled "Apparent Anachronisms" which he appended to the play (in *Complete Plays with Prefaces,* 3: 472-81).

21. Although one can give a multitude of good reasons for the failure of the historical dramas written by the great English poets of the nineteenth century, many plays may have failed because they consciously cultivated too specialized a form of theatricality: I refer to those plays written with specific acting stars in mind, for instance Keats's *Otho the Great,* written for (though never acted by) Edmund Kean, or Browning's *Strafford,* written for W. C. Macready.

22. *Complete Plays with Prefaces,* 3: 456-59 (Act IV).

23. Büchner, 1: 37 (II.iii).

24. *Seneca's Tragedies,* ed. F. J. Miller, Loeb Classical Library (London: William Heinemann, 1917), 2: 432 (ll. 291-92).

25. Quoted in Bevington, *From "Mankind" to Marlowe,* pp. 13-14.

26. *Tudor Drama and Politics* (Cambridge: Harvard University Press, 1968), pp. 97-105, 156-60, and 55-63 respectively.

27. "What Is Shakespeare's 'Henry VIII' About?" *Durham Univ. Journal,* n.s. 9 (1948): 54.

28. *Shakespearean Meanings,* pp. 49-50.

29. For an exhaustive description of what is traditional and what is unique in Margaret's cursing, see Wolfgang Clemen, *Kommentar zu Shakespeares Richard III* (Göttingen: Vanden-

hoeck und Ruprecht, 1957), pp. 78-94. According to the terminology I have used in this chapter, Margaret's whole role in this scene — even when Shakespeare develops this role beyond that of his predecessors — is a ceremonial one.

30. Anticipations of the historicism which *Götz* introduced into European literature can surely be found in earlier texts if we look hard enough. Among all writers before the eighteenth century, Shakespeare may well have come closest to rendering the pathos of one age giving way to another. Thus, David Riggs has recently read *Henry VI* (especially *Part I*) as dramatizing "the gradual deterioration of heroic idealism between the Hundred Years' War and the Yorkist accession" (in *Shakespeare's Heroical Histories* [Cambridge: Harvard University Press, 1971] p. 97), while a generation earlier Tillyard had presented an attractive image of *Richard II* as a confrontation of "two ways of life" — the "celestial medievalism" represented by the title character and the harsh new Renaissance order of his successor (in *Shakespeare's History Plays*, pp. 287-95). George Dekker (in conversation with me) locates a similar confrontation in *Antony and Cleopatra*, which he sees as recording the transition from a national to an imperialistic order. However well Shakespeare intuited the workings of the modern historical imagination, one must recognize that the framework of thought which enables us to notice occasional insights of this sort in his work is itself a product of the revolution created during the eighteenth century by figures such as Herder and the early Goethe (and of course Vico before — though unbeknownst to — them). For an explanation of the relation of *Götz* to Herder's ideas (and to Herder's conception of Shakespeare) see Friedrich Sengle, *Das historische Drama in Deutschland,* 2d ed. (Stuttgart: J. B. Metzlersche Verlagsbuchhandlung, 1969), pp. 35-41.

31. "Es kommen die Zeiten des Betrugs. . . . Die Nichtswürdigen werden regieren mit List, und der Edle wird in ihre Netze fallen" (Goethe, 4: 175 [V.xiv]).

32. For a fine account of how Scott found a means of accommodating the conflict of values that accompanies historical change within the novel, see Donald Davie, *The Heyday of Walter Scott* (London: Routledge and Kegan Paul, 1961), especially the section on *Waverley,* pp. 22-38.

33. *The Disinherited Mind,* 3d. ed. (New York: Barnes and Noble, 1971), pp. 37-63.

34. "Ich weiss wohl, dass Politik selten Treu und Glauben halten kann, dass sie Offenheit, Gutherzigheit, Nachgiebigkeit aus unsern Herzen ausschliesst" (Goethe, 4: 379 [I.ii]).

35. Note, for instance, the lady's reply when she is told about the political unrest in her domain: "Es wird nichts zu bedeuten haben, wenn man sich nur vernüftig gegen die Menschen beträgt und ihnen ihren wahren Vorteil zeigt" (Goethe, 5: 193 [II.v]).

36. Goethe, 5: 213-14 and 195-97 respectively.

37. See *The King's Two Bodies: A Study in Mediaeval Political Theology* (Princeton: Princeton University Press, 1957), pp. 24-41.

38. *Edward II,* ed. H. B. Charlton and R. D. Waller (1930; reprint ed., Gordian Press, 1966), p. 113 (II.ii. 9-10). It could be argued that *Edward II* contains a public realm of sorts — a composite of the various political points of view voiced by different characters. Yet these characters, like the king himself, all live in their private, quite egocentric, worlds. Whether we accuse the play of lacking coherence or credit it with achieving complexity through this juxtaposition of points of view, the context that emerges is scarcely "public" in the Shakespearean sense I employ as a model in this chapter — which is only to say that *Edward II,* for all its deeply moving qualities, offers a very different experience from, say, *Richard II.*

39. *Poems of Shelley,* p. 37. The quote is from the "conspiracy" half of Chapman's two-part play (III.iii. 140-43).

40. *Shakespeare's Heroical Histories,* p. 13.

41. The biographical play was a recognizable subgenre in Elizabethan times, as Irving Ribner has demonstrated in detail (see *The English History Play,* pp. 193-223). Like modern biographical plays, such Elizabethan examples as the anonymous dramas about Thomas Cromwell and Thomas More attempt to defend the actions of their respective heroes; yet by assuming what Ribner calls "the formula of *de casibus* tragedy" (p. 212), these plays are able to avoid denouncing the public realm and instead to put the blame for their heroes' downfall on the capriciousness of Fortune. Needless to add, Fortune provided a politically "safe" means by which an audience could vent its hostility on those who persecuted its martyrs.

42. "Am furchtbarsten aber erscheint dieses Dämonische, wenn es in irgend einem Menschen überwiegend hervortritt. Während meines Lebensganges habe ich mehrere teils in der

Nähe, teils in der Ferne beobachten können. Es sind nicht immer die vorzüglichsten Menschen, weder an Geist noch an Talenten, selten durch Herzensgüte sich empfehlend; aber eine ungeheure Kraft geht von ihnen aus, und sie üben eine unglaubliche Gewalt über alle Geschöpfe, ja sogar über die Elemente, und wer kann sagen, wie weit sich eine solche Wirkung erstrecken wird? Alle vereinten sittlichen Kräfte vermögen nichts gegen sie..." (Goethe, 10: 177 [*Dichtung und Wahrheit*, pt. 4, bk. 20]).

43. *Queen Christina, Charles XII, Gustav III,* tr. Walter Johnson (Seattle: University of Washington Press, 1955), p. 62 (act III).

44. "Welcher Schulmeister hat nicht von Alexander dem Grossen, von Julius Cäsar vordemonstriert, dass diese Menschen von solchen Leidenschaften getrieben und daher unmoralische Menschen gewesen seien? woraus sogleich folgt, dass er, der Schulmeister, ein vortrefflicherer Mensch sei als jene, weil er solche Leidenschaften nicht besitze und den Beweis dadurch gebe, dass er Asien nicht erobere, den Darius, Poros nicht besiege, sondern freilich wohl lebe, aber auch leben lasse. — Diese Psychologen hängen sich dann vornehmlich auch an die Betrachtung von den Partikularitäten der grossen, historischen Figuren, welche ihnen als Privatpersonen zukommen" (Hegel, Suhrkamp ed., 12: 48).

45. "Lorsqu'on met sur la scène un simple intrigue d'amour entre des rois, et qu'ils ne courent aucun péril, ni de leur vie, ni de leur Etat, je ne crois pas que, bien que les personnes soient illustres, l'action le soit assez pour s'élever jusqu'à la tragédie. Sa dignité demande quelque grand intérêt d'Etat, ou quelque passion plus noble et plus mâle que l'amour, telles que sont l'ambition ou la vengeance, et veut donner à craindre des malheurs plus grands que la perte d'une maîtresse. Il est à propos d'y mêler l'amour, parce qu'il a toujours beaucoup d'agrément, et peut servir de fondement à ces intérêts, et à ces autres passions dont je parle...." (Corneille, p. 67).

46. *Le Fanatisme ou Mahomet le Prophète* in *Oeuvres complètes* (Paris: Garnier, 1877), 4: 123 (II.iv).

47. *All for Love,* ed. Vieth, p. 13.

48. For instance, in Georg Lukács's various essays on nineteenth-century novels, Ian Watt's *The Rise of the Novel* (Berkeley: University of California Press, 1957), and Lionel Trilling's essay "Manners, Morals, and the Novel" (in *The Liberal Imagination* [1950; reprint ed., New York: Doubleday, 1953], pp. 200–215). Note Claudio Guillén's comment, "The idea that the modern novel is a product of the bourgeoisie rests on a notoriously convincing analogy not between two sets of hard data, but between two 'pictures' and two systems" (*Literature as System* [Princeton: Princeton University Press, 1971], p. 418). Insofar as I have been concerned, throughout this book, with what I earlier called "the transactions between imaginative literature and the external world," I have been drawing analogies between what Guillén would call two (or more) "pictures" or systems. His statement of what he takes to be the task of the literary historian — "to identify the careers of these different [literary, social or linguistic] systems in historical time, to discover those that prevailed, and to listen to the dialogue between them" (p. 419) — is close to what I take the task of the present study to be.

49. Note the following sentence from Hannah Arendt's *The Human Condition,* to whose analysis of the changes in the conception of private and public in Western history this whole section is deeply indebted. "The astonishing flowering of poetry and music from the middle of the eighteenth century until almost the last third of the nineteenth, accompanied by the rise of the novel, the only entirely social art form, coinciding with a no less striking decline of all the more public arts, especially architecture, is sufficient testimony to a close relationship between the social and the intimate" (Chicago: University of Chicago Press, 1958), p. 39. Historical drama, at least as Shakespeare and Corneille wrote it, obviously belongs to what Arendt calls "the more public arts."

50. Edmund Gosse, quoted by Aline Mackenzie Taylor in *Next to Shakespeare: Otway's 'Venice Preserv'd' and 'The Orphan' and Their History on the London Stage* (Durham: Duke University Press, 1950), p. 40; this book also contains a detailed account of the history of the play's reception. Since Gosse's observation, as Taylor shows, had already been anticipated by eighteenth-century critics of the play, it is clear that the "shift" from the public to the private realm had begun within a generation after the writing of the play. For Taylor's discussion of the public import which Otway's audience would have seen in the personal injury (the loss of a mistress to a senator) which Pierre experienced, see pp. 50-51.

51. *The Revolution of the Saints* (1965; reprint ed., New York: Atheneum, 1969), p. 234.

52. *The Herculean Hero in Marlowe, Chapman, Shakespeare and Dryden,* p. 118.

53. See, for example, G. Wilson Knight's essay "Myth and Miracle," in *The Crown of Life* (1947; reprint ed., London: University Paperbacks, 1965), pp. 12-13; E. M. W. Tillyard, *Shakespeare's Last Plays* (London: Chatto and Windus, 1938), pp. 20-22; Charles R. Lyons, *Shakespeare and the Ambiguity of Love's Triumph* (The Hague: Mouton, 1971), p. 186 and pp. 189-90; and the two full-length studies of the play, Julian Markels, *The Pillar of the World,* pp. 171-76, and Janet Adelman, *The Common Liar: An Essay on "Antony and Cleopatra"* (New Haven: Yale Univesity Press, 1973), pp. 164-68. Adelman's book provides not only a most precise account of the relation of the play to the late romances but also the most convincing explanation of what makes *Antony and Cleopatra* unique within the Shakespeare canon as a whole. The antitheses between public and private and between history and romance which operate so powerfully in this play are paralleled by what Rosalie L. Colie (in a fine analysis which did not appear until my study was complete) calls an antithesis between "Attic" and "Asiatic" styles of language (and life!) within the work (*Shakespeare's Living Art* [Princeton: Princeton University Press, 1974], pp. 176-207).

CHAPTER FIVE

1. *Corneille et la dialectique du héros,* p. 268. Note Doubrovsky's italics in his statement that "le théâtre de Corneille n'est pas un théâtre qui se greffe *sur* l'histoire; c'est un théâtre *d'*histoire; non un théâtre qui *utilize* l'histoire, mais qui la réfléchit" (same page).

2. *Foundations of Historical Knowledge* (New York: Harper and Row, 1965), pp. 222-25.

3. *The Idea of History* (1946; reprint ed., London: Oxford University Press, 1969), p. 30.

4. *Social Change and History* (New York: Oxford University Press, 1969). For Nisbet's definition of history "in the sense of the concrete, the particular, and the temporal," see p. 268; the concept of change, which Nisbet associates with terms such as "growth" and "development," is the subject of the book as a whole.

5. William Dinsmore Briggs, *Marlowe's Edward II* (London: David Nutt, 1914), p. xcv.

6. Hardy, p. 330 (pt. 3.I.i).

7. *Tamburlaine the Great,* ed. U. M. Ellis-Fermor (1930; reprint ed., New York: Gordian Press, 1966), p. 85 (Pt. 1.I.ii. 173-74).

8. *Language as Symbolic Action* (Berkeley: University of California Press, 1968), p. 86.

9. Racine, p. 769 (I.i).

10. *Essays in English and American Literature* (Princeton: Princeton University Press, 1962), p. 9.

11. For detailed descriptions of what precisely Brecht did to Marlowe's text, see Hans Werner Grüninger, "Brecht und Marlowe," *Comparative Literature* 21 (1969): 232-44, and Ulrich Weisstein, "The First Version of Brecht/Feuchtwanger's *Leben Eduards des Zweiten von England* and Its Relation to the Standard Text," *Journal of English and Germanic Philology* 69 (1970): 193-210.

12. "Die Auffassung des Menschen als einer Variablen des Milieus, des Milieus als einer Variablen des Menschen, das heisst die Auflösung des Milieus in Beziehungen zwischen Menschen, entspringt einem neuen Denken, dem historischen Denken.... Das historisierende Theater ... wirft sich ganz und gar auf das Eigentümliche, Besondere, der Untersuchung Bedürftige des so alltäglichen Vorgangs" (*Schriften zum Theater* [Berlin: Suhrkamp, 1957], p. 86).

13. *The Idea of History,* p. 50.

14. *The Oxford Ibsen,* 4: 584.

15. "Die Wolken hängen am stillen Abendhimmel wie ein ausglühender Olymp mit verbleichenden, versinkenden Göttergestalten" (Büchner, 1: 72 [IV.v]).

16. "The earth's youthful dream has been dreamt ... and according to the sign it would almost seem to me that we are standing at the entrance to a new time" (in *Sämtliche Werke,* pt. 1, vol. 3, p. 114 [III. 1. 1914 and ll. 1919-20]).

17. "The century is not ripe for my ideal" (*Don Carlos* in *Werke,* ed. Kutscher, 3: 217 [III.x. 3078-79]).

18. *The Sense of an Ending* (New York: Oxford University Press, 1967), p. 31.

19. *Complete Plays with Prefaces,* 2: 308.

20. P. 341 (scene 2).

21. "Galileis Verbrechen kann als die 'Erbsünde' der modernen Naturwissenschaften betrachet werden.... Die Atombombe ist sowohl als techniches als auch soziales Phänomen das klassiche Endprodukt seiner wissenschaftlichen Leistung und seines sozialen Versagens" (Brecht, 8: 204-5.

22. One might cite M. H. Abrams's recent book *Natural Supernaturalism* (New York: Norton, 1971), which interprets English and German romantic literature and philosophy within the context of Western thought as a whole, as a powerful contribution toward such a study. Kenneth Burke's various analyses of hierarchical thinking provide invaluable rhetorical tools for such a study; see, for example, "A Metaphorical View of Hierarchy," in *A Rhetoric of Motives* (1950; reprint ed., with *A Grammar of Motives,* Cleveland: Meridian, 1962), pp. 661-66.

23. For studies that stress the dialectical nature of each of these plays, see Burckhardt, *Shakespearean Meanings,* esp. 145-46; Doubrovsky, *Corneille et la dialectique du héros,* pp. 185-221; and Egon Schwarz, "Die Wandlungen Friedrichs von Homburg," in *Festschrift für Bernhard Blume* (Göttingen: Vandenhoeck und Ruprecht, 1967), especially p. 120.

24. Abrams, pp. 197-324.

25. Corneille, p. 902 (I.i).

26. P. 904 (I.ii).

27. P. 957 (V.iii).

28. Racine, p. 403.

29. P. 412 (I.i)

30. Napoleon thought the play's resolution sentimental until he heard an actor who "prononça le *Soyons amis, Cinna,* d'un ton si habile et si rusé, que je compris que cette action n'etait que la feinte d'un tyran, et j'ai approuvé comme calcul ce qui me semblait puéril comme sentiment" *(Mémoires de Madame de Rémusat,* ed. Paul de Rémusat [Paris: Calmann Lévy, 1880], 1: 279).

31. Sigurd Burckhardt, "*Egmont* and *Prinz Friedrich von Homburg:* Expostulation and Reply," in *The Drama of Language* (Baltimore: Johns Hopkins Press, 1970), pp. 94-100.

32. Brecht, 8: 205.

33. Reinhardt's productions are described in detail by Ingeborg Strudthoff, *Die Rezeption Georg Büchners durch das deutsche Theater* (Berlin: Colloquium Verlag, 1957), pp. 52-55 and 105-9, and by Wolfram Viehweg, *Georg Büchners "Dantons Tod" auf dem deutschen Theater* (Munich: Laokoon, 1964), pp. 56-68 and 181-90. Viehweg lists the cuts made by Reinhardt to shorten the political and philosophical discussions and to stress the more overtly "theatrical" actions (pp. 56-60).

34. "Im 'Egmont' sei die Partie des griechischen Chors unter die zwei Liebenden, unter Klärchen und Albas Sohn verteilt. *Diese* stellten denselben vor; das eigentliche Volk sei, wie gewöhnlich, ohne Teilnahme" (Goethe, 4: 568)

35. Brecht, 11: 382-407.

36. *Shakespeare: A Marxist Interpretation,* trans. Sonia Volochova et al. (New York: Critics Group, 1937), p. 76.

37. *Shakespeare und die Tradition des Volkstheaters,* p. 364.

38. For an analysis of the considerable body of commentary on Shakespeare's attitude to the crowd, see Brents Stirling, *The Populace in Shakespeare* (New York: Columbia University Press, 1949), pp. 64-96.

39. *Angel with Horns,* p. 58.

40. For a virtuoso interpretation of the speech from this point of view, see Kenneth Burke, "Antony in Behalf of the Play," in *The Philosophy of Literary Form,* revised ed. (New York: Random House, 1957), pp. 279-90.

41. *Romanische Literaturstudien: 1936-1956* (Tübingen: Niemeyer, 1959), p. 774.

42. Pp. 776-77.

43. For the conservative imagination of T. S. Eliot during the years after his conversion, creating a "sympathetic" crowd in *Murder in the Cathedral* did not occasion the dramatic or ideological problems it would have for a more liberal mentality in our time: as medieval villagers (significantly the group is made up wholly of women), they exist simply to observe, comment

upon, and suffer the changes and oppressions of the political world which the play as a whole seeks to discredit and transcend. Their famous lines "For us, the poor, there is no action, / But only to wait and to witness" (*Complete Poems and Plays,* p. 177) portray a crowd whose passivity evokes a sympathy closer to pity than to the admiration we feel for the active and heroic crowds of *Die Weber* and *Fuenteovejuna.*

44. *Schriften,* 1: 182.

45. Robert B. Pierce, *Shakespeare's History Plays: The Family and the State* (Columbus: Ohio State Univesity Press, 1971), p. 242.

46. *Civilization and Its Discontents,* p. 44.

47. Racine, pp. 433-34 (II.vi).

48. Racine, p. 403.

49. "Bruderfeindschaft ist überhaupt eine durch alle Zeiten der Kunst fortgreifende Kollision, die schon mit Kain beginnt, der den Abel erschlug" (in *Werke,* Suhrkamp ed., 13: 271).

50. Gerald Else, *Aristotle's Poetics: The Argument* (Cambridge: Harvard University Press, 1963), p. 413.

51. Büchner, 1: 30 (I.vi) and 38 (II.iii) respectively.

52. Kolve, *The Play Called Corpus Christi,* p. 204.

53. *Shakespearean Meanings,* pp. 166-67.

54. Racine, p. 452 (IV.ii).

55. Büchner, 1: 15-16 (I.ii), 17-20 (I.iii), and 43-45 (II.vii) respectively.

56. 1: 62-63 (III.ix) and 63-64 (III.x) respectively.

57. Racine, p. 468 (V.vi).

58. P. 416 (I.ii).

59. P. 414 (I.i).

60. Pp. 446-48 (III.viii).

61. See *Collected Writings,* ed. David Masson (Edinburgh: Adam and Charles Black, 1890), 10:46-52, and 11:54-59.

62. The "we" here refers to the modern Western literary intellectual, whose perceptions of the world have been influenced by a composite of not always compatible ideologies, many of which (above all, Marxism) subordinate the role of the individual to "larger" forces. The statement by Henry Kissinger quoted at the head of this section displays a traditional conception of power (note, for instance, the distinction he makes between a man and his office) quite antithetical to that held by the literary intellectual. Could it be that we (though not necessarily the thoroughgoing Marxist) attribute power to forces rather than individuals through our despair over the great gulf that separates us from the centers of power?

63. "Die grossen politischen Verbrecher müssen durchaus preisgegeben werden, und vorzüglich der Lächerlichkeit. Denn sie sind vor allem keine grossen politischen Verbrecher, sondern die Verüber grosser politischen Verbrechen, was etwas ganz anderes ist" (Brecht, 9: 369).

64. See the section "Levels of Reality" in Chapter 1 (note 29).

65. "Né voglio sia reputata presunzione, se uno uomo di basso et infimo stato ardisce discorrere e regolare e' governi de' principi; perché, così come coloro che disegnono e' paesi si pongano bassi nel piano a considerare la natura de' monti e de' luoghi alti, e per considerare quella de' bassi si pongano alto sopra monti, similmente a conoscere bene la natura de' populi bisogna esser principe, et a conoscere bene quella de' principi bisogna esser populare" (*Il Principe e Discorsi,* ed. Sergio Bertelli [Milan: Feltrinelli, 1960], p. 14).

INDEX

191